3

72/-

How Communist China Negotiates

How Communist China Negotiates

by ARTHUR LALL

 Columbia University Press

NEW YORK AND LONDON 1968

Arthur Lall, formerly Ambassador to the United Nations and
Head of the Indian Delegation, is Adjunct Professor of Government
at the School of International Affairs, Columbia University.

Copyright © 1968 Columbia University Press
Library of Congress Catalog Card Number 67-29051
Printed in the United States of America

Preface

THE INVOLVEMENT of the People's Republic of China in world affairs is already considerable, and will increase. The Peking government now has diplomatic relations with over forty-five countries; it has negotiated border treaties or agreements, and treaties or agreements of friendship, with a number of countries.

The Peking government's most notable negotiation thus far has been the protracted conference on Laos of 1961–1962, which resulted in the only international agreement as yet to have been signed by both the Secretary of State of the United States and the Foreign Minister of the Peking government. The records of the Laos Conference have not yet been published. Nor has the inside story of the negotiations become widely known, because the crucial issues of the conference were worked out in a series of unpublicized meetings among the heads of six of the delegations at the conference—the United States, the Soviet Union, the United Kingdom, Communist China, France, and India. It was my good fortune to be one of the six delegates who participated in these core negotiations on Laos.

Clearly, the intricate and instructive story of the Laos negotiations should be told and should be analyzed in the context of the Chinese Communist theory of international relations. Such is the primary purpose of this book. To provide a broader perspective, I have also included general observations on the nature of the Chinese presence at international conferences and on the background and training of the Peking government's negotiators. Another supplementary chapter briefly analyzes three bilateral negotiations which led to agreements between the Peking government and three Asian states. These negotiations further reveal China's international conduct, particularly in dealings involving smaller states with which China has had traditional ties.

The preparation of this book has been facilitated in numerous ways by the ready support and assistance of Dean Andrew W. Cordier of the School of International Affairs at Columbia University, to whom I express my warm gratitude. I am also especially indebted to my Columbia colleagues Doak Barnett and Donald Klein, both of whom were good enough to read the manuscript and make invaluable suggestions. I of course remain responsible for the contents of the text.

ARTHUR LALL

New York City
August 31, 1967

Contents

How Communist China Negotiates

CHAPTER I

The Nature of the Chinese Presence in Negotiation

THE MOST RECENT of the rare manifestations of the nature of the presence of the People's Republic of China at multi-governmental negotiations with non-Communist states occurred at the Fourteen-Nation International Conference on the Settlement of the Laotian Question, which was held at Geneva from May 16, 1961, through July 23, 1962.

The delegations to the conference assembled in the spacious high-ceilinged council chamber of the Palais des Nations, the European headquarters of the United Nations. This distinguished conference room is dominated by the massive figures and forms of the murals and ceiling paintings of José Maria Sert, and this dominance is heightened by the somber glows of the browns, grays, silvers, and golds which the artist favored for such works. But when the Laos Conference met, the room's normal accent was challenged by the intrusion of a yet more serious and massive presence: the delegation of the Peking government, numbering some fifty men and women, all dressed in drab olive khaki uniforms buttoned up to the neck. This single delegation not only filled the quota of a half dozen chairs reserved for it, as for each of the other thirteen delegations, but occupied almost a full quarter of the tiered seats in the galleries along the four walls of the room. If all the fourteen countries invited to the conference had come with delegations as large as that from Peking, no room at the Palais des Nations would have been large enough for the meetings. As it was, the Chinese delegation was by far the biggest in the room. The average delegation mustered a half dozen persons, and only three delegations other than the Chinese—those of the United States, the Soviet Union, and the United Kingdom—went barely into double figures. The personnel of all the thirteen delegations other than the Chinese filled just half the seats in the room. Consequently, the uniformed block of Chinese delegates was overwhelmingly the dominant presence at the conference.

Mao Tse-tung and other leaders of modern China have displayed an inordinate degree of pride in the size and population of their country. In the years when Mao and his colleagues were moving toward consolidation of their power over the mainland he frequently made such statements as the following: "China, the centre of gravity in Asia, is a large country with a population of 475 millions." [1]

In another of his writings Mao demurs at the nexus between overpopulation and revolution adduced in Dean Acheson's letter of July 30, 1949, which transmitted to the President the China White Paper of 1949; [2] he states: "It is a very good thing that China has a big population. Even if China's population multiplies many times she is fully capable of finding a solution; the solution is production." [3]

In commenting on some aspects of the "cultural revolution" *Renmin Ribao* (the *People's Daily*) carried a remarkable editorial on June 8, 1966, which extolled the separateness of thought of the new China:

Some people say: "The 700 million Chinese are all critics." . . . The fact that "700 million people are critics" is a thing stupendous, it is an epoch making event. This in itself shows that the thinking of our 700 million people has been emancipated, that they have risen to full height and that they are no longer slaves of the old culture and old ideas of imperalism and the exploiting classes.[4]

In connection with this pervading consciousness of bigness we should note also such phrases as "the great leap forward." Mao's own use of this and analogous phrases predates by many years the economic efforts in the late fifties that are associated with it. In his report to a meeting of the Central Committee of the Communist Party of China held in December 1947, he said, "During the eleven years 1937–47 the membership of our Party has grown from several tens of thousands to 2,700,000, and this is a very big leap forward." [5]

During the civil war in China Mao frequently told his men to concentrate a superior force in numbers against the enemy. In the same report from which the above statement is taken he said, "In every battle concentrate an absolutely superior force (two, three, four and sometimes even five or six times the enemy's strength), encircle the enemy forces completely." [6]

The lesson of numbers in human confrontations has been thoroughly grasped by the modern Chinese leaders. It is a weapon that is ready at hand, and its use has been extended to the negotiating table. The presence of about fifty Chinese in the room at the Laos Conference was a factor to which the other delegations had to adjust themselves, and it cannot be said that this was a factor completely without psychological effect.

It is, of course, not the case that the large size of the Chinese delegation was to be explained only by the impression of power the Peking government sought to make at Geneva. Part of the explanation was the nature of the composition of the delegation: it included, for example, representatives of Chinese publicity media.

Two other factors probably also have a direct bearing on the size of the Chinese presence at such conferences. One is that the Chinese government undoubtedly takes advantage of such rare opportunities as the Laos Conference to give its personnel some experience of observing and dealing with the officials of Western and other states. The second relevant factor could be the prevailing insistence of the Chinese Communists, as a tactic of dealing with issues, on intensive discussion by groups of party members before views are formulated for presentation to those who take decisions. From his early days as a leader Mao has stressed the importance of this procedure. In December 1929 he wrote a comprehensive resolution for adoption at a conference on the Communist Party organization in the army, in which he stated:

Party organisations at all levels should not make decisions without due deliberation. . . . The rank-and-file Party members must discuss in detail directives from the higher bodies in order to understand their significance thoroughly and decide on the methods to carry them out.[7]

It was not only during meeting breaks at Geneva that groups in the Chinese delegation, heads bent closely together, would be engaged in earnest discussion; whenever I took a draft proposal to the Chinese delegation at their own quarters it would be passed from hand to hand among a group of four or five senior members of the delegation who would rapidly discuss it among themselves before their spokesman (or -men) commented. Deputy Foreign Minister, Chang Han-fu, who was the working head of the delegation, would be the first to read the proposal. His face would show no reaction. Since there was no sign of a negative response, at my first meeting of this kind I thought that my proposal—into which much thought had gone both in regard to content and wording—was acceptable or, at any rate, was being sympathetically received. I was mistaken. Chang Han-fu raised a few points after discussing my proposal with his colleagues. Then he said something to the interpreter, who took over and, in rapidly delivered Harvard English, stated a long list of objections, some of them quite fundamental. I argued in favor of my draft. Ch'iao Kuan-hua, now a Deputy Minister, answered, "Mr. Lall, I know you mean well. You think you can persuade the Americans to accept your proposal. We know them better than you. We dealt with them for a long time after the War. They went back on all the promises they made to us through General Marshall. They won't accept your proposals."

"But you don't accept them either!"

Chang Han-fu broke in: "We've not said we don't accept them. We've told you that many improvements could be made. Why should we accept them in their present form when, as you can see now, they can be improved? Don't you think our suggestions are good? Then, do you think the Americans will accept them? We don't think they will. Here is fresh tea. Please let us have some."

A willowy and lovely Chinese girl had brought several pots of fresh tea and Chinese cookies. We drank the tea and turned to talk about the Chinese ballet and some new Chinese writers. Before I left I returned to my proposals. Again the Chinese talked among themselves. Ch'iao laughed in a high mocking tone. "Show it to them with the improvements we have suggested. We tell you they will say, 'No.' But we appreciate what you are trying to do. We will always discuss the matter with you." Three senior members of the delegation, led by Chang Han-fu, saw me to the front door, where another bunch of smiling, more junior Chinese waited to escort me to my car. Always they operate in groups.

A negotiation is an important matter when the United States and several other "capitalist" countries are ranged on the other side, and when Asian neutrals or nonaligned countries are present and must be duly considered. Besides, following the Mao dictum, there have to be enough members for each level in the hierarchy to hold its own discussions on the issues remitted to it. In 1954, too, their delegation at Geneva had been large and to Bandung in 1955 they took an enormous delegation. Moreover, at any conference there are times when each delegation must be represented at several simultaneous informal discussions, and to each of these the Chinese depute several diplomats. Though the major reason for this could be that it enables the delegation to function on the basis of intra-delegation discussion at each level of consideration of an issue, it certainly enables the closely knit Chinese to assure themselves that no single member has talked or otherwise behaved in ways that could embarrass his government.

The first time that Chang Han-fu informed me that he wished to come and see me I expected him to be accompanied by Ch'iao and their interpreter. I asked for tea to be set up for four—my guests and myself—in my suite at the Hotel du Rhône, but I had underestimated my Chinese guests. Six of them arrived. Fortunately the hotel responded with speed, which was to their advantage. Their small Swiss tea cakes were in great demand; several plates full were quickly devoured. The interpreter, whom now I occasionally see looking out at me from the pages of the *New York Times* as he accompanies—a pace or two behind—Chou En-lai or Ch'en Yi while they walk with a visiting head of government who uses English, especially enjoyed these Swiss delights: perhaps not a taste within the narrow sanctions of the cultural revolution, but one, that it was good to see him indulge.

In some situations there are advantages in negotiators meeting in two-man confrontations, with no one else present. In group dis-

cussion several shades of positions may emerge, and then, which are
the most important? Presumably those stressed by the leading member of the group, but, as every seasoned diplomat knows, this is not
always true. So, negotiating with a group can leave issues unclear. On
the other hand, when two negotiators have come to understand each
other's idiom and style they can explore with each other the various
nuances of the positions of their governments—to the extent that they
are permitted to do so. Each is in better control of the situation than
at group discussions, and each gives the other the important sense that
he alone is the trusted protagonist, that he alone can understand and
faithfully convey the situation to his government. The present Chinese technique is not conducive to the building of this kind of high
rapport between trusted negotiators.

Rarely, the Chinese will depart from this technique. Chou En-lai
met Jawaharlal Nehru alone, and during his visit to Ceylon in 1965
he had a tête-à-tête with Mrs. Sirimavo Bandaranaike, then Prime
Minister of Ceylon. But such meetings have been exceptions and have
not always produced the kind of results that might have been expected. Indeed, in Chou's meeting with Nehru he apparently said
things that were understood differently from the position maintained
by the Chinese regarding some issues relating to the Sino-Indian
border.[8] Perhaps the Chinese are now so attuned to the group
method of meeting that it is wiser not to meet them à deux: even a
highly skilled diplomat does not function at his best in a procedure
which he rarely uses and to which he has grown unaccustomed.

Not only does the group method of diplomacy deprive the Chinese
of the advantages of the art of diplomacy at its apogee—the deft
probing of a specific situation by a pair of diplomats—but they also
lose the benefits of a technique that contributes to the smoothing of
general relations between states. For example, the fact that the Permanent Representatives to the United Nations of two states develop
an excellent personal relationship by cultivating each other, visiting,
dining together, meeting informally in the United Nations delegates'
lounge, in their homes, and elsewhere, forges an additional link between their two states. They are even able to function as a team,
which might make valuable contributions in situations involving not

only their own countries but also others. If, however, the Permanent Representative of one of these countries were unable to visit his colleagues alone, then such close and beneficial personal terms could not develop.

At Delhi, in the period when relations with Peking were still excellent, the Chinese Ambassador was the most left out individual among the chiefs of Mission. There was great receptivity of, and interest in, China, even among those diplomats whose countries had not established diplomatic relations with the Peking government. But the spontaneous social mobility of the individual members of the large Chinese diplomatic mission was drastically restricted by the norms that had been established for them.

At the Laos Conference a long series of most delicate negotiating encounters took place in private meetings of the heads of a small group of delegations in which many of the crucial issues before the conference were talked through to agreement. For these secret sessions, to which we will return with greater specificity in later chapters, the cochairmen of the conference (the Foreign Ministers of the United Kingdom and the Soviet Union, or their deputies) had enjoined that only the heads of the selected delegations were to be in attendance. In spite of this clear injunction, from the very first meeting the Chinese delegation stuck to its own practice of representation by four diplomats and two interpreters. This encouraged one or two other delegations to resort to multiple representation at these meetings. There were also other informal gatherings of groups of delegates at which the Chinese invariably came in larger numbers than any other delegation.

On several of my visits to the Soviet cochairman it happened that a meeting of the Socialist delegations at the conference—those of China, North Vietnam, Poland, and the Soviet Union—was concluding. The large Chinese delegation that would emerge, headed by Ch'en Yi or Chang Han-fu, would itself fill two over-size Soviet limousines. Again the Chinese had been present in force, faithfully adhering to the injunctions of Mao Tse-tung.

While the Chinese diplomats retain their formation as a large group apart, which never breaks up into its individual components, they are by no means reserved or unfriendly. Within the pattern of joint action, the Chinese diplomat is generally charming, responsive, hospitable, and even approachable. I was very frequently the guest of Ch'en Yi or Chang Han-fu at their villa at Versoix near Geneva. Much exquisite Chinese food was served with liberal toasts in *mao tai,* a fiery drink that my Chinese colleagues, especially Deputy Minister Ch'iao, would urge me to swallow in one gulp—"Gambay, gambay!" (bottoms up), he would cry. Almost invariably I was the sole guest on these occasions.

In addition to these small dinners, teas, or lunches, Marshal Ch'en Yi held two large receptions to which a surprisingly large assortment of persons was invited. On each of these occasions there was an air of heightened interest, expectancy, and a certain degree of elation among the miscellany of guests. And each occasion became an informal press conference, with the members of the press corps surrounding the Marshal. He was at his most genial, thoroughly enjoying himself. He answered almost all questions at length and with immense verve. He enjoyed arguing his case with his interlocutors, but he curtly dismissed a few questions. For example, to a question on the subject of relations with the Soviet Union he replied: "The Soviet Union and China are great fraternal Socialist states. Next question, please."

CHAPTER II

The Background and Training of Chinese Negotiators

THE BACKGROUND AND TRAINING of Chinese negotiators and diplomats are of obvious interest and are relevant to an understanding of their modes of functioning in relation to the representatives of other countries.

To begin with, the Chinese negotiators are all avowedly members of the Chinese Communist Party, and they are more open about this affiliation than their Russian and Eastern European counterparts. Of course, one assumes and correctly so, that the leaders and most members of Soviet and Eastern European delegations to political negotiations are members of the Communist Party, but they seldom mention the fact. Indeed, less senior members of such delegations have been known to deny membership in the Party—though this could be a tactical gambit in an attempt to get an interlocutor, especially if from the West, to feel that he or she can talk frankly. However, it is asserted that sometimes non-Communist diplomats are attached to the delegations of Soviet and Eastern European countries.

The Chinese delegate, on the other hand, tends to say with pride: "I am a Communist." Certainly at the Laos Conference Chang Han-fu and his colleagues frequently professed their political beliefs to me without any element of reserve.

Not a great deal is known about the training of Chinese diplomats in general, but it can safely be assumed that the basic training of Chinese negotiators includes what is prescribed for members of the Chinese Communist Party cadres. An insight into the training of cadres is provided by the *New Phrases Dictionary,* published in Shanghai in 1951 and 1954, which in the 1954 edition defines "cadre" as follows:

Cadre: generally speaking, it means a worker in a state institution. Persons who work in state institutions or a department of production, capable of unifying and leading the masses to carry out Party and government policies and directives, to implement duties and programs promptly under the leadership of the Party and higher-level government institutions are cadres.

. . . the cadre must possess revolutionary character and revolutionary working manner, be capable of cementing ties with the masses and taking the lead actively. In other words he must be capable of being the tutor of the masses and in turn being the pupil of the masses.[1]

As Franz Schurmann puts it, a cadre has to be both "expert" and "red." The combination of qualities is an uneasy one, and during the last decade and a half the "reds" and "experts" have competed for leadership in economic affairs,[2] and, more recently, in political affairs.

The training of Chinese Communist cadres is impressively thorough. Enormous emphasis is placed on the need to "study," and this study is both systematic and practical.[3] Much of it is arranged through programs of in-service education of cadres. The general framework for these programs was established by a Central Committee resolution in 1942, which states: "The sphere of in-service cadre education should include professional, political, cultural, and theoretical education." Professional education to attain on-the-job proficiency is stated to be "the primary task in education and study." Professional Party education covers the following five areas of study: (1) investigation and research relating to the assigned duties; (2) research on the relevant Party polices, regulations, directives, and resolutions; (3) research on concrete experiences arising in the work of the relevant department; (4) research on the historical background of each department's work; and (5) research on the scientific principles pertinent to a full knowledge of each department's work.[4]

Political education focuses not only on theoretical works on Communism and Marxism but also on the attainment of proficiency in the

writing of political reports and articles. Cultural studies, the third element in cadre education, covers some areas of what we would call the
field of humanities together with such additions as "New Democratic
Culture." Theoretical education is directed toward a study of Marxism-Leninism, the philosophy of dialectics and historical materialism,
political economy, and "Scientific Communism." This part of the
study is based on extensive readings from the original texts of Marx
and Lenin, of course in Chinese translation. In general, the objective
is to instruct the Chinese Communist cadre members in accordance
with Liu Shao-ch'i's dictum in the 1962 edition of *How to be a Good
Communist,* which says: "We Communist Party Members cannot
divorce theoretical study from ideological cultivation. We must re-
form ourselves and steel our proletarian ideology not only in revolutionary practice but also in the study of Marxist-Leninist theory." [5]

We must assume that the Chinese negotiators have all received, as
a basic training, this four-part education as cadre members.

Though the Chinese Communist Party has gone to some pains to
avoid the development of a party composed too largely of the intelligentsia, a situation that prevailed for some time in the Soviet Union,
the leaders of the delegation to the Laos Conference were almost entirely from this stratum of Chinese society. Marshal Ch'en Yi, the
Minister of Foreign Affairs of the Peking government and vice
premier of the State Council,[6] was educated partly in Paris in the
early twenties. Before that he had gone to a university in China and
pursued an interest in classical poetry. Immediately on his arrival at
Geneva for the Laos Conference, Ch'en Yi visited the grave of Vol-
taire and as a tribute to the French philosopher he wrote a poem in
the Chinese classical manner. This done, he turned his attention to
the mundane affairs of the conference. This elegant gesture to the
memory of a great intellectual could come only from one who himself
was steeped in an intellectual tradition.

Immediately after his return from Paris, Ch'en Yi joined the Communist Party of China and his career in it was largely in the military
and ideological fields. In 1928 he was appointed secretary of the
Army Party Committee.[7] In the same year he was elected to the Second Special Committee of nineteen members of the Communist

Party, and sat alongside Mao Tse-tung and Chu Teh. At the beginning of 1941 he was appointed acting Commander of the new Fourth Army.[8] On November 16, 1948, the Communists appointed a General Front Committee to meet the needs of the crucial Huai-Hai campaign of the civil war. Ch'en Yi was one of five members of this committee, with Teng Hsiao-p'ing as secretary. Thus Ch'en Yi, an intellectual and something of a poet, has also had an outstanding career as a military leader in China.

Chang Han-fu, the senior vice minister of Foreign Affairs and Ch'en Yi's deputy at the Laos Conference, went through the Tsinghua University in Peking and then came to the United States, where he did graduate work at Columbia. His early professional career was mostly that of a newspaper editor. There is an interesting point of coincidence in the backgrounds of two delegates at the Laos Conference. When Chang Han-fu was serving as the head of the Department of Foreign Affairs of the Shanghai Military Control Commission in 1949, Ambassador Chester Ronning (who was deputy to Foreign Minister Howard Green at the Laos Conference), then a less senior Canadian Diplomat, applied to Chang for his permit to leave China, and Chang granted the permission and facilitated Ronning's departure. The two met again twelve years later at the Laos Conference.

The third member of the Chinese delegation was Ch'iao Kuan-hua. Ch'iao, too, is a member of the educated intelligentsia. His knowledge of Western languages is fairly good but not as great as that of Chang. However, his many conversations with me were rich with indications of a well-educated and cultivated person. Another prominent member of the Chinese delegation was Wang Ping-nan, then Chinese Ambassador to Poland and now a vice minister of Foreign Affairs. Wang is rather a dour man and is very much an intellectual. Huan Hsiang, then Chargé d'Affaires at London and for some time a student at the London School of Economics, was also a member of the delegation. Since a great deal of work was done in English, he helped on the drafting committee. Again, Huan is an intellectual but unlike Wang was always cheerful and often ebullient. The two interpreters —Ch'en, the senior one who came and went with Marshal Ch'en Yi, and Chi, the younger one who ate so many Swiss cakes—were both

Harvard men. The secretary-general of the delegation was a man whose education was entirely Chinese. He smiled affably and his demeanor was always friendly, but he said little and I was unable to form any impression as to whether his background was patrician or working-class. There were at least two members of the delegation who could speak Hindi.

Chang Han-fu and Ch'iao Kuan-hua are married to formidably intellectual sisters, Kung P'u-sheng and Kung P'eng, respectively. Both are graduates of Chinese universities and the former also studied abroad, receiving an M.A. from Columbia University. Both are prominent figures in the Foreign Ministry itself and Kung P'u has served on the executive council of the All China Democratic Women's Federation. These accomplished, charming, and intellectual women were present at Geneva for the Laos Conference with their husbands.

Though we are able to learn a fair amount about the basic background and training of Foreign Service officers in their capacity as members of the Communist Party of China, little is known about the additional training given them specifically for their duties as diplomats. However, some facts have come to us from a Chinese Foreign Service officer who defected in 1964. Tung Chi-p'ing left his post at Bujumbura, the capital of Burundi in Central Africa, in May 1964. In his article in *Look* of December 1964, Tung stated that he had received his higher education at the Institute of Foreign Languages at Shanghai, where he studied for four years. He said that he worked hard at the Institute but there was no formal graduation because this form of certification is regarded in modern China as a bourgeois affectation. However, he did have to pass a series of examinations. Tung's case does not give us enough information for general classifications. We may note, however, that he does not appear to have received special training in subversion or even in wooing foreigners.

The kind of training that Tung received, while it gives us some indication of the education provided for young men and women entering the Foreign Service, does not necessarily throw any light on the background of the present generation of Chinese negotiators at various international conferences. Ch'en Yi, Chang Han-fu, Wang Ping-nan, Ch'iao Kuan-hua, Huan Hsiang, Li Ch'ing-ch'üan (the Chinese

Ambassador at Bern and a member of the delegation to the Laos Conference), and Ch'en, the senior interpreter who was also a senior counselor in the Foreign Ministry, were all men who had received a more or less conventional education plus undoubtedly a thorough grounding in Marxism-Leninism-Maoism, with little or no special training in foreign affairs. The impression left with me after two or three scores of private meetings with the Chinese delegates was that they were much more interested in China internally, Chinese economic development, Chinese cultural movements, and China's relations with some of her immediate neighbors, than in international affairs as a whole. Of course, to this catalogue of interest certainly must be added their constant preoccupation with the policies of the United States, particularly in Asia.

The above tentative conclusion of a very strong China-ward orientation is borne out by an interesting fact Chang Han-fu revealed to me. He said (and we must remember that all these statements were made in the presence of at least four of his colleagues) that normally cabinet ministers, vice ministers, and other senior officers of the Ministry of Foreign Affairs at Peking are required to spend four months each year in the countryside, where they work among the people. This four-month period far from the governmental machinery at Peking is not a continuous one, though. The practice is to go out to the country to work on rural problems several or even many times a year so as to fulfill the quota of four months. Clearly the effect of this system on members of the Foreign Office must be profound. In particular, it makes them grapple directly with the internal problems of China and probably gives those problems a greater reality than the generally much more theoretical issues of China's foreign policies and programs.

Much more than this cannot yet be said about the molding of the Peking government's diplomats, or about the details of their functions and their place in the governmental system. Our knowledge about that system itself is meager. Franz Schurmann says:

Though we know the general structure of government, it is often difficult to say how structure and function are related. . . . Nevertheless, by making inferences from scattered evidence and by comparison with Soviet government, on which the state administration of Communist China is modeled, one can gain a general idea of the workings of government and of the main administrative trends.[9]

Lack of knowledge and the natural tendency to apply preconceived norms might well explain some of the conjectures regarding China. Thus, certain sections of the press may report, on a prominent Chinese leader, something such as this: "X has not been seen or heard of in Peking for the last three months. Has he fallen from favor? Who has taken his place? Does this denote a rise in the influence of Y and Z?" Frequently these speculations may be misplaced because the Chinese leader X could be in the country doing a large part of his annual stint of rural work!

Chinese journals and spokesmen keep to themselves the intricacies of their governmental system. However, in spite of our lack of full knowledge we are able to point to certain basic characteristics of the Chinese negotiator. He is well educated and highly trained to analyze situations and events in terms of practical Chinese Marxism, and in this sense he is a staunch Communist. He also is generally prone to analyze whenever confronted with an issue; he is highly China-oriented—often jingoistically so—and is fundamentally more concerned about the needs and aspirations of China than anything else. Since he has not yet developed a realistic world perspective, it is easier for him, drawing on his brand of revolutionary Marxism, to prescribe the course which he believes the world should and ultimately will follow. Some of these characteristics will alter when China comes fully into contact with the world through all the channels that now exist, including primarily the large complex of international organizations which has come into being in our era.

CHAPTER III

The General Approach and Attitude
of Communist China
toward International Negotiation

THE GENERAL ATTITUDE of the Chinese Communist government toward international negotiation has not, as far as can be ascertained,
been set down in one pronouncement or directive. It is to be gleaned
from a number of wide-ranging authoritative statements contained in
Mao Tse-tung's writings and other documents extending through
Marshal Lin Piao's article, "Long Live the Victory of the People's
War" in September 1965. Thereafter arrives the confusing period of
the wide variety of statements made in connection with the "Great
Proletarian Cultural Revolution" of 1966–1967, which it is premature to assess. We will look at the basic Chinese approaches, through
1965, under two headings: (1) philosophical principles and ideological directives, and (2) views on processes of negotiation.

*Philosophical Principles and Ideological Directives Bearing on Inter-
national Negotiations and Relations*
    Marxism-Leninism as interpreted by Mao is the basic philosophi-
cal framework in which the Chinese negotiator functions. How, then,
does the Chinese negotiator regard Marxism-Leninism? In the first
place he must necessarily accept Mao's dictum that "it is definitely
not doctrinairism but Marxism-Leninism to regard Marxist-Leninist
theories and principles as a guide to revolutionary action but not as
dogmas." [1] This thought has been frequently repeated by Mao and

has been referred to by other Chinese Communist authorities. Ch'en Po-ta in his work entitled *Mao Tse-tung on the Chinese Revolution* tells us that Mao's writings are the crystallization for China, both ideological and theoretical, of the Russian October Socialist Revolution and also a crystallization of the dynamic power of Marxism-Leninism. This Chinese Marxist illustrates that dynamic power by the following citation from Lenin:

We do not regard Marx's theory as something final and inviolable; on the contrary, we are convinced that it has only laid the cornerstones of the science which Socialists must advance in all directions if they do not want to lag behind the march of life. We think that an independent elaboration of Marx's theory is especially necessary for Russian Socialists, since this theory provides only general guiding principles which, in particular, are to be applied differently to England than to France, differently to France than to Germany, differently to Germany than to Russia.[2]

And, he stresses, Mao had applied Marxism differently to China.

A more recent statement of the Chinese attitude toward Marxism appears in Mao Tse-tung's well-known speech of February 27, 1957, "On the Correct Handling of Contradictions Among the People." Mao says:

People may ask: since Marxism is accepted by the majority of our people in the country as the guiding ideology, can it be criticized? Certainly it can. . . . Marxists should not be afraid of criticism from any quarter. . . . Plants raised in hot-houses are not likely to be robust. Carrying out the policy of letting a hundred flowers blossom and a hundred schools of thought contend will not weaken but strengthen the leading position of Marxism in the ideological field.[3]

However, this dictum is, as we knew, not fully translatable into reality within the actualities of the Chinese system. But it would probably be incorrect to argue, from the sad end to which the policy of letting a hundred flowers blossom came, that the principle of internal criticism, within this Communist hierarchy, is entirely inoperative.

A major difficulty in assessing Chinese attitudes arises from the fact that, steeped in Mao's thinking, the Chinese leaders appear to have accepted the fundamental role of contradictions in every sphere of life, policy, and action. Though we see on the one hand a relaxed

attitude toward the tenets of Marxism-Leninism, there are at the
same time very much in operation the contradictions of fears, intoler-
ance of any form of revisionism or deviations from what Mao himself
has come to regard as orthodox Marxism-Leninism.

This point of the ambiguity of the fundamental role of theory be-
devils all attempts to understand fully the precise nature of the current Chinese stance both in internal affairs and in regard to international affairs and Chinese foreign policy.

For example, what precisely do the Chinese mean by coexistence
between states? On the face of it, Chinese adherence to the concept
has been stated clearly enough. Thus, in the important letter sent on
June 14, 1963, by the Central Committee of the Chinese Communist
Party to the Central Committee of the Soviet Communist Party, the
Chinese said: "Since its founding, the People's Republic of China,
too, has consistently pursued the policy of peaceful coexistence with
countries having different social systems, and it is China which initiated the Five Principles of Peaceful Coexistence." [4] Yet, "coexistence" is a severely limited concept for the Chinese. The same important letter goes on to state: "In the application of the policy of peaceful coexistence, struggles between the Socialist and imperialist countries are unavoidable in the political, economic, and ideological
spheres, and it is absolutely impossible to have 'all-round cooperation.' " [5]

What then is the scope of peaceful coexistence, as the Chinese envisage this concept in its applications to international life? The same
letter of the Chinese Party throws some light on this question:

The application of the policy of peaceful coexistence by the Socialist
countries is advantageous for achieving a peaceful international environ-
ment for Socialist construction, for exposing the imperialist policies of
aggression and war and for isolating the imperialist forces of aggression
and war. . . . It is wrong to make peaceful coexistence the general line
of the foreign policy of the Socialist countries. In our view the general
line of the foreign policy of the Socialist countries should have the following content: . . . to strive for peaceful coexistence on the basis of
the Five Principles with countries having different social systems and oppose the imperialist policies of aggression and war; and to support and
assist the revolutionary struggles of all the oppressed peoples and nations.[6]

Thus, while there is to be coexistence, there are two important sets of caveats (or contradictions). First, "Imperialist policies of aggression and war" are to be opposed. The question arises, what is an imperialist policy? For example, is extensive aid to an Asian or African country by the United States an imperialist policy of economic aggression? The answer is that the Chinese leaders at Peking consider that it is for them to decide whether this is so or not. The second important caveat is that the general line of the foreign policy of the Socialist countries must support and assist the revolutionary struggles of oppressed peoples and nations. Who decides which peoples are oppressed? Again, the answer is that the Chinese leaders decide.

It would seem, then, that in the matter of coexistence too the Chinese faithfully stick to their dogma of the existence of contradictions. In practical terms there can be simultaneously both coexistence with an entirely different system of society and bitter opposition to a form of society that is trying to develop along Socialist lines. Thus, the Chinese Communist government was aiding the government of the Imam of Yemen and was constructing roads and a harbor in that country. There was nothing in common between the Chinese Communist regime and the theocratic regime in Yemen; nevertheless, considerable cooperation had been instituted.

Similarly there is close cooperation with Pakistan, and assistance, both military and economic, is given to it although the systems of government and society in Pakistan and China are dissimilar, and all Communists in the former state are in jail. After Premier Chou En-lai's visit to Rawalpindi at the end of June 1966, the *Agence France-Presse* reported that the Chinese Premier had given his host, Marshal Ayub Khan, the assurance that China, holding to the principle of "not exporting revolution," will never create difficulties for the regime of the Pakistan president; i.e., it will not assist in "revolutionary struggles" of Communists or others in spite of the general line of support or assistance for such struggles proclaimed by the Central Committee of the Chinese Party. Furthermore, the French News Agency adds that Premier Chou did not raise any objections to Pakistan's continued adherence to CENTO and SEATO.[7] The cooperation between Pakistan and China seems to reach the dimensions of a virtual military agreement so that pratically Pakistan is now in the interesting position of being in military alliance with Communist China on the one hand, and the United States and other Western states on the other. From the point of view of China's otherwise seemingly rigid concepts this represents a flexibility in the implementation of policy which few states can rival.

On the other hand, in regard to Yugoslavia, a Socialist state, and India, which deems itself to be advancing along the road to Socialism (but democratically, in the Westminster sense of the word), the Chinese and their close friends make accusations such as these:

The big bourgeois-landlord government of India has not only mortgaged India's economy, independence and sovereignty to the imperialists . . . it has, in fact, made close alliance with the more reactionary regimes in Asia, e.g., the Japanese militarists, Chiang Kai-shek gangsters, "Malaysian" neo-colonialists and the right-reactionary forces in Indonesia, in order to serve the U.S. imperialist global strategy of world domination.[8]

Again we see an arbitrary decision by the Chinese leaders that India, whatever may be the nature of its government, is reactionary and therefore there is no room for coexistence with it. Facts play only a subsidiary role in this conclusion, as is clear from the so-called facts in the citation above. For example, though relations between Pakistan and Indonesia are closer, more varied, and more cooperative than those of India and Indonesia, it is India that is castigated for her close relations with Indonesia while Pakistan is accepted as a country with which coexistence is to be practiced in the highest degree, and there is no derogatory mention of her relations with Indonesia.[9]

Another example of a major contradiction in foreign policy is furnished by Peking's oft-repeated insistence on the solidarity of the Socialist countries, on the one hand, and its sharp and uncompromising denunciation, on the other hand, of the policies of the Soviet government and Yugoslavia, which surely cannot assist in achieving "relations of friendship, mutual assistance and cooperation among the countries in the socialist camp in accordance with the principle of proletarian internationalism." [10]

Regarding the effect that contradictions have on action, Mao Tsetung has declared that there is a distinction between contradictions with "the enemy" and those among the people. Contradictions among the people can be resolved by peaceful means; however, contradictions with the enemy are another matter.

A line must be drawn "between us and our enemies," says Mao, but, "among the people" matters can be resolved by "distinguishing between right and wrong." [11] "The enemy" today is an imperialist (e.g., the United States), or a revisionist (all the Communist states that think differently from Peking), or a reactionary (e.g., India and Japan), but not friendly states, whatever the political, social, or economic forms they encourage or prohibit. The decision on which countries are enemies is made in Peking, as is also the category of enemy to which individual states are to be relegated.

These decisions, though in one sense arbitrary, are also in another sense based on considerations much deeper than the tenets of the reigning ideology at Peking. Those considerations are China's security, vital interests, and the image that Peking is creating of China's place in the community of nations, taking into account her characteristics, both real and potential, as a great power. With a number of smaller countries in her neighborhood (e.g., Burma, Cambodia, Ceylon, Nepal, Pakistan, and Afghanistan) China has developed and assiduously cultivated close and cooperative relations. On the other hand, with the bigger powers in her neighborhood—those which she regards as potential or real rivals, such as the Soviet Union, Japan, and India—her relations have steadily deteriorated as her own power on the mainland has appeared to grow.

The facts indicate that, philosophical tenets notwithstanding, a basic attitude among the Chinese leaders is to decry, denigrate, and, if possible, humiliate countries that are rivaling, or may rival, China in Asia. Of the smaller countries in Asia (e.g., Thailand and the Philippines), she castigates only those that have close and operative alliances with the United States and therefore are, in a sense, a projection in Asia of the great power of the United States.

At times some Sinologists, while quite correctly emphasizing emulation of China's past position in Asia as an important motivation in her present desire to regain international importance, have somewhat overstated China's historic role in Asia. The impression is sometimes given that China was the center of Asia. While this was certainly so in regard to Eastern Asia and parts of Southeast Asia, it was never so, throughout a recorded history of several thousand years, in regard to the vast population (as great, if not greater than that of China) and the great territory of South Asia. Indeed, in Asia it was India that was the purveyor to China not only of Buddhism but of her metaphysics and epistemology.[12] Moreover, politically there was, of course, never any tribute paid by the Indian system to the Chinese.

Indeed, has there not been a certain degree of misunderstanding of the nature and the implication of the so-called tribute payments to important personages in Asia? It is traditional for a lesser ruler in Asia to show his respect for an obviously more powerful ruler or personage by offering him expensive gifts. It is not only the feudatories, let us say, of the Maharana of Udaipur who would offer such gifts to their overlord. Presentations would also be made to him by other neighboring independent chiefs because of the general standing of Udaipur in Rajasthan. Such payments did not establish Udaipur as the overlord of all other states in Rajasthan. To take a different kind of example, when Sir Thomas Roe came to India as the Ambassador of James I of England, at the beginning of the seventeenth century, he brought expensive presents, including jewelry and gold, for the Moghul Emperor at Delhi. These gifts were regarded as "nazarana" or tribute. It would have been expected of Sir Thomas Roe to make such gifts periodically and indeed he did so, even with some regularity. The average Moghul courtier would of course have regarded such gifts as constituting, in some sense, evidence of the supreme authority and power of the Moghul Emperor over the British Queen. However, not too much emphasis should be placed on such courtly demonstrations in assessing the real political relationships of states in Asia.

Nevertheless, they may be said to create a certain historic pattern, which, in our time with the spread of the idea of equal sovereign states, carries over as a certain degree of expectation of friendly relations without, of course, any presentation of gifts or so-called tribute. In this sense China has expectations in certain parts of Asia. Moreover, she has deftly turned to her own advantage the major aftermath of British imperial policy in South Asia.[13] It is apparent that in condemning the Tashkent Agreement and in general encouraging animosity between Pakistan and India, the Peking government is following a policy of acting to promote what it regards as its own national interests in Asia.

At the same time, the leaders in Peking are well aware of the susceptibilities of the modern nation state. It would not be in China's national interest to make it a general practice to flout these susceptibilities. And Peking realizes that it would be unwise and inappropriate to continue, in this era, traditional Asian symbols of hierarchies among states. China is generally punctilious in her relations with many of the smaller Asian countries and takes great pains to avoid any indication of interference in their internal affairs. Of course, excluded from this benign treatment are those states in Asia that have allied themselves with the United States or are clearly associated with the Soviet Union, such as Mongolia, as well as certain larger states, such as India, Japan, and now Indonesia.

Here again the Chinese philosophy of contradiction intrudes. Chinese leaders often talk in terms of Asian solidarity, but Chinese policies do not promote such soldiarity. Her leaders would respond to such a charge by saying that those Asian countries which are under the influence of non-Asian powers (the United States, the Soviet Union) are no longer to be treated as Asian states. In this category she arbitrarily places all countries in Asia of which she does not approve. Presumably these states are, to the Peking government, examples of a contradiction of the present trend in Asia of throwing off imperialism and neocolonialism.

If the theory of contradictions constitutes a major difficulty in identifying a stable philosophical basis for China's international relations, another major philosophical difficulty is posed by the problem of semantics. What exactly does the Chinese leadership mean when it affirms that China supports unconditionally the Indonesian Communists or the struggles of the people of the Congo (Leopoldville)? [14] Indeed, what is meant by the phrase that the People's Republic of China "firmly support[s] the revolutionary struggles of all oppressed peoples and nations, and resolutely opposes great-power chauvinism and national egoism." [15] Again, what do the Chinese mean when they state "should United States imperialism dare to attack China, either on a limited scale or in full strength, the only result will be total annihilation of United States aggressors." [16] Frequently the Chinese refer to the annihilation of their enemies or the enemies of their friends.

Let us examine the two Chinese concepts of "firm support" and "annihilation." One of the fullest of Peking's recent statements on foreign policy is contained in the lengthy Joint Statement issued by Chou En-lai and Mehmet Shehu when the Albanian leader visited Peking in May 1966. We have already referred to the staunch support this statement affirms for certain sections of the people in Indonesia and Africa. It does likewise for "the people of the Dominican Republic, Peru, Colombia, Guatemala and Venezuela in their armed struggle for national liberation." [17] But, in point of fact, in spite of these strong words, the Chinese have not given any tangible support to the Indonesian Communists. They stood by and let several hundred thousand such Indonesians be massacred. It is also extremely doubtful that any form of tangible Chinese support is given to the people of Venezuela. In the same Joint Statement the Chinese speak of their firm support for "the American people's struggle against the Johnson Administration's aggression in Vietnam; they firmly support the American Negroes' struggle against racial discrimination and for freedom and equal rights." [18] There is probably no tangible Chinese assistance coming to groups in the United States. Thus, the word "support" in many cases, when used by the Peking government, seems to mean more "moral" than any other form of support.

The word "annihilation" seemingly has a very important place in Maoism. Mao's own early writings often speak of annihilating the enemy. An inner-party directive issued by him on September 16, 1946, entitled "Concentrate a Superior Force to Destroy the Enemy Forces One by One," states, "The effects of this method of fighting [concentration of a superior force] are first, complete annihilation, and second, quick decision." [19] Mao goes on to state that "only complete annihilation can deal the most telling blows to the enemy, for when we wipe out one regiment, he will have one regiment less, and when we wipe out one brigade, he will have one brigade less." [20]

These clear statements create unambiguously the impression that by annihilation Mao means complete destruction of the enemy; and this would also be the normal meaning of the word in the context in which it is used by Mao. However, immediately after the portion of the directive cited, Mao goes on to state, "Only complete annihilation can replenish our own forces to the greatest possible extent. It is now not only the main source of our arms and ammunition but also an important source of our man-power." [21]

Thus, while we were led to believe that by annihilation Mao Tse-tung meant complete physical destruction (the wiping out of the enemy), a twist in the meaning occurs (perhaps this is another contradiction!) and we learn that annihilation is more akin to complete alteration of the nature of the enemy so that he may be brought into the Maoist fold. This analysis does not suggest that the Maoist meaning of the word "annihilation" makes the process in any way an acceptable one; however, it brings out the important point that the meaning given by Maoism to the word is not the meaning normally associated with it.

When it comes to the statements of leaders other than Mao, the shifting nature of the meanings of key words tends to increase, thereby aggravating the semantic problem in understanding China's basic attitudes in international affairs. A case in point is the much discussed Lin Piao article entitled "Long Live the Victory of the People's War." [22] Secretary of State Dean Rusk referred to this article in the following terms:

This strategy involves the mobilization of the underdeveloped areas of the world—which the Chinese Communists compare to the "rural" areas—against the industrialized or "urban" areas. It involves the relentless prosecution of what they call "people's wars." The final stage of all this violence is to be what they frankly describe as "wars of annihilation."

It is true that this doctrine calls for revolution by the "natives" of each country. In that sense it may be considered a "do-it-yourself kit." [23]

This statement was made after several distinguished scholars had thrown some light on Lin Piao's meaning. Professor Doak Barnett, in answering questions following his statement at the hearings before the

Senate Committee on Foreign Relations on March 8, 1966, had suggested that the article told revolutionaries in other countries to be self-reliant and not to rely on concrete external support. He added, "I think, in effect, one thing they are saying to the Vietnamese in this speech was 'this is an important revolution, keep it up, but you have got to do it yourself essentially.' " [24]

Shortly after the Secretary of State's statement, another scholar, Professor Donald Zagoria, told the Senate Committee the following about Lin Piao's statement: "Far from giving notice of any intention to intervene aggressively, Lin Piao is rationalizing Peking's unwillingness to go to the aid of the Vietcong, in a struggle which—let there be no doubt—the Chinese Communists regard as just and which is taking place on their very borders." [25]

What precisely does Lin Piao mean? The Secretary of State has seen in his words a strategy that involves the relentless prosecution of "people's wars." He also sees in it a do-it-yourself formula. These two elements in the Lin Piao statement, though not exactly incompatible, verge on the Chinese penchant for contradiction. How can there be a really relentless war against those in power if relatively unarmed people are left to do it themselves? Professor Zagoria points out that even when there is such a "people's war" on their very borders, and when the Chinese regard it as an entirely just war, they still find hortative rationalizations for refusing to extend any significant tangible assistance. Indeed, Lin Piao himself is unclear about the nature of Chinese support and assistance. In an important paragraph on what China will do, he says that in revolutionary wars waged by oppressed peoples China invariably gives "firm support and active aid." Then, as if to correct the impression that China will go headlong in assisting revolutionary peoples in their wars, he says, "Every revolution in a country stems from the demands of its own people," and revolution cannot be imported. Immediately after this statement Lin Piao sums up his sermon on aid by stating: "But this does not exclude mutual sympathy and support on the part of the revolutionary peoples in their struggle against the imperialists and their lackeys. Our support and aid to other revolutionary peoples serves precisely to help their self-reliant struggle." [26] Starting from the concept of active aid, Lin Piao seems to slip to mutual sympathy coupled with an undefined form of support, and his position is left swinging between the two poles of a contradiction.

Stated another way, the poles of contradiction obviously allow for considerable flexibility in Chinese foreign policy, even though the starting point might often look menacingly firm. It is this flexibility that allows China, in spite of seemingly uncompromising barrages of words, to negotiate on certain international issues. We will see this phenomenon at work when we examine the course of events in the long negotiations on Laos in 1961–1962.

The negative or intransigent pole may be regarded as a psychological haven to which the Chinese leaders can retreat when international situations are not being resolved in some manner acceptable to them. Indeed, we find evidence of this in the Great Socialist Cultural Revolution of 1966–1967. Having seen several recent setbacks to movements they favored, e.g., those in Indonesia and Ghana, and, somewhat earlier, the defeat of the Bandaranaike government in Ceylon, the Chinese have tended at home to retreat to a very hard position. Thus, an important editorial in *Chieh-fang-chün pao* (*Liberation Army Daily*), dated July 7, 1966, states, "In the sharp clash between the two world outlooks, either you crush me, or I crush you." [27] The editorial goes on to say, and this is a departure from more sober Chinese thinking, which lies nearer the other pole:

Mao Tse-tung's thought . . . is also a powerful invincible weapon of the revolutionary people the world over . . . once the world's people master Mao Tse-tung's thought, which is living Marxism-Leninism, they are sure to win their emancipation, bury imperialism, modern revisionism and all reactionaries lock, stock and barrel, and realize communism throughout the world step by step.[28]

These sentiments might be described by the Chinese themselves as chauvinism, in their more sober moments when they look at issues from nearer their other pole.

What, I believe, emerges from a consideration of the spectrum of meanings between the poles of Maoist thinking is that we must be careful not to draw conclusions from looking exclusively at those words that cluster around one or the other pole. We must not expect to find fixed and verifiable meanings even in seemingly rigid statements. That applies whatever the direction of such statements. Statements which may reasonably be construed to mean that China would not intervene in a particular war must be read alongside statements that tend to give the opposite meaning. In practice, Peking's "aid" may become tangible as it did in the Korean War or it may remain exasperatingly threatening or tangible only to the extent of being pin-pricking as it was in the Indo-Pakistani conflict of 1965. This faculty that Peking has developed, of using the same words to cover a long spectrum of meanings, adds considerably to the difficulty of negotiation with China. One fundamental factor in negotiation is the need to discover the minimal requirements of each party to the negotiation. In the case of Peking it is especially difficult to make this discovery. It is a closely guarded secret. However, if Peking desires agreement, at the opportune moment the secret will be revealed.

Another attitude that is relevant in connection with negotiating with China is the Maoist doctrine that there is no middle road. This doctrine has, I believe, come to be stated with more and more clarity and yet, at any rate in the short term, it is difficult to see that Chinese actions match the doctrine. The editorial of the *Liberation Army Daily* cited above states plainly, "It will not do to sit on the fence; there is no middle road." [29]

But it is important to see how this doctrine has developed and been put into practice. One of Mao's earliest statements on this matter was contained in a major article entitled "On New Democracy," with which he initiated, in January 1940, a new publication entitled *Chinese Culture*. He said:

In the international situation of today, the "heroes" in the colonies and semi-colonies must either stand on the side of the imperialist front and become part of the force of world counter-revolution or stand on the side of the anti-imperialist front and become part of the force of world revolution. They must stand either on this side or the other, for there is no third choice.[30]

In this statement Mao takes a specific situation, that which exists in the colonies and the semi-colonial world, and he tells those who aspire to national leadership to decide whether they are for or against colonialism. This challenge has not been unusual. Time and again in India, during its struggle for independence, there took place a separation of the real national leaders, such as those in the Congress Party, from those who called themselves "Liberals" and who seemed willing to temporize and compromise with the British. To those who espoused the national struggle, the liberals appeared to be searching for an impossible third way.

However, farther on in his article "On New Democracy," Mao Tse-tung found another and wider application for this doctrine:

As the conflict between the socialist Soviet Union and the imperialist powers becomes further intensified, it is inevitable that China must stand either on one side or on the other. Is it possible to incline to neither side? No, this is an illusion. All the countries in the world will be swept into one or the other of these two camps, and in the world today "neutrality" is becoming merely a deceptive phrase.[31]

Here, again, let us note that a special confrontation is the starting premise: the conflict between the Soviet Union and the "imperialist" powers. But what happens when this first premise shifts, as is now the case? What happens when, on July 19, 1966, "Commentator" says in *Renmin Ribao:* "Vice-Premier Ch'en Yi exposed the U.S.-Soviet collusion," [32] and toward the end of the comment the writer says of the alleged joint efforts of the United States and the Soviet Union to set up peace talks on Vietnam, "although this duet has proved a flop because you [the Soviet Union] exposed and disgraced yourselves, it nevertheless seems that you are not reconciled to its failure and will continue to make other efforts." [33]

In short, according to the Chinese, Soviet-American confrontation is being replaced by cooperation and collusion. In this Chinese view Mao's first premise disappears. Indeed, Chinese wrath with the Soviet Union is undoubtedly all the greater because the Soviets are, in their eyes, making it possible for other countries to adopt not only a third way, but a fourth, a fifth, and an *n*th way. The more this becomes possible the more strident become Chinese criticisms of the Soviets and, simultaneously, in an attempt to strengthen their own determination, the more unconditional becomes the Chinese doctrine of "no third choice." This explains the forthright all-encompassing statement made in June 1966 in *Chieh-fang-chün pao.* When an *ex cathedra* policy is handed down the line, it tends to crystallize and become even more dogmatic than it was when enunciated by its creator. As early as 1948 Liu Shao-ch'i wrote, "American imperialism has become the bastion of all the reactionary forces of the world; while the Soviet Union has become the bastion of all progressive forces . . . these two camps include *all the people of the world*—of all countries, classes, sections of the population, parties and groups." [34] This statement by Liu Shao-ch'i goes so far in its adherence to Mao's more restrictive doctrine (at that time) that it expresses itself in terms of the kind of hyperbole that tends to flourish in a hierarchical society, and Communist China has continued, though in unfamiliar guise, to be such a society.

Though the doctrine of "no third choice" continues to be sounded, it is difficult to believe that the top leadership considers the doctrine to correspond with the present facts of various kinds of polycentrism in the world situation. And, indeed, even before the loosening of bloc ties was as clear as it is today, when pressed on such issues the answer of fairly important Chinese Communist leaders has not accorded with some of the uncompromising formulations of the doctrine.

For example, I asked Chang Han-fu, the orthodoxy of whose Communist credentials cannot be doubted, whether, in the Chinese view, a country such as Sweden that has evolved a system containing a high degree of social security and other Socialist characteristics would one day undergo a Communist revolution and become Communist. Instead of saying, as I expected him to, that the day would come when this would be so, he replied: "This is a matter which the Swedish people must decide entirely for themselves." I pressed him further: "But I suppose you feel that they will see how much better your system is and will voluntarily adopt it?" Again he said that this was entirely a matter for the Swedish people. Then I asked whether, in the Chinese view, the countries of Asia would, on seeing the successes of China and learning of its state of development, choose the Chinese Communist way. Again his reply was: "This too is a matter entirely for decision by the people of the countries concerned." I then asked an omnibus question: "Do you, then, believe that the example of China and other Communist countries will lead non-Communist countries to choose Communism?" He replied: "This too is for those countries to decide." My final question was: "Will there be violent revolutions in all these countries leading them to Communism?" Chang Han-fu's reply was: "That too is for them to decide. We do not believe in exporting our revolution."

Of course, we must not interpret these remarks of Chang Han-fu as indicating that he does not adhere to other basic tenets of Communist doctrine such as the inevitability of the spread of Communism. What his remarks probably imply is that for fairly long periods to come there will be, in practice, other choices open to the nations of the world, which means that for a while there are third, fourth, etc., choices open to them. Of course, in regard to the inevitability of the historic process, it is not only Communism that has believed in the ultimate universal spread of its own doctrine. Several prominent religious creeds for long periods of time have upheld the same basic philosophy. What is important is how those who hold these philosophies of inevitability act in their relations with those who think or believe differently.

Are the Chinese willing to act differently while maintaining their position that Communism (of their own brand) must inevitably win? In brief, are they willing to seek viable compromises with the rest of the world? On this question the facts must speak for themselves and we will come to the facts in later chapters. At this stage we are looking at Chinese attitudes and principles bearing on international negotiation and need only note that, in spite of the fact that it must be increasingly apparent to the Chinese that the conditions for the acceptance of one type of revolutionary society by the whole world are becoming increasingly less favorable, there has been no official abandonment of the doctrine of "no third way."

The Chinese have managed to fit into this rigid posture the doctrine of the *Panch Shila* (the Five Pillars of Coexistence), particularly in their relations with certain Asian states. We will see this doctrine at work in Peking's negotiations with Burma, Ceylon, and Nepal, which will be reviewed later in this work. However, adherence to the *Panch Shila* and to the ten principles of the Bandung Conference (1955) do not amount, in the last analysis, to a break with the basic "no third way" doctrine. This is easily demonstrable. Thus, while the doctrine of coexistence between the Chinese way of life and others is said to cover all non-Communist ways of life, in fact Peking applies it highly selectively. Any state that has close and friendly relations with the West tends to be excluded by Peking from the purview of coexistence. Whatever the theory may be, Peking does not talk of coexistence with such Asian states as Thailand, Malaysia, the Philippines, or even Singapore, and now there is no coexistence with India or Indonesia. The countries to which the status of coexistence is extended are presumably adjudged by Peking to be those that, at least in some degree, "lean" to its side. Of course, Peking's method of assessing whether a state so "leans" in not necessarily acceptable to other countries. A state may regard itself as neutral or nonaligned, but Peking may argue that since strict neutrality is (in its view) impossible, such a state is in fact leaning either toward the Chinese or in the opposite direction. This is why such an important nonaligned state as India, which played the major role in developing the modern posture of nonalignment, is not regarded as nonaligned by Peking, whereas other states that have not even declared themselves as nonaligned are lauded by the Chinese as stoutly "independent and neutral" states, because of the evidence of their "leaning" toward Peking.

Chinese doctrine has pronounced itself on the possibility of compromise with the "imperialists." One of Mao's most important statements on this matter was made to a meeting of Communist cadres in Yenan after his return in October 1945 from Chungking, where he engaged in forty-three days of negotiations with the Kuomintang. In his report Mao made an analysis of the situation at the end of World War II. He said:

The world after World War II has a bright future. This is the general trend. Does the failure of the Five Power Conference of Foreign Ministers in London mean that a third world war is about to break out? No. Just think, how is it possible for a third world war to break out right after the end of World War II? *The capitalist and the socialist countries will yet reach compromises on a number of international matters because compromise will be advantageous.*[35]

Six months later, Mao wrote a brief note appraising the international situation (April 1946). In this note he stated that the forces of world reaction were preparing a third world war but that the democratic forces could overcome the dangers of war. Then he added:

Therefore, the question in the relations between the United States, Britain, and France and the Soviet Union is not a question of compromise or break, but a question of compromise earlier, or compromise later. *"Compromise" means reaching agreement through peaceful negotiation.* "Earlier or later" means several years, or more than ten years, or even longer.[36]

The above citations are obviously of great importance in regard to Peking's basic attitude in its relations with the non-Communist world. Though the spread of Communism may be a long-term inevitability (in their view), it would seem that a shorter-term inevitability is the reaching of compromises; and these are to be attained by peaceful negotiation. Furthermore, this shorter-term inevitability is conceived as involving parleying or negotiating for even more than ten years, i.e., about as long as Mao could clearly foresee. Mao does not tell us how long the compromise, once reached, would last, but presumably this duration would be considerably longer than the already long period required to reach agreement.

We must not come to an overly optimistic conclusion. Mao goes on to state that the kind of compromise he has in mind does not mean compromise on all international issues, for that would be impossible as long as the United States, Britain, and France continue to be ruled by "reactionaries." However, as if not to make too strong a disclaimer, he then says, "This kind of compromise means compromise on some issues, including certain important ones." [37]

There is, thus, reason to believe that according to Chinese Communist doctrine some scope exists in international affairs for compromises to be arrived at through negotiation. The various actual cases of negotiation and agreement with Communist China, which will be analyzed in succeeding chapters, may be regarded as working illustrations of Mao's doctrine regarding negotiation and compromise.

Finally, in regard to their negotiating attitudes, we should note that the Chinese see no incompatibility (though, of course, there is a contradiction in their terms) between reaching agreement to coexist peacefully with other states and the continuance of revolutionary people's wars in various parts of the world. In what is still one of its major refutations of the position of the Soviet Communist Party, the Central Committee of the CCP, in a letter of June 14, 1963, stated:

> In recent years, certain persons have been spreading the argument that a single spark from a war of national liberation or from a revolutionary people's war will lead to a world conflagration destroying the world of mankind. What are the facts? Contrary to what these people say, the wars of national liberation and the revolutionary people's wars that have occurred since World War II have not led to World War. The victory of these revolutionary wars has . . . greatly strengthened the forces which . . . defend world peace.[38]

And it is, of course, only in conditions of peace that there can be peaceful coexistence, which, as the Chinese letter goes on to state, is one of the three cardinal aspects of the foreign policies of the Socialist countries.

The Chinese, then, hold the view that as long as the Vietnam war (for example) remains a "struggle of national liberation" it will not develop into a world war. They further seem to believe that support and assistance given to the nationalists involved in such a struggle will also not lead to a world war. Secondly, it would appear to be in line with their doctrine that nothing should be done to change the character of such conflicts into international or world wars.

However, these doctrinal positions must not be taken to mean that a national liberation movement can never become a larger war. One determinant in this regard is, in fact, implied in the last citation from the letter of June 1963: if a "war of national liberation" or a "revolutionary people's war" were to change into a war of aggression against other countries, then, of course, the whole argument advanced to substantiate the view that national liberation or revolutionary wars could be contained would cease to be applicable. This would undoubtedly be so if any overt actions of one or the other side extended the fighting to other countries. In the case of Vietnam it is clear that the Chinese would regard an attack on their country as such as extension. It is not clear that they would regard such extension to have taken place if there were a full-scale attack on North Vietnam. On the one hand, their view, and that of Hanoi, is that North and South Vietnam are one country and are therefore involved in one national movement. On the other hand, the Democratic Republic of Vietnam is spoken of as an independent sovereign state. It is relevant also that South Vietnam has its own "national" liberation movement. There is the possibility then, that in certain circumstances, a full-scale attack on North Vietnam would be regarded as an attack on the Socialist state known as the Democratic Republic of Vietnam, and that such an attack would have the effect of internationalizing the war to an unpredictable degree. Those circumstances would probably arise if North Vietnam were subjected to a full-scale attack and if it became clear, at any stage, that the attack were likely to defeat North Vietnam totally, thus posing a threat to Chinese security.

Chinese Views of Processes of Negotiation

Mao has quoted with enthusiastic approval Stalin's view on the interrelationship of theory and practice: "Theory becomes aimless if it is not connected with revolutionary practice. Practice gropes in the dark if its path is not illumined by revolutionary theory." [39] But little has been said by the Chinese leaders on the actual processes of negotiation, or on its "revolutionary practice." However, some of their general remarks on the importance of certain procedural and structural elements are applicable to the processes of negotiation.

How do the Chinese look at an issue with which they must deal? One of Mao's typical and important directives appears to be relevant. He has said, "A comprehension of the whole makes it easier for one to handle the part . . . because the part belongs to the whole." [40]

True, Mao Tse-tung laid down this rule of strategy primarily in regard to military situations. But it is the kind of formulation that the political leaders of China are not likely to overlook in other international confrontations.

Mao has repeatedly and at length stressed the relationship between the whole and its parts. This has many applications in Peking's strategy. For example, we have observed the Chinese view of the relationship between wars of liberation and the overall world situation. In their negotiating strategy too the Chinese constantly try to assess the wider relationships surrounding the issues directly involved.

Secondly, the importance of a detailed analysis of issues—a tactic that greatly influences negotiations—is also strongly stressed by Mao. Berating some of his commanders for their erroneous tactics in the war with the Kuomintang, Mao charged them with ignorance of Marxism-Leninism and reminded them, "Lenin said that 'the most essential thing in Marxism, the living soul of Marxism,' is the 'concrete analysis of concrete conditions.' " [41]

This meticulous attention to concrete details has been adopted by the Chinese in the conduct of international negotiations. Mao has repeatedly emphasized this aspect of his tactics. Writing in April 1944, he said, "Treat all problems analytically instead of negating everything." [42] And again in the following year he said, "He who makes no investigation and study has no right to speak." [43] These injunctions impose exacting disciplines on Chinese negotiators. They work hard to conform to Mao's dictum, and this generally helps them to gain an impressive mastery of the issues and situations that are under negotiation.

In regard to the general bearing of the Chinese Communist cadres, Mao has strongly stressed the importance of discipline. It is likely that an additional reason to those mentioned in Chapter I for the large Chinese delegations at negotiations is to ensure that the following two-way maintenance of discipline is enforced: "It is necessary to educate Party members on matters of Party discipline so that the general membership will on the one hand observe the discipline themselves, and on the other see to it that the leaders observe it as well." [44] Chinese delegations invariably create the impression of a strongly maintained discipline in all respects.

Another characteristic of Chinese tactics in international negotiations is to affirm dogmatically that their side is right and the other is wrong. This attitude is enshrined in Mao's statement: "The right and wrong sides over a controversial issue should be clearly established without compromise or equivocation." [45] Again, he has said, "We must firmly uphold truth, and truth requires a clear-cut stand." [46]

Mao has also frequently spoken of just and unjust wars and Chinese support for just wars and opposition to unjust wars.[47] The sense that the Chinese have that they are always on the side of right and justice is a view that, as we shall see, they make explicit in the course of negotiation.

Finally, the Chinese are not averse in certain circumstances to reaching decisions by majority vote. Decisions of this kind have been mentioned explicitly in connection with internal and Party situations. Mao has at least twice stressed that in the Party the minority must subordinate itself to the majority.[48] Though restricted, the role of the voting procedure is of greater significance in China than it appears to be on the surface. For example, there have been elections to leadership positions in the Central Committee of the Party,[49] and to the national committee of the Chinese People's Political Consultation Conference.[50] It may be that these elections are generally unanimous, by consensus. Undoubtedly, it may be assumed that the Communist Party Politburo makes a selection of those who will be put up for office. In this high Party organ, whose deliberations are completely secret, presumably the rule that the minority should submit to the majority prevails. The precise voting procedures of China are kept in the background. Analogously, in international negotiation the Chinese will fight hard in formal, informal, and in backstage meetings to win acceptance of their point of view. But if they fail and find that they are in the minority, then, at some stage they find it possible to adopt a position in line with what can be presented as a general consensus. In short, in international negotiation, they strongly prefer a procedure of consensus to be adopted because no matter what concessions they might make backstage, this rule formally excludes the possibility of their being shown as having "lost" in the negotiations.

If not much more can yet be said with any certainty on the preferences or predilections of the Peking government in regard to negotiating procedures, this is sufficiently explained by, first, the relatively small number of full-scale international negotiations in which that government has been involved and, secondly, our lack of detailed knowledge of the structure of the government of China and more so of the relationship of its structure to the way in which it functions.[51]

CHAPTER IV

The Peking Government and the Convening of the International Conference on Laos, May 1961

THE AGREEMENTS concluded at the 1954 Geneva Conference included those on the cessation of the hostilities in Laos, a final declaration dealing with Cambodia, Laos, and Vietnam, and a Laotian declaration setting out some of the elements of a neutral policy. The agreement on the cessation of the hostilities in Laos—as in the other two areas of Indochina—assigned duties to an international supervisory commission consisting of India (as chairman), Canada, and Poland. The commission was to inform the members of the Geneva Conference on various stated circumstances. Such communications were to be made through the chairman of the commission. It seemed appropriate to the Indian government that it should send those communications to the cochairmen of the Geneva Conference—the Foreign Ministers of the Soviet Union and the United Kingdom—for transmission to the states that had been present at the conference of 1954. This *modus operandi* became the established convention, and thus the cochairmanship of the Geneva Conference of 1954 came to be institutionalized.

In 1958 the government of Laos asked the international supervisory commission to cease functioning in the kingdom. The situation in the country deteriorated, and it became clear that Laos was no longer able to maintain the independence and neutrality that had been written into the 1954 Geneva documents.[1] In these circumstances, on December 14, 1960, Prime Minister Nehru of India addressed a communication to the cochairmen of the Geneva Conference requesting them to reconvene the international supervisory commission for Laos.

It was at this stage that the Chinese government at Peking also reacted to the Laotian situation. On December 28, 1960, Foreign Minister Ch'en Yi addressed a letter to Foreign Ministers Gromyko and Home on the situation in Laos. The letter began with an attack on the United States and Thailand as aggressors in Laos. Marshal Ch'en Yi then demanded that the signatories of the 1954 Geneva Agreements and primarily the cochairmen of the Geneva Conference should take effective measures "to stop the actions of the U.S. government and its vassal the Thailand government, in violation of international law and the Geneva agreements." [2]

Marshal Ch'en Yi went on to state the motivation of China in raising this issue. He could have said simply that China, as a neighboring state and a signatory of the 1954 Geneva Agreements, was concerned about the situation in Laos. It is significant, however, that though he did mention these two factors he added that China "has to consider taking measures to safeguard its own security." Thus China frankly, and perhaps in a certain sense inadvertently, revealed that her attitude toward what goes on in states on her borders is in part, and perhaps mainly, dictated by her assessment of the requirements of her security, and the urge that national states have to protect their vital interests. This is, as one can readily understand, a point of view that is not uncommon. No state, most certainly no great state, is happy to see a powerful and potentially inimical state gain influence on its borders.[3]

Returning to the substance of the Laotian situation, Marshal Ch'en Yi's letter stated:

The Chinese government fully endorses the proposal put forward by the government of U.S.S.R. in its note to the British government dated December 22, 1960 and by Pham Van Dong, minister of foreign affairs of the Democratic Republic of Viet Nam, in his letter to the Co-Chairmen of the Geneva conference dated December 24, 1960, namely to convene a conference of the participants of the 1954 Geneva conference and resume the activities of the international commission for supervision and control in Laos so as promptly to stop the U.S. government's intervention and aggression in Laos and restore peace there.[4]

What is of significance, apart from the expected attack on the United States, is that Marshal Ch'en Yi endorsed the proposal to reconvene the Geneva Conference; in other words the Chinese were in favor of a return to negotiation and, moreover, they were in favor of international supervision in Laos on the terms of the 1954 agreements. It should be noted that though relations between China and India had been deteriorating, China raised no objection to the supervisory commission in which India had the key role of chairman.

The situation in Laos at that time was virtually a struggle between, on the one side, a "right wing" led by Prince Boun Oum and General Phoumi Nosavan and supported by the United States, and on the other, the Pathet Lao supported by North Vietnam and the Soviet Union. The "Centrists" or neutral elements were in a period of eclipse. Prince Souvanna Phouma was in exile in Phnom Penh. It is of interest that Marshal Ch'en Yi's letter of December 28, 1960, did not contain a plea in behalf of the Pathet Lao; the letter asked the cochairmen to take action to contact the "legal government of Laos headed by Prince Souvanna Phouma." And, finally, Marshal Ch'en Yi said that if the commission were not to resume its activities promptly the Chinese government "requests that the co-chairmen promptly convene a conference of the participants of the 1954 Geneva Conference so as jointly to seek effective measures to stop the actions of the U.S. government in violating the Geneva agreements and intervening and committing aggression against Laos." [5]

On January 1, 1961, Prince Sihanouk, the Chief of State of neighboring Cambodia, following up a proposal he had made in September 1960 at the General Assembly of the United Nations that both Laos and Cambodia be neutral, proposed that an enlarged Geneva Conference on the Laos situation be convened consisting not only of the participants at the 1954 Geneva Conference, but, in addition, other states interested in the issue. The new members of the conference were to be the three states on the international supervisory commission (India, Canada, Poland), and the neighboring states of Burma and Thailand. This proposal was immediately received favorably by Nikita Khrushchev.

Following on the heels of those revisionist acts, on January 14, 1961, Ch'en Yi addressed his second letter to Foreign Ministers Gromyko and Home, in which he stated: "The Chinese government agrees to this positive proposal of his Royal Highness Prince Sihanouk and believes that such a conference, if it could be convened, will certainly help to seek ways to safeguard the Geneva agreements and restore peace in Laos." [6] The letter closed by asking for steps to bring about "the early convocation of such a conference."

About the same time—on January 7, 1961—the United States Department of State issued a statement on the problem of Laos.[7] That statement did not mention the various calls that had been made to reconvene a Geneva Conference on Laos; nor did it, understandably enough, contain any mention of the Chinese reaction to those calls. It set out in full the United States policy of assisting Laos to maintain its independence and concluded by saying, "In the spirit of the Geneva Agreement which ended the war in Laos in 1954, and with the full cooperation and at the request of all successive governments, the United States has worked toward these objectives." [8]

In its recital of Laotian events toward the end of 1960 and at the beginning of 1961, the State Department made no accusation against Peking of Chinese assistance to the Pathet Lao, which was up in arms against the Boun Oum government. The statement said, "Following the withdrawal from Vientiane of Communist forces, the Soviet and Vietnamese Communists continued an extensive airlift of war matériel, including personnel, to rebel forces in the interior of the country." [9] It is of some significance that in this critical period in Laos there was no evidence that neighboring China was directly assisting the Pathet Lao.

On February 2, 1961, at a mass rally at Peking, Ch'en Yi stated that the solution of the Laotian problem lay in "establishing, in accordance of the aspirations of the Laotian people, an independent and unified, peaceful and neutral Laos which enjoys national amity." [10] He thus set out the objectives of a conference on Laos in terms simi-

lar to those favored by Cambodia and India and which later came to
be very widely supported. He also said that "China has always
adopted a policy of nonintervention in the internal questions of
Laos," [11] thereby disavowing any interest in direct involvement in
Laotian affairs. Meanwhile, the United Kingdom, which had been ap-
proached several times by the Soviet government and informally by
other governments for the reconvening of the Laos Conference,
rather tardily accepted that proposal. On March 23, 1961, a British
aide-mémoire was addressed to the Soviet government in reply to
that government's note of February 18, 1961. The British note suggested that in the first instance the cochairmen should issue an immediate request for a de facto cease-fire in Laos. If this could be accomplished the international supervisory commission should be reconvened to verify the effectiveness of the cease-fire. The British note accepted the Soviet suggestions that a conference on Laos be convened
and supported Sihanouk's proposal for enlarging its membership.[12]

On the same day (March 23, 1961), President Kennedy made a
statement on Laos to the American people. This statement revealed
two points of great significance in relation to China. The first is that
the President identified the Soviets and Communist North Vietnam as
suppliers of "increasing support and direction from outside" to the
Pathet Lao. He did not mention the Chinese in this connection. Secondly, President Kennedy stated, "All we want in Laos is peace, not
war—a truly neutral government, not a cold-war pawn—a settlement
concluded at the conference table, not on the battlefield." [13] He also
supported "the British proposal of a prompt end of hostilities and
prompt negotiations." [14] Actually, as we have seen, the proposals for
negotiations came from other sources and had been accepted by
many states, China among them. Moreover, the United States' objective for Laos was stated by President Kennedy in terms very similar
to those that had been declared earlier on behalf of Peking by Marshal Ch'en Yi.

On the face of it then, it appeared that both the United States and
China were in favor of cessation of hostilities and a peaceful and neutral Laos, these latter ends to be attained by conference negotiation
and not by armed conflict. This convergence of the objectives of the

United States and China in regard to a country in Southeast Asia is of profound significance, both in itself and as an indication of the possibilities for settlement of other grave problems in the region.

The Soviet reply of April 1, 1961,[15] to the British note of March 23, 1961, was on the whole responsive, particularly to the procedures suggested for attaining a cease-fire and a peaceful settlement of the Laotian situation through an international conference. This paved the way for the issue by the cochairmen, Foreign Ministers Gromyko and Home, of three important messages on April 24, 1961. Each of them contained elements that are relevant to an understanding of China's approach to negotiation, bearing in mind that if China had objected to the contents of any of these important messages the conference could not have been convened.

The first of these messages was addressed to the various elements involved in the military conflict in Laos, and it called for a cease-fire before the convening of the international conference at Geneva on May 12, 1961. Significantly the message called "on all Military Authorities, Parties, and Organizations in Laos to cease fire." [16] At the time of the issue of the message there was a government headed by Prince Boun Oum, which was recognized by the Western powers; there was the Souvanna Phouma government, then in exile but still recognized by several countries, including nonaligned ones such as India and Burma, as well as the Soviet Union; there were also the Pathet Lao, who were, on the whole, advancing in Laos and had come to control about half the territory of the kingdom. In addition, there were other fighting groups such as the Meos and some of the generals whose adherence to one side or the other was not entirely firm. Instead of specifying some of these groups as governments and others as insurgents or irregulars, the cochairmen wisely adopted a formula that, while it indicated that some of the parties to the conflict were of an authoritative character ("Military Authorities"), avoided the problem of the relative status of these authorities; and they also included in their phrase "parties and organizations." The wisdom of this formula lies in the fact that the Chinese could claim that the Pathet Lao was one of the Military Authorities while the Western powers could claim that the Military Authorities were solely those of the Boun Oum government while the Pathet Lao and the neutralists or Centrists were merely parties and organizations. Since all sides could find plausible interpretations of the cochairmen's phrase their assent to a cease-fire became ensured. The Peking government raised no objection to this appeal to the Laotian factions.

The second of the cochairmen's messages of April 24, 1961, was addressed to the government of India, requesting it to reconvene at Delhi the International Commission for Supervision and Control in Laos. The reconvened commission was to "discuss the question of the tasks and functions which should be allotted to it after the cease-fire in Laos," and it would "present an appropriate report to the co-Chairmen who will consider the Commission's report and give it directions on going to Laos to carry out the work of controlling the cease-fire." [17] Furthermore, the cochairmen, in their message on a cease-fire, had called "on the people of Laos to cooperate with the International Commission for Supervision and Control in Laos and to render it assistance when it arrives in the country on their instructions, in exercising supervision and control over the cease-fire." [18] The above injunctions of the cochairmen involved activities of a Commission consisting of three outside powers on the territory of a host country (Laos). China could have assailed this move as a scheme to intervene in the domestic affairs of Laos and subvert its independence; and, covering itself by such an accusation, it could have refused to send representatives to the proposed negotiating conference on Laos—if it had been truly opposed to a peaceful settlement by negotiation with "the imperialists." However, China refrained from such a step and thereby indicated its willingness, and perhaps its desire, to resort to negotiation instead of leaving this issue to be decided by the force of arms. This indication of an attitude that favored negotiation did not mean that China was unwilling, at the same time, to take a strong line regarding the Laotian situation. A *Renmin Ribao* editorial of February 25, 1961, after referring to a declaration of Souvanna Phouma that there could be no compromise with the saboteurs of Vientiane (the Boun Oum group) stated:

The Chinese people warmly welcome and fully support this stern and just stand of the people and Government of Laos. The Chinese people are fully convinced that as long as the Laotian people remain united and persist in struggle, they will, with the support of the peace-loving countries and peoples, surely smash all the schemes and tricks of U.S. imperialism and realize the independence, peace and neutrality of Laos.[19]

The above words of an authoritative Chinese source raised a semantic problem, as is often the case with Chinese pronouncements. They could be interpreted to mean that China had no interest really in a peaceful settlement of the Laotian question. But this would not be an interpretation that fitted all the surrounding facts. For one thing, the same *Renmin Ribao* editorial quotes from a statement made by Vice Premier Ch'en Yi on February 22, 1961, as follows: "The Chinese government holds that the sole correct way to peacefully solve the Laotian question and to ensure the peace and neutrality of Laos lies in convening an enlarged meeting of the Geneva conference, as proposed by Prince Sihanouk." [20] Secondly, we have seen in Chapter III that the phrase "the support of the peace-loving countries" does not necessarily mean tangible defense support. Besides, there are other aspects of the new Chinese philosophy that seem to be reflected in the Chinese statement before us: first, there is the strong emphasis placed by Mao Tse-tung on what is right; [21] a second relevant factor is the revolutionary or activist character of the new Chinese system. These two clues add up to the posture that the right must be determined and once determined it must be achieved. If it cannot be achieved peacefully, then it must be achieved by other means. In short, the willingness of Peking to negotiate does not mean an abandonment of alternative means, if the circumstances should warrant their use. This characteristic of states to go along with possibilities of negotiation while retaining their capability to resort to force is not uncommon.[22]

The third message sent out on April 24, 1961, by Foreign Ministers Gromyko and Home was addressed to the governments of fourteen states: Burma, Cambodia, Canada, the Chinese People's Republic, the Democratic Republic of Vietnam, France, India, Laos, the Polish People's Republic, the Republic of Vietnam, Thailand, the Soviet Union, the United Kingdom, and the United States. All these states had previously been sounded and had agreed to participate in an international conference on Laos. The cochairmen now invited each of the fourteen countries to send its delegation to Geneva to begin work on May 12, 1961, and they stated that their intention was that the participating countries would be represented by their Ministers of Foreign Affairs.[23] In this message it was stated that the government of Laos had agreed to the conference. To the Chinese, the Soviet Union, and other countries, the "government of Laos" was an entirely different entity from the "government of Laos" recognized by the United States and other Western powers. Besides, there was a strong faction, perhaps at that time militarily the strongest of all in Laos—the Pathet Lao—that was not recognized as a government. In these circumstances, the Chinese might well have said that they would not go to a conference that would be attended by the Boun Oum "rebels." However, they did not raise this objection. Similarly, the United States, knowing that an invitation would also be issued to the Souvanna Phouma government, which it did not recognize, did not raise objections to this course. Furthermore, the United States was aware not only that an invitation would be issued to the Souvanna Phouma government but that the Pathet Lao—which did not claim to be a government—would also be invited to participate in the Geneva Conference, but, because of the facts of the situation, the United States did not make this an obstacle to negotiation.

Thus the cochairmen of the Geneva Conference took a wide view of what constituted "the government of Laos" as a party to the international conference on Laos. Both the Peking government and the United States responded not by announcing adherence to this wide view but by raising no great objection to it. This crucial concurrence in the issuing of invitations to the actual parties to the conflict, without getting bogged in questions of relative status among those parties, was one of the primary factors that made it possible to reach agreement on the convening of the Laotian Conference.

On the day following the dispatch of the three messages by the cochairmen, the American Department of State issued a statement containing the following remarks:

The U.S. welcomes this development which we hope will bring about a peaceful settlement in Laos. As the U.S. has made clear in the past, the first essential step is that a cease-fire be put into effect prior to the convening of the conference. The U.S. will, therefore, observe the situation in Laos very closely . . . should a verified cease-fire be brought about, the U.S. hopes to see emerge from the conference the peaceful, united, and unaligned Laos of which President Kennedy spoke on March 23.[24]

The United States thus made it clear that while it raised no objection to peaceful negotiation the Laos Conference would have to be preceded by a verified cease-fire. This was not an easy condition to satisfy because of both the forest-covered and mountainous terrain of Laos and the lack of any clear lines between the military contestants in many parts of the country. Moreover, time was short. In accordance with the message of the cochairmen of April 24, 1961, the three countries on the International Commission convened in Delhi on April 28, 1961, and on May 1 sent their report to the cochairmen. On May 6, 1961, the cochairmen sent their instructions to the commission. Those instructions stated that the basic task "consists in fixing the cease-fire in Laos in accordance with the understanding reached by the belligerent parties and in exercising supervision and control over the cease-fire." [25] The commission left Delhi immediately after the receipt of this order and attempted to accomplish its job. Meanwhile, the delegates to the Laos Conference had arrived in Geneva to begin work on May 12. However, no cease-fire had yet been verified by the International Commission. The opening of the conference became a matter of doubt. Fortunately, on May 12, 1961, a report was received from the commission, stating, "The commission are satisfied that a general *de facto* cease-fire exists." However, the commission admitted that there had been breaches of the cease-fire but explained them as follows: "Such breaches as have been informally complained of are either due to misunderstanding, or to factors such as the terrain, the nature of disposition of forces, both regular and irregular, of all parties." [26] The reference to breaches raised doubts for the United States and the conference was not able to convene on May 12. It was not until a further message was received from the commission and until backstage persuasions convinced various governments that genuine efforts were being made to stabilize the cease-fire, that the conference opened—four days later than the date set for it, on May 16, 1961.

The United States had won its point about a cease-fire, but the

Chinese view of what the commission should achieve was different from that of the United States. Premier Chou En-lai had made this clear in a message addressed as early as January 14, 1961, to Pham Van Dong, the Prime Minister of North Vietnam. The New China News Agency, on January 15, 1961, reported Chou En-lai as saying:

Regarding the question of resuming the activities of the International Commission for Supervision and Control in Laos, Comrade Ch'en Yi pointed out in his letter of December 28, 1960 to the co-Chairmen of the Geneva Conference that the most urgent task of the Commission now is to adopt effective measures at once to stop the interference by the U.S. and Thailand governments in the internal affairs of Laos, and to effect the withdrawal from Laos of all the military personnel and equipment of the U.S. and Thailand.[27]

Again, in a message to Prince Sihanouk on February 11, 1961, Chou En-lai stated that "even for the purpose of reactivating the International Commission for Supervision and Control in Laos, it is necessary first to convene an international conference of the countries concerned, which will make new provision on the tasks and functions of the Commission in the light of the new situation." [28] It is clear from the course events actually took that the Chinese maintained some flexibility in regard to the matter of the functions of the commission. This flexibility moreover occurred in a context in which a firmer adherence to their own point of view might have been expected: the growing military success of the Pathet Lao forces.

All in all, the convening of the International Conference on Laos entailed movement by the Peking government from some of its previously stated positions. Those positions had included the important one that the United States and Thailand, which, in their view, had intervened in the affairs of Laos, should withdraw. The movement by the Peking government would appear to indicate that prior stipulations, even when pressed internationally by Peking, for embarking on negotiation are not necessarily rigidly adhered to. This, of course, is not a very different attitude from that of most governments. Parties to a negotiation generally strive, before the commencement of such negotiation, to enter upon it in conditions that they regard as favorable to their own cause. It does not follow, however, that they will not enter into negotiations on somewhat less favorable conditions. The Laos Conference of May 1961 was no exception to this rule. Both the United States and the Peking governments sat down at the conference table knowing that there had not been full compliance with their prior conditions or stipulations.

CHAPTER V

The Negotiating Confrontation at the
Opening of the Laos Conference

WHEN the Laos Conference finally convened on May 16, 1961, it immediately became clear that the main confrontation of positions would be between the United States and the Peking governments, which had brought the largest delegations to the conference, though the Chinese outnumbered the Americans by about two to one.

After a largely formal opening statement by Prince Sihanouk of Cambodia in the early evening and a few procedural formalities, the meeting was expected to adjourn. But it turned out that Marshal Ch'en Yi was insistent on speaking. So that the very first session of the conference should not be converted into a solo debut by Peking, Lord Home (as he was then), the Foreign Minister of the United Kingdom and a cochairman of the conference, made the first substantive statement. His fairly long speech did not bear directly on any known Chinese position: the United Kingdom, with its greatly changed status after World War II, is not likely to be in direct confrontation with China in the foreseeable future, its position in Hong Kong notwithstanding. The only reference to China was an oblique one and was meant to safeguard the diplomatic position of the United States and other friends of the United Kingdom. Lord Home said:

The 1954 conference took place on the understanding, expressed in the final communiqué of the Berlin meeting of the Foreign Ministers which preceded it, that—and I quote—"Neither the invitation to, nor the holding of the conference should be deemed to imply diplomatic recognition in any case where it has not already been accorded." In our view, the same considerations apply to the present conference.[1]

No one questioned this view and it created no issue in the work of the conference. Home's statement ended well after 7:30 P.M., but still the Foreign Minister from Peking was anxious to speak. Though it was late, there was a readiness to meet his wishes: if he spoke then, the text of his remarks would be made available in time to facilitate the formulation of the United States reaction when Secretary Dean Rusk came to speak on the following day.

However, the mere fact that Ch'en Yi insisted on speaking on the opening day of the conference was in several ways significant and indicative of China's negotiating stance. First and foremost, that China took the floor before the Soviet Union was a striking departure from the usual procedure when Russia is present along with a number of other Communist states. At the United Nations and at other international conferences, the Soviet Union is almost invariably the first speaker among the Communist states. China, by reversing this practice, was clearly indicating that it was in no sense subordinate to a "Soviet Line." Secondly, Marshal Ch'en Yi was also implying that since Laos is an Asian issue it is, so far as the big powers are concerned, more a matter for China than for the others. He was therefore asserting the right to speak first. Home, it might be said, spoke before him simply because he had the honorific position of cochairman; his speech was therefore, in a sense, ex officio.

The major impression which the burly Marshal Ch'en Yi created was one of confidence, strength, and sureness of purpose. He did not do this by deploying any techniques of oratorical emphasis. He spoke calmly, though in full voice.

His statement placed the United States in clear confrontation with his country. His speech of some forty minutes contained eighteen direct references to the United States, and, in addition, many more innuendoes. Seventeen of these direct references were critical, mostly highly critical, while one was favorable though tinged with sarcasm. The technique of the presentation was threefold. First, Ch'en Yi sought to identify the United States as the main culprit in the Laotian situation and to criticize it as much as possible. Secondly, he played up the good deeds and right approach of Peking. For example, he said,

The Chinese Government has consistently pursued a foreign policy of peace and made unremitting efforts to safeguard peace in Southeast Asia and the world. . . . The Chinese Government has consistently supported Southeast Asian countries in their just cause of practicing a policy of peace and neutrality, safeguarding national independence and opposing interference and aggression from outside.[2]

The third element of Marshal Ch'en Yi's technique was a show of reasonableness. Thus, he stated that

the Delegation of the Chinese Government is ready to work jointly with the delegations of *all* the other countries participating in this conference to make contributions to the peaceful settlement of the Laotian question. . . . Provided *all* the countries participating in this conference have the sincerity to truly settle the question, there is no reason why our conference cannot achieve positive results.[3]

On the substance of Marshal Ch'en Yi's negotiating position four points stood out in particular. The first of these he stated thus: "The Chinese Government has consistently stood for the peaceful settlement of the Laotian question on the basis of the 1954 Geneva agreements." [4] The context of this statement was that many Laotian and other Asian leaders had been stressing the importance of complete compliance with the 1954 agreements. Marshal Ch'en Yi, then, took the position of aligning himself with this view—a position that would, first, win widespread support in Asia, and, secondly, indicate China's respect for existing international agreements. The second substantive point of importance in Marshal Ch'en Yi's statement was praise for the work of the International Commission for Supervision and Control in Laos. He said, "The International Commission for Supervision and Control in Laos, in pursuance of the directives of the co-Chairmen of the Geneva Conference, has begun its work, and our enlarged Geneva Conference is eventually taking place here after breaking through the various obstacles. All these are gratifying." [5] It was a noteworthy display of flexibility that Ch'en Yi, in spite of previous Peking stands against sending the International Commission to Laos till its functions had been defined by the conference, should praise the

work it had embarked on in Laos prior to the convening of the conference, more especially as it was known that the Chinese government
is highly suspicious in general of the concept of "control and supervision" by foreign powers.

The third point of significance in Ch'en Yi's statement was his criticism of the United States for having "refused to take part in" the
1954 agreements, though it participated in the first Geneva Conference. The Marshal went on to develop his view of the implications of
the United States' refusal to participate in the 1954 agreements:

The U.S. Government issued a unilateral declaration to the effect that it
would refrain from the threat or the use of force to disturb these agreements; yet even this promise was very soon repudiated. Before the ink on
the Geneva Agreements had dried, the United States hastily rigged up
the so-called Southeast Asia Defense Treaty Organization.[6]

This was an attempt, by interpreting the facts to suit the view advanced, to castigate the United States as having acted both in disregard of the 1954 agreements, and, secondly, to introduce into Asian
affairs a largely non-Asian presence. Ch'en Yi pointed out that more
than half the members of SEATO were not Southeast Asian countries. He was appealing to the Asian sentiment in favor of liberation
from outside intrusion.

The fourth point in Ch'en Yi's statement was his stressing that "the
internal problems of Laos must be settled, and can only be settled, by
the Laotian people themselves. The people of Laos, like all the other
independent nations of the world, have the right to choose their path
according to their own will." [7] He then referred to certain agreements
in Laos between Souvanna Phouma and Souphanouvong, to the effect
that Laos should follow a line of peace and neutrality, and added,
"These propositions reflect the Laotian people's desire for the realization of national harmony and democratic unity, and for the preservation of their national independence. The Chinese government has
consistently supported, and will continue to support, this desire." [8]
Peking, was, in short, the champion of Laotian independence and
neutrality.

Finally, and as a counterpart to Laos' own desire for independence
and neutrality, Ch'en Yi held that the participants at the conference

should assume a joint obligation to ensure the independence and neutrality of Laos with no foreign power being permitted to use force or the threat of force against Laos, or being permitted to use aid as a means to violate the neutrality of Laos and interfere in its internal affairs. He then made his point specific: "The military personnel of the U.S. and of the other countries which are interfering in Laos with U.S. support must be withdrawn." [9] In this statement of the obligations to be assumed by the international community in regard to Laos, Ch'en Yi did not specifically mention any military elements from North Vietnam, which were generally held to be in Laos, but his general formulations could, indeed, cover them as it would all other foreign armed personnel. Ch'en Yi was silent on the problem of the introduction of military equipment into Laos. On this matter, however, the Chinese delegation later expressed views that will be discussed elsewhere.

The next morning, the first speaker was Dean Rusk, the Secretary of State of the United States. His technique was one of much greater restraint than that of Ch'en Yi. This was deliberate, for he referred to Ch'en Yi's statement and said, "I shall comment upon his remarks with the restraint enjoined upon us by Prince Sihanouk." [10]

However, while Ch'en Yi had been blatant and had named the United States critically seventeen times, whereas Mr. Rusk adhered to his promise of restraint and referred directly to the Chinese only twice, there was a certain degree of similarity in the techniques that both used. Ch'en Yi had named the United States as the main culprit; Dean Rusk was far more subtle: "The real threat to peace in Southeast Asia is not from South to North, nor from across the Pacific Ocean. The threats are from North to South, and take many forms. If these threats should disappear SEATO would wither away, for it has no purpose but to maintain the peace in Southeast Asia." [11] By implication this made it clear enough that the major culprit in Southeast Asia was none other than China.

Dean Rusk put this point into ideological context by going on to state: "We cannot settle this argument in this conference, for it involves commitments of the Communist world . . . just as it involves the commitments of free peoples who are determined to perfect and cherish their freedoms." [12]

Finally, in regard to negotiating techniques, the Secretary of State responded to Ch'en Yi's show of reasonableness by saying:

We note the statement made by the representative from Peiping that he is ready to work jointly with the delegations of all the other countries participating in this conference to make contributions to the peaceful settlement of the Laotian question. We ourselves are prepared to work diligently to discover whether there is agreement in this conference on the question before us.[13]

In this part of his statement Mr. Rusk did not go so far as to say explicitly that the United States would work with all the other delegations, and thereby he perhaps safeguarded the United States' position of reserve toward certain countries with which it does not have diplomatic relations. He did, however, imply that there would be such joint work in trying to arrive at an agreement.

In spite of the direct confrontation between the United States and China, there appeared to be a certain degree of parallelism and potential agreement in the substance of these two statements.

True, the first point of substance advanced by Rusk was the full fixing of an effective cease-fire in Laos. He said:

An effective cease-fire is a prerequisite to any constructive result from our proceedings. A failure of a cease-fire would result in a highly dangerous situation, which it is the purpose of the conference to prevent. I would urge that the Co-Chairmen take this up immediately in order that the situation be clarified, and the ICC given the necessary authorizations and instructions.[14]

Later in his statement Mr. Rusk reverted to the importance of maintaining the cease-fire. But in some measure this was not different in spirit from Ch'en Yi's approbation of the work of the ICC; that work was directed entirely, at that time, to fixing the cease-fire. Therefore, on this point there was a closer parallel between the American and Chinese points of view than appeared on the surface.

The next point of substance raised by Mr. Rusk was to draw attention to the absence from the conference table of a representative of the Boun Oum government of Laos. Mr. Rusk referred to it as "The Royal Laotian Government, empowered by the King and Parliament" and said it was "the only authority resting upon that nation's constitution, and the means established by law for registering the wishes of its king and people." [15] He expressed the view that this matter required the immediate attention of the cochairmen so that the participants at the conference "may have the benefit of the participation of the government of the very country which we are discussing." [16] This position was, if not the same as that of the Chinese, its counterpart, expressing the expected complementary attitude. Ch'en Yi had mentioned the Centrists (under Souvanna Phouma) and the left wing with Souphanouvong; and now Dean Rusk was mentioning the other essential participant, the right wing. Privately all delegates were agreed that it was necessary to have all three Laotian wings represented at the conference table. [17]

Mr. Rusk then proceeded to deal with the core problems before the conference. He spoke of one aspect of these problems as "insuring a genuinely neutral Laos." [18] He went on to say, "Almost every nation here has expressed itself in favor of a neutral Laos." [19] Certainly, Ch'en Yi had just spoken in favor of a neutral Laos. Therefore, at least superficially, there was agreement between the United States and Peking on an important point before the conference. But Mr. Rusk went on to state that there would have to be a definition of the concept of neutrality that all the conference participants could support in its application to Laos. Neutrality in the classical sense of nonalignment was not enough, though that too was necessary. The agreed definition would have to "include positive assurance of the integrity of national life." [20] While Ch'en Yi had not used those words, we have seen that he had spoken approvingly of Laotian national harmony, unity, and the preservation of national independence and had pledged Chinese support for the desire of the Laotian leaders to take their country in this direction. [21] There appeared to be enough overlap in the thinking of the Foreign Ministers of Washington and Peking on a concept of neutrality for Laos to make agreement a probability.

But the matter of neutrality demanded further clarification, and later in his statement Mr. Rusk returned to it. *All* foreign military personnel would have to be removed from Laos; the United States wanted no military bases in Laos and had no desire to send military equipment into the country. There would have to be agreement on these matters. We have noted that Ch'en Yi also emphasized the withdrawal of foreign forces and stressed nonalignment (which would preclude military bases). Here, too, there appeared to exist a considerable degree of agreement between the two points of view. On the question of military equipment Ch'en Yi had been silent, but he had not expressed a view opposed to that of the United States.

Mr. Rusk then came to his concluding thought on neutrality:

Finally, neutrality must be consistent with sovereignty. It involves safeguards against subversion of the elements of the state, which is organized, directed, or assisted from beyond its borders. In the end, we must find a way to let the people of Laos live their own lives under conditions of free choice, and under conditions which permit the continuing exercise of choice, to adapt institutions, policies, and objectives to the teachings of experience.[22]

Here again, though Mr. Rusk had spelled out his view in considerably greater detail than Marshal Ch'en Yi, the latter too had asserted that the people of Laos had the right "to choose their path according to their own will." He had also said, "The international aspect of the Laotian question is to create the necessary international conditions under which the people of Laos will be really able to realize their aspirations free from outside interference." [23] Thus both the United States and Peking, in addition to "classical neutrality," desired a truly independent Laos exercising its own choice as to the kind of life and institutions it wanted.

Next, Mr. Rusk came to the machinery for "maintaining and safeguarding" Laotian neutrality, and here his statement drew the outlines of a scheme of which there had been no parallel in Marshal Ch'en Yi's discourse. He pointed out that the control machinery created in 1954 had proved inadequate and that it must now

have full access to all parts of the country, without the need for the consent of any civil or military officials, national or local . . . it must be able to act on any complaints from responsible sources, including personnel of the control body itself, responsible civil and military officials in Laos, the governments of negotiating countries, and of the members of this conference.[24]

He proposed that the control body should act by majority rule. "In short, pledges and promises must be backed by effective controls, effectively applied to maintain a genuinely neutral Laos." [25]

Since conceptually there appeared to be little difference in regard to neutrality and independence for Laos, the nub of the negotiating confrontation between the United States and China would be contained in the problem of controls in Laos. Ch'en Yi had welcomed the presence of the Control Commission in Laos, but Dean Rusk had asked for clear-cut and effective capabilities for the commission to ensure compliance with the solemn pledges of the states that they would respect the neutrality and independence of Laos.

The emerging confrontation between the United States and China at the conference was highlighted when Foreign Minister Gromyko made his first statement, on the same day as Mr. Rusk's first statement, and did not embark on a full-scale attack on United States policies in Southeast Asia as Ch'en Yi had done. He was critical of the focusing of United States attention on the problem of the cease-fire but he did not express this criticism in extreme terms. Indeed, Mr. Gromyko used his intervention mainly to present to the conference the drafts of the Soviet proposals for (1) an international declaration on the neutrality of Laos, and (2) an agreement on the withdrawal of foreign troops and military personnel from the territory of Laos and on the mandate for the international commission. Gromyko only once mentioned the strong Chinese statement and he did so as follows: "The Deputy Prime Minister and Minister of Foreign Affairs of the People's Republic of China, Comrade Ch'en Yi, quite rightly mentioned in his very colorful intervention that Laos can no longer be in the sphere of activity of SEATO." [26] The description of Ch'en Yi's intervention as "colorful" was nearer to tactful dissociation from its tone than to approval.

How did the other members of the conference react to the United States–Peking confrontation as it was shaping up? Most of the major delegations virtually ignored it. The statement of Foreign Minister Couve de Murville of France made no mention of either the United States or the Chinese statement. V. K. Krishna Menon, speaking for India, mentioned both statements in passing but steered clear of their confrontation. However, Ung Van Khiem, Foreign Minister of North Vietnam, on May 19, 1961, delivered a strong statement, which included a full-scale attack on American policies on Vietnam. He did not devote nearly as much attention to the Soviet and Chinese speeches, particularly the latter. He supported the "fully constructive" proposals introduced on May 17, 1961, by Andrei Gromyko for the solution of the Laotian question, and dealt briefly with the Chinese statement supporting the proposals for the liquidation of SEATO and the removal of the remnants of the Kuomintang Army in Laos. On the whole, the North Vietnamese kept their distance from the Chinese while they fully supported the Soviet statement.

The opening speech of the Burmese Minister for Foreign Affairs contained no reference to previous remarks, but the statement of Nhiek Tioulong, the Foreign Minister of Cambodia, on May 22, 1961, was extremely interesting from a negotiating point of view and at the same time was indicative of the directions in which unaligned thinking in Southeast Asia was tending. Nhiek Tioulong made a series of references to past speakers. On the whole, these references were made broadly in chronological order, but he took the Indian statement, the seventh to be delivered, out of its place and, indeed, gave it absolute priority with the following reference: "We should also express our appreciation to our very active friend Krishna Menon, the discreet and talented conciliator." [27]

After paying "sincere homage" to Lord Home, the Cambodian Minister referred to the Chinese statement (Ch'en Yi had in fact spoken immediately after Home) and said:

We greet with pleasure the constructive character of the statement made by the Chief of the Delegation of the People's Republic of China, Marshal Ch'en Yi, who, while reaffirming vigorously the well known position of his great country, has put out his hand to his adversaries and did so to a greater extent than the latter might have thought possible.[28]

The Cambodian representative next noted "the remarkable statement of M. Couve de Murville, head of the French Delegation, who feels just as we do." [29] He then referred to the American Secretary of State (though Mr. Rusk had spoken before the French delegate) as follows:

We also appreciate the fact that the honorable Head of the U.S. Delegation, Mr. Dean Rusk, has admitted that neutrality is not only a negative political conception and does not consist in keeping its distance between the two blocs, but the sovereignty of Laos should be respected and subversion directed or assisted from the outside should cease and all foreign military personnel should be evacuated from Laos.[30]

Nhiek Tioulong said that there was nothing in this conception that Cambodia would not approve, but he added, that "if wise counsel should be followed, it should be followed also by those who receive as well as those who give. Then we should insure a return to peace." [31] There was a slight element of sting in this last comment on the American statement.

Regarding the Soviet statement, the Cambodian Foreign Minister said:

We also applaud the principles contained in the draft declaration presented by Mr. Andrei Gromyko, in the name of the Soviet Delegation, in accordance with which all participants reaffirm the undertaking to respect sovereignty, independence, unity and territorial integrity, not to intervene in the internal affairs of this country. We also approve that part of the draft which proposed a rapid evacuation—30 days, I believe—of all the units of military personnel and foreign units from Laos.[32]

The Cambodian Foreign Minister's next sentence was particularly significant: "There is a striking concordance in the statements of the two leading statesmen on the terrain of general principles." [33]

In this sentence the Cambodian Foreign Minister not only focused attention on the common ground between the United States and the Soviet Union; by designating Secretary of State Dean Rusk and Foreign Minister Gromyko as the two leading statesmen present, he placed them ahead of the Vice Premier and Foreign Minister of the Peking government. By doing so he counterbalanced his tribute to the Chinese statement.

Nhiek Tioulong then made some comments on the United States view of controls to secure the neutrality of Laos: "We hope that concept of the control situation, proposed by Mr. Rusk, is not the last word of the author." [34] Turning to the Soviet proposals, he added, "However, the mechanism of control proposed by the Soviet delegation . . . perhaps goes a bit too far in the other direction. . . . We should try to find a just solution somewhere at mid-point, which would prove acceptable to all." [35] This meant that hard bargaining lay ahead of the conference and it had better get down to it. Taken altogether, the Cambodian statement was a deft attempt at delicate balancing, which kept all the main participants in the center of the stage without picking any of them as the leading actor or hero. This was Southeast Asian nonalignment in its veritable and inevitable essence: no great power, or large state, is to be overly encouraged, and none among them is to be definitely preferred to the others. This might be exasperating to one power or the other, but it makes sense in Southeast Asia where too close an embrace by any great power would surely jeopardize both the independence and the peace or, in the final analysis, the territorial integrity of the small states that make up the mosaic of the area.

CHAPTER VI

Was the Sino-American Confrontation
at the Laos Conference Negotiable?

WITH THE LINES DRAWN in a fairly clear manner in the opening statements of delegates, the major question that loomed at Geneva was whether the pattern of confrontation that had emerged was, in fact, negotiable—and particularly in as much as it had to do mainly with the attitudes of the United States and the Peking governments.

Marshal Ch'en Yi was quick to show that his delegation intended to maintain its earlier initiative: he was the first of the major participants to take the floor for the second time. On May 24, 1961, he made his second statement on behalf of the Peking government. The main negotiating tactic of this statement was to attempt to isolate the United States delegation. In this vein Ch'en Yi asserted that "the Delegates of Britain, France, and many other countries hold that the 1954 Geneva Agreements should be maintained as a basis, but the United States Delegate pushed aside the International Commission for Supervision and Control set up under these agreements, made unjust criticism against it and attempted to create some new international bodies instead." [1] The purposes of this differentiation between the Western participants was, at least, to show that China did not regard the others as being as difficult as the United States.

Ch'en Yi then referred with approval to parts of the statements of India, Burma, and Cambodia that had been critical of any solution imposed on Laos from the outside through onerous and interfering controls. He went on to claim that the representative of Laos had approved the position of the Chinese delegation. This "approval" was not given by Quinim Pholsena, the representative of Prince Souvanna Phouma—and the Peking government regarded him as the Prime Minister of Laos—who had not mentioned the Chinese proposals. It was Phoumy Vong Vichit, the representative of the Pathet Lao, who had said, "I quite agree with the point of view of China, and of the Soviet Union, and in accordance with which the solution of the Laos question should be based on the Geneva Agreements of 1954." [2] He was thus stretching the facts in making his claim regarding the attitude of Laos.

Marshal Ch'en Yi welcomed the Soviet proposals and also referred in very favorable terms to the speech made by the Foreign Minister of North Vietnam. The only speeches he did not refer to were those of the Polish and Canadian delegates. Thus he had found something favorable to say of almost all the speeches except that of the United States.

The second significant aspect of Ch'en Yi's statement was its vigorous emphasis on maintaining the independence of Laos. Here he injected strong criticism of the United States on the ground that its point of view, if implemented, would encroach upon that independence. This stress on safeguarding the national independence of a small country would tend to be favored by most of the countries at the conference.

Also, from the point of view of a conference that most participants regarded as a reconvening—with a slightly enlarged membership—of the Geneva Conference of 1954, it was a sound tactical move to stress that the basis of agreement should be that which had been accepted at the 1954 conference. Ch'en Yi contended, for example, that the Soviet proposals won the support of the Chinese delegation because they were based upon the 1954 Geneva Agreements.[3] Of the United States' position he said, "In contrast, the proposals of the U.S.[4] are in contravention of the 1954 Geneva Agreements: they obliterate the demarcation between the international and the internal aspects of the Laotian question, and are actually aimed at putting Laos in international condominium." [5]

In the above context Ch'en Yi commented on what he designated as the United States view of "the people's national and democratic movements." He said:

The United States ruling circles have always described the people's national and democratic movements in various countries as aggressive activities organized from without. By guarding against "threats from within" and "subversion from other elements of the state" is actually meant suppressing the Laotian people's national and democratic movements and eliminating the patriotic forces in Laos. This constitutes a bare-faced interference in the internal affairs of Laos.[6]

The attack on the United States position regarding the nature of controls necessary to ensure Laotian neutrality was rounded off with the following rather patronizing phrase: "We advise the U.S. Delegation to think it over well." [7]

Did this mean that China was opposed to all control and supervision in Laos? This question, which had certainly been raised in the minds of the other delegates by what Ch'en Yi had said, was answered by him as follows in a later part of his statement:

The Chinese Delegation is in favor of necessary international supervision and control. We deem that it is not necessary to reorganize the present International Commission. As for the terms of reference of the Commission, they should be, of course, properly readjusted in accordance with the new conditions. In readjusting the terms of reference of the Commission, a sharp distinction must be drawn between the internal and international aspects of the Laotian question, and interference in the internal affairs of Laos is absolutely impermissible, since Laos is a sovereign state.[8]

Thus the Chinese delegation sought to assure the conference that it was not taking an extreme position that would have done away with all international supervision and control.

Returning to the United States position, Ch'en Yi adopted a more conciliatory approach:

For the present, there is a great divergence between us and the U.S. Delegates on the definition of neutrality and the question of international machinery. However, we are after all sitting at the same conference table. Provided that there is sincerity for a peaceful settlement of the Laotian question and earnest discussions conducted by seeking for the facts and reasoning, it is still possible to reach unanimous agreement.[9]

But the Chinese delegate seemed to feel he had to reiterate some of his criticisms of the United States. Somewhat later in his intervention he castigated the United States for what he described as its interference in the internal affairs of Asian countries: "I wish to repeat: the peace and security of Southeast Asia can be assured only by putting an end to United States aggression and intervention, and abolishing [the] SEATO military bloc in the peaceful areas in Southeast Asia." [10]

In reference to the other countries at the conference we have noted the passing but friendly remarks made by Ch'en Yi. Toward the end of his statement, after holding that "the Soviet proposal should be taken as the basis of discussion and agreement at the Conference," he said: "The delegates of certain other countries have put forward their own proposals for the settlement of the Laotian question, and, in the course of questions and consultation, we will give serious study and consideration to all those parts of them which are constructive." To the members of the conference this was also an invitation to make further proposals.

Finally, Ch'en Yi stated that any solution of the Laotian question must not run counter to the following principles:

(1) It must be based on the 1954 Geneva Agreement. (2) It must respect the independence and sovereignty of Laos. (3) It must strictly insure the neutrality of Laos. (4) It must draw a sharp distinction between the internal and the international aspects of the Laotian question. The internal problems of Laos can only be solved by Laotians themselves. Any international agreement must not interfere in the internal affairs of Laos. (5) All the participating nations must take part in and strictly abide by the Common Agreement.[11]

On the first of the above principles advanced by Ch'en Yi there was already wide agreement at the conference, for the most part explicit but not so in the case of the United States. Since the United States had been unable formally to adhere to the 1954 agreements, it was not appropriate that they should make explicit, at any rate at the start of the conference, their willingness to go back to those documents. However, since its close allies, Britain and France, had expressed, both at the conference and informally to other delegates, their conviction that the new agreements for Laos would have to be in line with those of 1954, it was assumed at the conference that the United States did not object to the substance of this position.

As to the second principle put forward by the Chinese, the United States and other countries had expressly stated a similar approach to a settlement. This was also true of the third principle regarding neutrality, in which the words "must strictly insure" were reassuring. However, as to how this strict insurance would be worked out would be a matter of much debate, which would also raise issues of compatibility with the fourth Chinese principle, which was broadly acceptable to the nonaligned delegations at the conference but did not yet have a clearly formulated counterpart in the United States statement.

The fifth principle for the first time made explicit a sincere hope of the other conference members. Clearly, Marshal Ch'en Yi's main purpose in advancing this principle was to ensure that the United States would sign the agreement and be bound by it.

Delivered between Ch'en Yi's aforementioned statement of May 24 and Averell Harriman's statement of May 31 was a brief statement by Deputy Foreign Minister Giorgi Pushkin of the Soviet Union, in which very interestingly the Soviet delegate focused the attention of the conference on the common ground that had thus far emerged. In his reading it was now agreed by all that there must be an independent, sovereign, and united Laos with a neutral status; that the Geneva Conference decisions of 1954 must serve as a basis for working out the new settlement; and that the Laos problem had two aspects, the international and the national and that "the Conference must review and decide the international aspect." [12]

Pushkin also explained further the main concepts contained in the draft proposals that had been submitted to the conference by Foreign Minister Gromyko. These explanations, read with the Soviet proposals, very deftly drew attention to a potential compromise solution in regard to the withdrawal of foreign military personnel and the functions of the International Commission. According to the Soviet proposals the commission would have three functions: first, to supervise and control the cease-fire; secondly, to supervise and control the withdrawal of foreign military personnel; and thirdly, under the instructions of the cochairmen, to investigate any case of the introduction in Laos of foreign military units or personnel. Since in the draft proposals the Soviet Union had allowed only thirty days for the withdrawal of military personnel from Laos, and since presumably the cease-fire would be quickly stabilized, it looked as if the Soviet Union was thinking of locating the International Commission in Laos for only a few months. This would have been unacceptable to many other participants in the conference. However, Pushkin, by mentioning article 12 of the Soviet proposals, set at rest this apprehension. That draft article stated that the cochairmen of the Geneva Conference and the government of Laos would decide the duration of the operations of the International Commission and that to this end they would "after three years hold due consultations thereon and notify their decisions to all the parties to the present Agreement." [13]

When, on May 31, Ambassador Averell Harriman spoke for the United States, he addressed his remarks entirely to the preservation of the cease-fire and to the more effective functioning of the International Control Commission (ICC). He asked that the other groups in Laos should give the ICC the same freedom of movement as General Phoumi of the right wing had given it. He quoted from the report of the ICC dated May 27, 1961, on its intended visits to various sensitive areas, and the lack of cooperation by the Pathet Lao. He insisted that the ICC should be given clear instructions by the conference to enable it to make widespread investigations of any complaints of violation of the cease-fire. To emphasize the importance that the United States attached to this issue, Ambassador Harriman said:

So let me repeat: My Government regards the issue now before us as bearing significantly on the question of whether the preconditions we have always insisted upon for participation in this conference shall be met. Beyond that, it is an augury on the ultimate question of whether the conference can create conditions for a unified, independent, and neutral Laos which we have all come here determined to try to achieve.[14]

On the next day Marshal Ch'en Yi delivered his response to Averell Harriman's statement. In style it was milder than his previous two statements. While he presented a version of the facts, as he saw them, to show that Laotian right-wing military elements were being air-dropped by United States planes behind the lines of the Pathet

Lao to create violations of the cease-fire, he did not in general use the language of invective. Regarding Averell Harriman's emphasis on the cease-fire as a necessary precondition, Marshal Ch'en Yi said: "In his statement yesterday, the United States delegate repeatedly stressed that an effective cease-fire was the pre-condition of this conference. We have to point out that such an agreement, in our understanding does not exist at all." [15] The Marshal contended that the United States was preventing the conference from proceeding to substantive discussions. He added, "This cannot but make people doubtful of the sincerity of the United States for the peaceful settlement of the Laotian question." [16] His formula for consolidating the cease-fire and moving on toward a settlement was the following: "We consider that the more progress our conference makes, the more it will help stabilize the cease-fire in Laos. . . . We hope that the United States will . . . join the other participating nations in serious discussion of the concrete proposals for the peaceful settlement of the Laotian question." [17] Finally, he pointed out that the Soviet Union had made proposals he had supported and that France had also advanced its proposals; then Ch'en Yi stated: "And we would welcome the United States of America to table its own proposals too." [18]

These views were not unreasonably expressed, and many delegates privately felt that some of them merited consideration. Ch'en Yi's closing sentence was also conciliatory: "There is no harm in different views being expressed at our Conference, provided that all of us have sincerity for a peaceful settlement of the Laotian question; we shall eventually be able to find the way to unanimous agreement through full consultation." [19] No delegate took exception to this closing note.

On June 5 and 6, 1961, certain important and even crucial developments took place that were relevant to the Laotian question. On June 5 Malcolm MacDonald, who was presiding at the session on behalf of Foreign Minister Home, drew attention to the communiqué that had just been issued in Vienna "after the historic meeting between President Kennedy and Prime Minister Khrushchev." He expressed the hope and belief that it would "help us in our work in this conference for a united, independent, sovereign and neutral Laos." [20]

In his statement to the conference on the same day, speaking for the Soviet Union delegation, Deputy Minister Giorgi Pushkin also drew attention to the Vienna meeting between Kennedy and Khrushchev and its favorable influence on the international situation. Ambassador Jean Chauvel, speaking for France on June 6, said he would like to associate himself "with what our Soviet colleague said yesterday of the Vienna conversations." [21] On the same day Chauvel introduced the French draft of a protocol on the control and supervisory aspects of a settlement of the Laotian question. In the light of these statements it looked as though the Vienna meeting had ushered in a new and constructive phase for the Laos Conference.

Averell Harriman responded to these statements on June 6, 1961. He quoted the communiqué issued after the Vienna summit meeting and chided the Soviet delegation for not heeding its injunction relating to the cease-fire in Laos. Ambassador Harriman then went on to state flatly,

As has been explained before, we are not prepared to engage in discussions of specific agreements or other documents concerning Laos, until the pre-conditions established for convening this convention have been met. . . . The Chairman of the Council of Ministers of the Soviet Union and the President of the United States have agreed that the conditions of an effective cease-fire should be met. We trust that this understanding will be promptly translated into action here in Geneva and in Laos.[22]

In addition to refusing to discuss, in existing conditions, the draft proposals submitted by the Soviet Union and France on the settlement of the Laotian question, Ambassador Harriman asked for adequate instructions to the International Control Commission in Laos, cessation of the hostilities on the ground, and full cooperation of the combatant parties with the International Control Commission.

How would the conference, and particularly the Chinese delegation, react to this refusal to discuss specific documents of the settlements of the Laotian question, particularly when it seemed that though the Laos cease-fire might be strengthened it would not succeed in stamping out every incident between the opposing factions?

It was not immediately apparent that Averell Harriman's speech, or rather the circumstances that had given rise to it, had resulted in a virtual deadlock. Malcolm MacDonald adjourned the meeting after Harriman's speech and announced that the next meeting of the conference would take place the following day, June 7, 1961.

In fact, no meeting was held on June 7, and no constructive thoughts were born in the discussions in the corridors. The two cochairmen of the conference, Foreign Ministers Gromyko and Home, who had left Geneva and had been functioning through their deputies, hastily returned. Further behind-the-scene consultations were held with the leading delegates,[23] but it looked as though the impasse could not be resolved. The Chinese were adamant that the cease-fire was in effect, that if breaches occurred they were the fault of the right-wing faction of Prince Boun Oum, and that no further action was required at Geneva to maintain the cease-fire. On the other hand, the United States delegation insisted on meticulous enforcement of the cease-fire and fresh instructions to the ICC.

After four days of continuous negotiation, on June 11 Gromyko and Home were able to agree on the following message from the cochairmen to the International Control Commission:

The two Co-Chairmen have received the reports of the International Commission for Supervision and Control in Laos, dated May 20, May 27, and June 5, and express appreciation of the information they contain. They understand that the Commission now intend to discuss with the parties proposals for making the cease-fire more effective. The Co-Chairmen call on the interested parties in Laos to respond to the appeal in their message of April 24.[24]

Lord Home read this brief and seemingly inconsequential message to the conference on June 12, 1961. It was, in fact, a most crucial document at the Laos Conference and is an example of the kind of slender bridge that hard-fought bargaining is sometimes able to build, and by so doing is able to salvage even a major and crucial negotiation from failure. In this statement the United States could claim that the cochairmen had conveyed their understanding that it was now intended to discuss with the parties how to make the cease-fire more effective. Moreover, the United States could say that there had been a reiteration of the cochairmen's appeal of April 1961, on which the Laos Conference had been called. On the other hand, the Chinese could claim, as they did privately, that the cochairman's message of June 11, 1961, to the commission amounted to nothing; in fact it had been thanked for information sent, and note had been taken of its efforts to strengthen the cease-fire; and, of course, the cochairmen could always repeat their previous appeal. The essential point was that both sides—the United States and the Chinese—could interpret the message in a manner that saved their own faces.

For the meeting of June 12, the Chinese Foreign Minister had inscribed his name as the first speaker. However, after Lord Home had read to the conference the cochairmen's joint message to the ICC, he asked whether there were any comments on what he had said. Ambassador Harriman raised his hand and was given the floor. As might have been expected, he said that "it was of prime significance" that the cochairmen had called on the interested parties to respond to their appeal of April 24.[25] He drew attention to the phrase in the joint message regarding proposals for making the cease-fire more effective and then read to the conference the full text of a letter dated June 8, 1961, from the ICC to the Laotian parties and drew from it the conclusion that on-the-spot visits by the commission were a necessity and that the commission counted upon "the promised cooperation of all the parties for making these visits."[26] He expressed the hope that the appeal of the cochairmen, and the activities of the ICC on the ground, would "in fact bring about the effective cease-fire which my Government has consistently sought, and which is a prerequisite to progress by this conference, and the other matters with which we must deal."[27]

Averell Harriman's fairly long statement raised a fresh storm among the Communist representatives. Gromyko made a firm protest and asked on what basis the place of the first speaker, the representative of the Chinese People's Republic, had been given to the United States, adding:

On what basis are you acting? [This was addressed to Lord Home, who was in the chair.] On a basis of some solidarity, NATO solidarity? But it is not a NATO Council. It is an International Conference on Laos. You and I did not agree on the discussion of any communication of both Chairmen. . . . It seems to me that if both Chairmen will act in such a manner, then we shall lack some organization here in the conduct of our Conference.[28]

Lord Home began, "Mr. Gromyko, I should be very distressed if we fell out, in any way," and went on to make an apologetic and conciliatory speech. It looked as if we could then go on to hear Marshal Ch'en Yi's speech. But at that point the delegate of Thailand raised his hand and there followed a long procedural exchange between him and Home, with the latter giving in point by point so that the Thailand delegate too went on to make a long statement.[29] During a period of an hour and a half Ch'en Yi and his vast delegation of some forty or forty-five men and women had looked on, some with anger, some with scorn, and the younger ones with amazement. Ch'en Yi's face was scornful and disdainful. Finally he took the floor at almost 1:00 P.M. (he refused to wait until after the lunch break).

To the surprise of the other delegations, the Chinese Foreign Minister passed in silence over Averell Harriman's intervention and gave only two brief sentences to the long intervention by the Thailand delegate. His first point was to show that, in spite of what he called "this attitude of the United States [which] has brought our conference to a standstill for several days," progress was being made because other delegations had begun to discuss proposals to solve the basic problems before the Conference. He pointed out that on June 6 the French delegate introduced a draft protocol on control and "the British delegate made comments on the Soviet and the French proposals. Although in many ways the view of the British and the French delegates differ from ours, we welcome them to join us in discussing matters of substance." [30] After a brief reference to the situation in Laos, he expressed the hope that the United States too would "seriously join the delegates of the other countries in a substantive discussion of the main question before us." [31] He added that that question was "whether the participating nations will work jointly to find the avenue to a peaceful settlement of the Laotian question." [32] Though he interspersed his plea that the conference should address itself in a business-like way to the precise tasks entrusted to it with accusations of United States interference in the affairs of Laos, his language, tone, and general presentation were on the whole mild.

Ch'en Yi then went on to comment in detail on the French proposals. He said that while there were some acceptable points in the French draft declaration, the protocol on the functioning of the International Commission for Supervision and Control was not at all acceptable because it did not respect the sovereignty and independence of Laos. He was forthright on this point: "The Chinese delegation has come to this Conference with [the] intent [of] respecting an independent and neutral Laos. The Chinese delegation will never be a party to the dirty business of preying upon the Laotian people and enforcing an international condominium over Laos in the name of the international control over its neutrality." [33]

The very next sentence of Ch'en Yi's statement revealed an important aspect of China's negotiating techniques: "Mr. Chairman, I wish to say frankly that we did not expect that the French delegate would propose such a draft protocol." [34] This was a subtle sentence; while appearing to chide France, it in fact singled out that country among the Western participants in the conference, and by so doing threw out a challenge to France, a challenge to take a position somewhat different from that of the other Western powers.

Ch'en Yi went on to contrast the French position with that of the United States. He charged that Secretary Rusk had advanced "a so-called new definition of neutrality and proposed to establish an international control machinery with supreme powers." [35] Asking France to reconsider its position, and expressing the hope "that the French delegate will cherish the position France occupies, in relation to the Laotian question," Marshal Ch'en Yi said, "We would like to assume that perhaps the French delegate has not fully recognized the serious consequences of the draft protocol he proposed." [36]

Why this view of the French draft protocol? By that time (June 12, 1961) two draft proposals to solve the Laotian problem had been presented to the conference: one by the Soviet Union on May 17, 1961, and the other by France on June 6, 1961. While the Russian proposals on control by the International Commission covered a page and a half and contained eight brief articles, the French proposals extended to three pages and were set out in eleven rather full draft articles. For example, French draft article 3 stated:

74 *Sino-American Confrontation*

The Commission and its teams shall have all the authority for investigation, inspection, and verification necessary for the performance of their duties, including authority to hear witnesses. To this end they shall, as of right, have free and unrestricted access by land, sea or air to all parts of Laos, and shall have full freedom to inspect, at any time, all aerodromes, installations or establishments and all units, organizations and activities which are or might be of a military nature. The Commission and its inspecting teams shall have access to aircraft and shipping registers, to manifests and other relevant documents relating to all types of aircraft, vehicles and river craft, whether civil or military, domestic or foreign, and shall have the right to check cargoes and passenger lists.[37]

Eight or ten articles in this vein added up to a very extensive system of supervision in Laos, on a basis of considerable autonomy for the commission and its teams. This the Chinese frequently described in private as nothing less than the re-imposition of foreign rule over Laos, and they stated that they could never be party to such a step, which they regarded as extremely retrogressive particularly in a state that had recently regained its independence from foreign domination.

To the Western delegates as well as to some of the nonaligned, Ch'en Yi's criticism of the French proposals again raised the question as to whether the Chinese were not trying to oppose all forms of international control in Laos. If so, then a primary need of the situation—at least so far as the Western delegates were concerned—would remain unmet, and the conference would produce high-sounding declarations with no practical value.

But the Chinese negotiators were not going to give the Western delegates the satisfaction of being able to blame China for refusing to agree to any control provisions in a Laotian settlement. Marshal Ch'en Yi, after his appeals and reproaches to the French, stated explicitly that China was in favor of international control and supervision in Laos: "We are in favor of necessary supervision and control in Laos by the International Commission, but in all its activities the International Commission should respect and not violate the independence and sovereignty of Laos." [38]

What was to be the purpose of supervision and control so far as China was concerned? The Foreign Minister of the Peking government explained the Chinese position in a one-sided and unsatisfactory manner: "What we should discuss here is how to stop United States intervention and exercise the necessary supervision and control." [39] Ch'en Yi immediately went on to interpret the Soviet draft of May 17, 1961, as meeting this requirement: "In this regard, the two documents put forward by the Soviet Union have precisely embodied this spirit." [40] In point of fact, however, the Soviet proposal did not mention the United States troops or military personnel in Laos. The Soviet draft declaration on the neutrality of Laos contained the following provision: "All foreign troops and military personnel now present in Laos shall be withdrawn within a specified period." [41] The control provisions of the Soviet proposals contained in the document they submitted on the withdrawal of foreign troops and military personnel from Laos stated the following: "Article 6. The International Commission shall supervise and control the withdrawal of foreign troops and military personnel as prescribed by Article 1 of the present agreement." [42] Similarly, article 3 of the Soviet proposal prohibited the introduction into Laos of "any foreign military units or military personnel." Thus it was quite clear that the Soviet interdictions were applicable to all foreign forces and that there was neither specification of United States forces nor any indication that the forces of only one country were present in Laos. Indeed, it was an implication of the Soviet language that foreign troops or personnel from more than one country were present in Laos.

However, Ch'en Yi, while finding the Soviet proposals to be acceptable, was clearly indicating that his delegation would direct its opposition solely to the United States presence in Laos. At the same time, it was also true that the Chinese in pressing this position were making it clear that they were not opposed to the application to Laos of a concept of international supervision and control. Indeed, Ch'en Yi stated immediately after making his unwarranted interpretation (to which we have drawn attention) of the Soviet proposals: "We support the Soviet proposals, though we are not against making reasonable adjustment of one kind or another, on the basis of these proposals." [43]

Moreover, Ch'en Yi disputed the British view that the Soviet proposals dealt only with the cease-fire and thereby lent his support to a larger concept of control operations in Laos. He pointed out that those proposals "explicitly provide that the International Commission should exercise supervision and control *over matters like* the withdrawal of foreign troops from Laos." [44] He went on to stress the need for the parties in Laos to agree to make effective supervision and control a reality. Without such agreement the commission would not be able to discharge its functions. Was this a feasible point of view, he asked, and in reply he stated:

We are glad to learn that the parties concerned in Laos already agreed, in principle, on June 7, that the International Commission would visit certain places for inspection. . . . We hope that, with further agreement reached among the three sides in Laos, the International Commission will make greater contributions toward stabilizing the cease-fire in Laos.[45]

These remarks by Marshal Ch'en Yi, while not fully satisfactory to the Western delegates, did go some way toward meeting the views of the nonaligned delegates, who, of course, discounted his interpretation of the Soviet proposals. This latter group of delegates, it must be remembered, was and is strongly anticolonial and tends to guard jealously the full independence of states, particularly of those states that have recently re-emerged from colonial status. The general approach of these delegates to the problems of Laos was that, first, there must be complete withdrawal of all foreign military forces and indeed of all foreign military pressures and, secondly, that the Laotians should be left to themselves to sort out their own affairs peacefully and without seeking military assistance from other states. In the process they should be assisted, to the extent they desired, by an International Commission, which would also act as a watchdog in their behalf. Moreover, Laos would be a full member of the developing system of international life through the United Nations and its own diplomatic and cultural relations with all countries.

Marshal Ch'en Yi's statement was assessed by the nonaligned delegates in the light of their general position. And, to a degree, Chinese negotiating techniques at the conference took into account the general susceptibilities of such states as Burma, Cambodia, and India.

After his exposé of the Chinese attitude toward controls in an independent Laos, Ch'en Yi made three further points, which would find some favor with at least the nonaligned states and perhaps, to a lesser degree, with other states at the conference.

The first of these points was to warn against bringing any pressure to bear on a government of Laos to sign a treaty unfavorable to itself, pleading the justification that such signature would in itself be an exercise of sovereignty. In this connection, Marshal Ch'en Yi made the pregnant statement: "In the past, the international treaties imposed by the Western big powers on weak or small countries all bore the signatures of the latter but, as I see it, this does not change the character of these treaties which impair the sovereignty of the weak or small countries." [46]

This point tied in naturally with Ch'en Yi's second one, which was that the SEATO treaty was incompatible with the sovereignty of Laos. He said, "In order really to attain the aim of respecting the independence and neutrality of Laos, the South-East Asia Treaty, which is incompatible to the neutral state of Laos, must be abrogated." [47] This point was of course not acceptable to the Western powers but was very much in keeping with nonalignment. One of Prime Minister Nehru's most basic tenets of nonalignment was precisely that military alliances and groupings tended to increase world tensions and were therefore to be eschewed. Indeed, he had especially deplored the SEATO arrangement in a speech in the debate on foreign affairs in the Indian Parliament on September 29, 1954:

We in India have ventured to talk about an area of peace. We have thought that one of the major areas of peace might be South-East Asia. The Manila Treaty [SEATO] rather comes in the way of that area of peace. It takes up that very area which might be an area of peace and converts it almost into an area of potential war. I find this development disturbing.[48]

The views of Cambodia and Burma were very close to those of India in regard to the SEATO arrangement. Ch'en Yi's stand, therefore, was one to which the nonaligned at the conference would not demur. As we shall see, however, though China almost throughout the Laos Conference seemed insistent that the SEATO alliance should be abrogated, toward the end it gave evidence of a certain pragmatic flexibility on this point.

Ch'en Yi's third point, touching on internal developments in Laos, was an interesting one. In regard to those developments, particularly since the right-wing forces, under Boun Oum and Phoumi Nosavan, were not doing particularly well against the left-wing Pathet Lao, it might have been expected that Ch'en Yi would strongly support arrangements that would give the left-wing elements a favorable position in Laos. On the contrary, Ch'en Yi referred to proposed talks between the three factions in Laos (right-wing, left-wing, and center) and said, "I am sure that the delegations of many participating nations share the Chinese Delegation's ardent hope that the high-level talks will shortly take place and speedily reach agreement on the formation of a united coalition government." [49] The significant point in the above quotation is contained in the last four words: "a united coalition government." In those words Marshal Ch'en Yi announced that Peking was in favor of a government of right, left, and center in which the non-left-wing elements (or non-Communist, on the assumption that the Pathet Lao were directed by Communists, though this was not admitted by Souphanouvong) would presumably hold a two-thirds majority. Ch'en Yi was not seeking to push the military advantages of the Pathet Lao to what might have appeared to be a logical conclusion when it came to formation of a government; he was not making an opening bid for a one-party left-wing government or even for a government in which this element would form a moiety.

It should be noted that another possible starting point for the Chinese might have been to ask for a purely neutral government, under Souvanna Phouma, whom they had consistently supported. In this way, though the Pathet Lao would have been excluded from the government, so too would have been the right wing. However, Ch'en Yi took the course that appeared to be dictated by the higher realities of the situation—the need to negotiate a settlement—and did not balk at that course, though to take it meant giving the non-Communists assured control of the government. This is a most interesting point and one that must not escape attention, more particularly as Laos, like Vietnam, is a direct neighbor of China and one could be led to expect that, at least at the beginning of the negotiations regarding Laos, China would have tried to bring into position a government ideologically more sympathetic toward itself. The attitude adopted, which seemed to be realistic, was one that led most of the delegates at the conference table to conclude that the Chinese delegate meant seriously to negotiate a Laotian settlement even if that settlement would not be especially to their liking. To put it another way, as long as Laos could be freed of the military influences and forces of a potential enemy, and as long as nonintervention in its internal affairs could be assured, China seemed willing to live with such an arrangement.

At the close of his statement, Ch'en Yi reinforced the feeling that was growing around some parts of the conference table as a result of this important intervention of June 12, 1961, by stating:

Of course, divergencies are unavoidable, when we discuss matters of substance. We will meet with difficulties of one kind or another. Nevertheless, Mr. Chairman, I agree with a statement made by Mr. MacDonald [Malcolm MacDonald, the British delegate] on June 6: "If we negotiate these matters with patience, tolerance and constructive resolution, we shall reach complete understanding." The Chinese delegation believes that there are all the conditions for our Conference to reach an agreement acceptable to all the parties concerned and thus set an example of easing international tension through negotiation.[50]

This was an important closing remark for several reasons. First, it affirmed a faith in the place of negotiation in international life. It could be seen as a calculated indication that the Peking government favored negotiation for the settlement of international disputes, and not only favored such course but proposed to participate in it. Secondly, it faced up realistically to the fact that there would be differences of view when we came to discuss matters of substance; and, with some idea of what those differences would be, Ch'en Yi still considered that it would be an attainable objective to work for an agreement acceptable to all the parties concerned. Thirdly, Ch'en Yi had the good sense to place in the center of the expression of his view certain remarks of the British delegate, thereby indicating that in essence his understanding of the process of negotiation was similar to that of the Western cochairman of the conference.

Indeed, Ch'en Yi's statement of June 12, 1961, was one of those that cemented the process of negotiation at the Laos Conference by making it clear that though China would use strong words in defense of certain positions, its general approach was in favor of meaningful negotiation. Of course it was wise to treat this conclusion, as one must all conclusions reached during the progress of a negotiation, as a tentative one. The very process of negotiation itself is such that at any given time, no matter what progress has been made in constructing a settlement, the whole situation remains precarious and provisional till the final loose ends are tied together to make the agreement full and complete.

CHAPTER VII

The First Fruits of China's Willingness to Negotiate

CH'EN YI'S STATEMENT of June 12, 1961, made it possible for the negotiators to move beyond the protracted debate that had really been on whether the conditions could be established—a cease-fire, willingness of the three factions in Laos to cooperate, and a mutual examination of basic positions at Geneva—for the conference to get down to substantive negotiation.

When the fifteenth plenary session convened on June 13, 1961, after hearing a brief statement from Phoumy Vong Vichit, the representative of the Neo Lao Hakxat, the conference listened to Foreign Minister Gromyko's exposition of the Soviet draft proposals (Appendix 1). As was to be expected, Andrei Gromyko supported Ch'en Yi's interpretation of the functions of the International Commission in Laos. "The Minister of Foreign Affairs of the People's Republic of China, Marshal Ch'en Yi, spoke very well on this matter," [1] he said.

In summing up his position, on the basis of Mr. Khrushchev's remarks to President Kennedy at Vienna,[2] Gromyko made the following statement, which incidentally bore on the position of Peking at the conference:

If agreement on the Laotian problem cannot be reached in our Conference—and in our view, conditions for such an agreement are available —let no one think that the Soviet Union, the People's Republic of China, and the Socialist countries as a whole will lose as a result of this, more than any other states represented at this Conference. This is not so.

Everyone will stand to lose, if the situation in Laos remains unsettled and therefore potentially dangerous.[3]

The Soviet Foreign Minister did not use the phrase "the Soviet Union and the other Socialist countries." He might well have done so, especially in view of the fact that there were three other Socialist states at the conference table. Instead he mentioned the People's Republic of China by name and lumped together the other Socialist countries of the world. Even in the Socialist camp, then, there was deference to the significant position of China. Moreover, this was an indication that the agreement of the Soviet Union alone among the Communist countries would not be regarded as sufficiently comprehensive to solve issues. The People's Republic of China, in its own and separate right, would have to be an assenting party.

After Mr. Gromyko's intervention the conference listened to a two-and-a-half-hour statement from V. K. Krishna Menon.[4] In that statement Krishna Menon explained, from the point of view of the country that had been given the duties of chairman of the International Commission, how he thought the control and supervisory functions should be carried out. And in launching upon this detailed statement he said, "We start from the basis of the 1954 Agreement and I am happy to think that whether it be the United States, United Kingdom or China, or the Soviet Union or the French, they have all agreed to the position that we start from the Geneva Agreement." [5] Here, then, was a statement that, in the Indian view, China had taken a position alongside the other great powers in finding a common basis for the work of the conference.

Similarly, when discussing the functions of the International Commission in regard to the external aspects of the Laotian situation, Krishna Menon said that the great powers thought alike: "Mr. Dean Rusk said that it is the policy of the United States Government. It has been said by the Russians and the Chinese, and by the British, and everybody else who really determine the affairs of the world." [6] Here there were two thoughts: first, a discerning of the existence of common ground between the other great powers and Peking, and, secondly, a special position for China among those "who really determine the affairs of the world." However, the Indian view was not entirely firm in ascribing a special position among the great powers to China. In discussing the possibilities of Laos' obtaining military equipment and military training facilities, Krishna Menon stated that Laos would look to the United States or the Soviet Union or France, "because there is no one else who is capable of giving." [7] He added that the British could probably give arms but they would be of a kind that would not suit Laos. Significantly, the Defense Minister of India did not mention China as a possible source of arms. This may have been an indication, at least in part, of the poor intelligence of the Indian government regarding the military strength of its neighbor to the northeast.

On June 15, 1961, Averell Harriman made a statement on behalf of the United States, his first intervention after Ch'en Yi's long statement of June 12. It was interesting that there was no direct reference whatsoever to that Chinese intervention. Ambassador Harriman did refer briefly to the aspersions some delegates had cast against other delegates and governments participating in the conference, and, while some of the Chinese statements came within the ambit of this general remark, Ambassador Harriman's silence on the Chinese intervention did *inter alia* perhaps indicate that he did not find himself in significant disagreement with the Chinese assertions regarding an independent neutral Laos or those on the need for serious negotiation among all the delegates at the conference table.

Averell Harriman suggested that the conference should set up working groups to examine the detailed proposals before it. This statement was, in fact, a most significant contribution to the progress of the conference: it indicated, in effect, that the United States, which had thus far considered the precariousness of the cease-fire in Laos to be an effective obstacle to substantive negotiation at the conference, was now willing to join in such negotiation. In one important respect, therefore, the United States was no longer in opposition to the stand of most of the other states at the conference, including China.

The conference did not immediately establish working groups, but it did continue detailed consideration of substantive proposals. On June 16 M. Chauvel, speaking on behalf of France, made a second detailed analysis of the French proposals (Appendices 3 and 5). On

June 19, 1961, James Barrington expounded Burma's views regarding substantive matters, and he was followed by Foreign Secretary Howard Green of Canada, who explained his government's position on those matters. He stressed that the conference should proceed as rapidly as possible with its discussions on issues of substance so as to reach early agreement. Howard Green was so keen on expediting the work of the conference that he asked that a comparative tabulation be made of the Soviet and French proposals so that the conference could discuss them with facility.

Representatives from the West, the Communist countries, and the nonaligned states had all by now engaged in discussion of substantive proposals, and this was what the Peking government had pressed for in its intervention of June 12. If no immediate tabulation was made of the various proposals before the conference this was because Averell Harriman, on June 20, 1961, supported my request (speaking for India) on June 19, 1961, that we should allow a little more time to pass so as to give other states an opportunity to submit their proposals. I did not then reveal that India would soon table comprehensive proposals on the Laotion question, but I was, of course, aware of this intention of India's and was personally engaged in preparing proposals for consideration by the conference.

On June 20 Averell Harriman introduced substantial amendments to the French proposals dealing with the functions of the International Commission in Laos. The general purpose was to strengthen the already rather comprehensive French text on the powers of the commission to control and supervise the implementation of the provisions in the proposed agreement that would establish the neutrality of Laos.[8]

As was to be expected, the United States proposals led to a Chinese rejoinder. Ch'en Yi took the floor on June 26, 1961. First he stated his agreement with critical references that had been made by the Soviet and Polish delegates on the American supplementary articles. Then the Peking delegate gave the conference his own views on the new proposals. He charged that the United States wanted to obtain the national defense secrets of Laos and "also to fix the strength of the army of Laos and the quantities and types of its armaments."[9]

Ch'en Yi went on to say, "As we all know, a country's national defense needs can only be determined by the Government of that country itself. This is the main indication of national sovereignty. The United States has indeed made a preposterous demand." [10]

In fact, in expressing the view stated above, Ch'en Yi indicated the gap between the Peking government's position and that to which the rest of the world community is attempting to move. The whole effort for arms control and disarmament, under the aegis of the United Nations, is based on the view that the level of armaments of a particular state is not a matter to be determined solely by that state. It was in principle clearly a wise proposal that Laos, which had seen so much warfare, should accept a limitation of armaments on its territory. This was all the more relevant in a country in which the warfare had been largely internecine. Ch'en Yi's view was not only a reflection of the isolation of China from major trends among other nations concerned about the military situation; it also indicated the importance that China attaches to its own national armament.

After concluding his remarks on this aspect of the United States proposal with the view that it was "absolutely impermissible," Ch'en Yi went on, in his immediately succeeding remark, to reveal another facet of Communist China's attitudes: "The Franco-American draft protocol cannot be the basis for our discussion, nor can it be compared and reconciled with the Soviet proposals. How can we lump together right and wrong and then strike a mean between them?" [11]

The dogmatic conviction of the Maoists that they—or those who support them—are right and others are wrong is, of course, a major stumbling block to the process of reconciling varying points of view on the international scene. We have already noted Mao's own dogmatism concerning right and wrong.[12] This attitude has continued to dominate Peking's thinking. In ideological terms the Chinese insist that theirs is the "correct" party.[13] For example, on May 10, 1966, Yao Wen-yuan, writing in Shanghai's *Jiefang Ribao,* quoted Mao Tse-tung's simplistic view of the truth: "Comrade Mao Tse-tung has taught us: 'We must firmly uphold the truth and truth requires a clear-cut stand.' " [14] Such citations from present-day Chinese thinking could be multiplied virtually endlessly, and Marshal Ch'en Yi was on the same wavelength when he made his statement about right and wrong at the Laos Conference on June 26, 1961.

He went on to ridicule the idea, which he saw in the Western proposals, of protection of the neutrality of Laos by the International Commission. What was his formula, then, for ensuring Laotian neutrality? He gave it to us in the following words:

In order to insure respect for Laotian independence and neutrality, the primary things that must be done are to conclude an international agreement with concrete contents, to abolish the SEATO bloc, and to make the United States and its followers undertake not to interfere in any manner in the internal affairs of Laos. The United States must sign the agreement and pledge not to violate the agreement, immediately after its conclusion, as it did in 1954.[15]

In point of fact this formula was neither revealing nor was it, to the extent that it made any points, fully implemented by the conference. Ch'en Yi asked for "concrete contents" but he did not reveal what those contents should be. However, in this way he gave his delegation a measure of flexibility, which was a wise negotiating move, even if by acquiring flexibility in a sense he contradicted his own previous assertion that no reconciliation was possible between the Soviet proposals and those of France and the United States.

As to the specific proposal made by the Chinese leader—that SEATO be abolished—we shall see later how even the most forthright and apparently adamant positions can be abandoned: in the event, SEATO was not abolished and yet China signed an agreement on Laos.

When Ch'en Yi went on to state that the purpose of the Franco-American proposals was to destroy the Neo Lao Hakxat he was indulging in what might be regarded in negotiation as permissible championing of a party involved in the situation under consideration. However, then he said, "The Chinese delegation reaffirms that it is resolutely opposed to the Franco-American draft protocol. I wish to point out unequivocally that any attempt to impose on Laos an international trusteeship, as provided in the draft protocol, will lead to no other result but rekindling war-flames in Laos." [16] These remarks introduced a blatant threat of the recrudescence of the use of force in Laos. While it is true that nations, when they negotiate, do not—the

Charter of the United Nations notwithstanding—renounce all possibilities of the use of force, it tends to vitiate the process of negotiation if
threats of force are brought strongly into the foreground. Such tactics
normally harden positions all around and increase the obstacles to
developments in the direction of agreement. Fortunately, at the Laos
Conference the vast majority of the participants did not echo Ch'en
Yi's hard language.

It might well be that Ch'en Yi's personal style was partly a result
of his own considerable military background. He had been Secretary
of the Army Committee of the Communist Party of China in 1928,[17]
and for many years he had been Commander of the New Fourth
Army during the civil war in China and the war against Japan.[18]

Recovering his diplomatic composure, Ch'en Yi proceeded immediately after his rather threatening remarks to state that "our Conference has all the conditions for reaching an international agreement on
the peaceful settlement of the Laotian question, *acceptable to all.*" [19]
It must have been clear to Ch'en Yi that if the agreement was to be
acceptable to all it would have to contain at least some of the concepts embodied in the Franco-American proposals. Since these words
were spoken a few seconds after his reaffirmation of resolute opposition to the Franco-American draft, Ch'en Yi was showing his capacity to make seemingly radical shifts of position, and by doing so was
diminishing the seriousness of the Chinese position in the negotiation.
There appeared to be in his statement some lack of intellectual
appreciation both of the contradictory meanings of his remarks and
of the effect that this indication of confusion would have on the attitudes of some of the other delegates toward China as a negotiator.

A little later in his intervention Ch'en Yi adopted the tactic of
seeming to take the negotiation to the brink of collapse. Referring to
the agreement, dated June 22, 1961, reached between the Laotian
Princes on the internal and external aspects of a unified Laos,[20] he
pointed out that it contained the following reference, so far as Laos
was concerned, to such arrangements as SEATO: "Not to recognize
the protection of any military alliance or coalition." He then added
this comment:

Secretary of State Mr. Dean Rusk, hastened to state that, "A declaration
of this sort could not affect the internal government arrangement as far

as SEATO is concerned." That is to say, no matter what decision the Laotians may make, and no matter what decisions our Conference may finally adopt, the United States still wants to treat Laos as a protectorate of SEATO.[21]

To this (his own) interpretation of the United States' position Ch'en Yi reacted strongly: "If the United States persists in this attitude, what is the meaning of our sitting here and discussing respect for Laotian neutrality?" [22] And yet only a few minutes later in referring to the functions of the International Commission Ch'en Yi could say, "I would request you all not to ignore the fact that, on this question, we have more common points than divergencies." [23] And nearer the close of his remarks he said that he had restated his views "not to widen the divergencies, but to seek unanimity. We are all rational people. We all hope for a peaceful settlement of the Laotian question." [24]

But before he made these closing remarks he tried to draw a distinction between exercising supervision and control over the withdrawal of foreign military personnel in Laos and the inclusion in the agreement of similar functions to discourage or prevent the introduction of foreign military personnel into Laos in the future. He advanced the view that if only the United States would withdraw its own forces and stay out of Laos, then the future would look after itself. This questionable differentiation between undoing a situation and taking steps to prevent it from recurring was again a manifestation of a certain lack of perception or an attempt to satisfy the conference with a naïve point of view, both being approaches that could not find favor with the majority of the negotiators.

This statement by Ch'en Yi, on June 26, 1961, with its internal contradictions, was a warning that the Laos Conference, which originally had been expected to sit for about six weeks, would try the patience of the negotiators for many a month. It would be some time before the Chinese would reveal which of their hardnesses were brittle and which unyielding. For the present, perhaps the Chinese themselves did not know—certainly this was the impression created by some of the confusions in Ch'en Yi's presentation to which I have drawn attention.

It was with some of these blurred nuances of the Chinese statement in mind that, speaking immediately after Ch'en Yi's intervention I said that we had heard enough to convince us that "the idea that the proposals of the Soviet Union and of France, as amended by the United States, should be tabulated and considered jointly as the basis of our future work . . . would be unrealistic." [25] We were convinced by this time that a fresh set of proposals, taking into account the Zurich communiqué of the three Laotian Princes (Appendix 9) and the sharp divergencies between the Western and the Soviet proposals, should be submitted to the conference.

CHAPTER VIII

A Setback in Negotiation

THE CONFUSIONS immanent in Ch'en Yi's last statement notwith-standing, it had looked as though the conference had at last got down to substantive negotiation. Three sets of proposals were now on the table and there had been some serious discussion of them. Moreover, on June 22, 1961, the leaders of the three factions in Laos had reached agreement at Zurich both on internal and external matters relating to their country [1] and thereby made a valuable contribution to progress at Geneva.

Though these indications clearly pointed in the direction of con-centration on substantive negotiation, a new difficulty arose and ob-structed progress at the conference for the next three weeks. On July 3, 1961, Phoui Sananikone, who had taken his seat on June 27, 1961, as the representative of the Boun Oum group in Laos, opened the proceedings of the conference. Phoui had been twice, though briefly on each occasion, the Prime Minister of Laos and was there-fore an authoritative spokesman for the group he now represented. Without presenting a formal proposal, and speaking in the tentative manner often adopted by Asian statesmen, even when they make definitive pronouncements, Phoui introduced an issue that was to stir up a procedural wrangle at the conference. He said:

There are two problems in this Conference. The first consists of putting effectively an end to hostilities in Laos, in order to bring back a state of peace wished for by all Laotians, and, I am sure, all the peoples of the world.

The second problem consists in granting the Kingdom a status of strict neutrality, respecting its independence and its sovereignty.

These two problems, although they have to be solved for the same country, nevertheless are quite distinct.

Why not approach them one after the other? Why not solve the first, before passing on to the second? [2]

Posed as a mere matter of procedure, this proposal raised an issue of fundamental importance: the return of peace in Laos would mean that the Pathet Lao and other factions would have to lay down arms. This could leave the Boun Oum group in control of the capital and other important areas, and since this group was known to be strongly pro-Western it might not agree to Laotian neutrality, thereby fundamentally altering the very basis of the conference on Laos.

Ch'en Yi was the next speaker, and he was now making his fifth major statement. As against this, the conference had heard one major statement from Dean Rusk, two from Andrei Gromyko, and two from Lord Home. Ch'en Yi did not immediately refer to Phoui's statement. On the contrary, he opened with remarks that illustrated how the very process of negotiation, assuming the existence of a will to continue with it, will often slowly generate movement from previous adamantine positions. Ch'en Yi began by saying that "through the debates of the past period, our Conference has made some achievements. We have come to know one another's stand and discovered that we have points in common on many questions." [3] This prologue put the conference into a different state of mind from that which had been induced by the broad sense of the first, second, and fourth statements by the Foreign Minister of the Peking government. For him to say that it had been discovered that there were points in common on *many* questions, when there were not, after all, more than a handful of important issues before the conference, could only mean that we could now move to the process of formulation of some parts of the texts of the Agreement and Protocol that would enshrine the new international treaties in regard to Laos.

Marshal Ch'en Yi went on to make a most interesting and important bridge between what he had previously stated to be irreconcilables. We have noted his total rejection of the Franco-American draft and his categorical statement of its irreconcilability with the Soviet proposals. Furthermore, right and wrong could not be lumped together.[4] Now he evolved an ingenious formula that would permit the possibilities of reconciliation of varying points of view. He put it this way:

In order to reach a generally acceptable agreement, the countries concerned, on the one hand, have to engage in earnest and serious discussions and distinguish between right and wrong on each issue; and on the other hand, have to show a conciliatory spirit for reaching agreement on a reasonable basis.[5]

In this view there needed to be no exclusion of one set of proposals or another. True, with the new Chinese formulation, the delegates at the conference could distinguish between what they thought right and wrong for each issue, but their objective would be conciliation and the reaching of reasonable agreements.

As to how this was to be done, Ch'en Yi said that the way was shown by a Chinese saying, which he quoted: "Seek common ground and reserve divergencies." [6]

He then praised the Zurich agreement between the three Laotian princes and said that "precisely because the three Laotian Princes have reached an explicit agreement on a policy of peace and neutrality for Laos, our Conference should all the more proceed to substantive negotiations on the question of the undertaking by the other participating countries to respect the independence and neutrality of Laos." [7] The Marshal was thus arguing that the question of peace and neutrality had been solved so far as the various factions in Laos were concerned, and that therefore the main task that remained was for the international community to make explicit its commitments to respect Laotian independence and the country's chosen status of neutrality.

With this in view Ch'en Yi made a formal proposal to the conference:

Embracing what was stated above, the Chinese delegation formally proposes that our Conference terminate its general debate and proceed to substantive negotiations on an undertaking to respect the independence and neutrality of Laos and reach a relevant international agreement.[8]

He closed by saying that the conference had "all the bright prospects for reaching agreement."

It is also noteworthy that in the course of his statement Ch'en Yi made a friendly conciliatory reference to what were by then known to be efforts of India and Cambodia to try to work out compromise proposals for the consideration of the conference. He said that "the delegates of certain neutral countries are preparing to advance their positive suggestions to begin more efforts by all." [9]

Poland, North Vietnam, and the Soviet Union immediately spoke in support of Ch'en Yi's proposal to consider first the formulation of an agreement regarding the independence and neutral status of Laos. Thus, the four Communist countries at the conference yielded a kind of primacy to China in permitting it to make an important proposal that they in turn supported. It would have been, on the basis of the United Nations' experience, more normal to expect such a proposal to emanate from the Soviet Union, and in this case more so because she was a cochairman of the conference, and arrangements relating to procedure were directly in the province of the cochairmen. However, China was given the position of spokesman.

An interesting sequel to Marshal Ch'en Yi's proposal was that Malcom MacDonald, speaking on behalf of the United Kingdom, said that his government wished to give very serious consideration to the Chinese proposal and to the suggestions of Phoui Sananikone. He did not express himself in favor of the latter suggestion, though it was known that the United States strongly favored it. In concluding his statement Malcolm MacDonald referred in a friendly manner to the statement of Marshal Ch'en Yi. His words were:

I only say, in conclusion, quoting Marshal Ch'en Yi, that we all bear a very heavy responsibility, around this table. . . . We in the British Delegation share fully the Marshal's sincerity of expression, that we all wish to play our parts constructively in establishing agreements which shall ensure the peace and happiness of the Laotian nation.[10]

At the next session of the conference the then Foreign Minister of the Republic of Vietnam; the Canadian delegate, Chester Ronning; and John Steves, speaking for the United States, all supported Phoui Sananikone's proposal and called for prior attention by the conference to strengthening peace in Laos and clarifying the role of the International Commission to this end. Indeed, Steves pressed the point strongly and referred sarcastically to the Chinese proposal. He said, "Why then have we been faced with this proposal, this patently calculated maneuver that the Conference divert its attention from the urgent business at hand, in order to discuss a hypothetical declaration of neutrality?" [11]

In spite of this strong and forthright support for Phoui's point of view by the United States, Ambassador Chauvel speaking for France did not support the American position. He chose the British line without mentioning it, stating that "it would be wise, I think, to give to our governments the time to take a general view, to take stock of the opinions expressed by the various countries in this Conference, and to draw from them the necessary conclusions." [12] These indications by the United Kingdom and France were of considerable importance, particularly in the context in which they were made. It was only the Communist countries that had supported the proposal of Marshal Ch'en Yi. The neutral states—Burma, Cambodia, and India—had made no statements at the conference on the Chinese proposal. Privately some of them had mentioned that they would favor giving priority to working out a declaration of the neutrality and independence of Laos. At the conference table itself Cambodia had outlined proposals it had considered tabling but had decided to withhold. These tentative proposals gave priority of consideration to the question of an agreement on the neutrality and independence of Laos. However, the significant fact had emerged that two leading Western powers had not immediately supported the United States on a most important question of procedure before the conference: for if priority were given to the Chinese proposal an agreement could be worked out with which the continuing presence of United States military personnel in Laos would be incompatible. It was clearly difficult for the United States to accept a procedure that would lead to this result without simultaneously ensuring that all other foreign intervention would not only cease but be curbed by a strengthened International Commission.

These considerations were all the more vital in the context of the internal situation as it was then developing in Laos. The agreement of the Princes in Zurich had not led to the formation of a coalition government, though this should have been its first logical consequence. On the contrary, while overt military action had not developed significantly in the country, hostile preparations were continuing. Furthermore, there was news of some defections from the Boun Oum group of forces to the Pathet Lao or to the Centrists. Even with the counterbalancing effect of strong United States support in equipment, finance, and skilled personnel, the right-wing groups were not gaining ground in the country. These considerations put what appeared to be a procedural wrangle at the Geneva Conference into a very different and foreboding perspective. A decision in favor of the Chinese proposals could conceivably further shift the balance of forces in the country in favor of the Centrists and the Pathet Lao. It must have been sorely trying to some of the participants that the British and French were unable to support the suggestions made by Phoui Sananikone.

Meanwhile, Giorgi Pushkin, speaking for the Soviet Union and referring to John Steves' remark about "a hypothetical declaration of neutrality," said, "I regret that the representative of the United States of America should treat with such levity a document as important as that concerning the neutrality of Laos." [13] And in regard to the proposal supported by the United States he added, "The Soviet Delegation categorically rejects such a procedure for the discussion of these problems, since it goes against the most elementary common sense." [14] This statement brought into the open the full magnitude and significance of the procedural issue that divided the participants around the conference table.

Marshal Ch'en Yi had returned to Peking and left in the Chinese seat his senior Deputy Minister for Foreign Affairs, Chang Han-fu. Meanwhile the other participants had got to know Chang Han-fu in informal discussions and on social occasions. He told me that he had studied at universities in the United States and had done graduate work at Columbia. His knowledge of English was more than adequate. He was able to respond directly without any hesitation to all points raised in informal discussion. (In formal discussions in and outside the conference, he, of course, always used Chinese.) Direct communication with him, because of his sound knowledge of English, was easier than with Marshal Ch'en Yi, whose French had worn off in the course of some forty years of uninterrupted revolutionary work in China.

Chang Han-fu spoke for a half hour on July 6, 1961, in support of Marshal Ch'en Yi's proposal and in opposition to the statement of the United States. It is interesting that he did not mention the statements of Phoui Sananikone or of the delegates of Canada, Thailand, and South Vietnam. He leveled his guns solely against the United States. The zenith of his attack was as follows:

The United States, on the one hand, is stepping up its aid, and the training of the troops of the Savannakhet group; on the other hand, it is carrying out all sorts of activities in an endeavor to exclude the Neo Lao Hakxat in forming a government of national union in Laos.

The United States Information Service went so far as to openly declare in Washington, on July 3, that "American support for any Laotian Premier would depend on seeing that the Pathet Lao and pro-Communist factions did not gain a commanding political majority in the coalition government." [15]

Chang Han-fu contended that this incontestably revealed that "the United States is deliberately preventing our Conference from making any progress so as to keep in step with the aforesaid act of intervention." [16] It must be remembered that Chang Han-fu was making his first statement, and it happened to be a major one, at the Geneva Conference. It was to be expected that he would stoutly maintain the Chinese position. But in doing so he had gone beyond the facts adduced by him in support of his own case. In the above citation from his remarks, the charge that the United States was endeavoring to *exclude* the Neo Lao Hakxat from a government of national union in Laos was not even borne out by his quotation from the USIS release. That release indicated that the United States would not be able to support a government in which the Pathet Lao had a commanding political majority. It did not say that the United States wished to exclude this group from the government. An alternative explanation of

Chang Han-fu's statement was that it was the Chinese hope that the Pathet Lao would in fact hold a commanding position in the coalition government. However, we should note that Chang Han-fu did call upon all the delegates to respect the Zurich communiqué,[17] which contained the following provision regarding a Laotian government of national union: "The Government of national union will comprise the representatives of the three parties and will have a provisional character." [18] While the communiqué does not state explicitly that the three parties would be more or less equally represented, that appeared to be the intention, and the communiqué had been generally understood in this manner. There was no immediate response to Chang Han-fu's statement and, in a state of deadlock, the thirtieth session of the conference was adjourned.

Meanwhile there was a report from the International Commission in Laos that bore on the problems confronting the conference. On the question of the cease-fire, the commission stated: "In spite of the alleged cease-fire violations during the last fortnight the Commission is satisfied that the cease-fire is generally being maintained throughout Laos. . . . The meeting of the three Princes at Zurich has proved beneficial both in improving the general atmosphere and in the proper maintenance of the cease-fire." On the political aspect of the situation in Laos the commission made the following observation: "Some progress at Geneva on the international aspects of the Laotian problem will have a salutary effect on both the local political and military situations in Laos." [19]

In an article entitled "Stalemate in Geneva," which appeared in the *Peking Review* on July 14, 1961, the Chinese explained the deadlock in characteristic terms:

The United States' refusal to discuss and negotiate on such a question of key importance exposes the fact that it continues to cling to its policy of aggression and intervention against Laos. It fears that once it has committed itself to an international obligation to respect the independence and neutrality of Laos, this will bind it hand and foot and keep it from engaging in further aggression and intervention against Laos. . . . While stalling the talks, as reports from Laos show, the United States has directed the Thai and south Vietnamese troops and Phoumi-Boun

Oum rebel forces to intensify their harassing activities against areas under the control of the Royal Laotian Government and the Neo Lao Hakxat, and they have taken some strong-points. The number of U.S. military personnel in Vientiane has increased to more than 1000.[20]

Meanwhile at the conference table Giorgi Pushkin again pressed for the adoption of Ch'en Yi's proposal to give priority to a declaration on the neutrality and independence of Laos. In support of this proposal he pointed out that even the French delegation had first submitted its draft proposals on neutrality while its protocol on control was brought to the conference two weeks later.[21]

Malcolm MacDonald had spent the previous four days or so consulting with the United Kingdom government at London and had returned with a compromise proposal that met the Chinese position half way. He did not put the weight of the United Kingdom behind the procedure backed by the United States, but suggested instead that the conference should discuss the two major topics on alternate days, beginning with neutrality and independence. In this way, if anything, the Chinese proposal was slightly favored over the proposal backed by the United States.

Informally the major delegations at the conference had been informed of the British proposal before it was made. The Polish delegate had a prepared speech for the session at which Malcolm Mac-Donald introduced his proposal. He took the floor and said that the British proposal, which would involve skipping from one subject to another, would reduce the conference to a state of chaos.

Averell Harriman, speaking for the United States, placed his main emphasis on the need to equip the International Commission thoroughly and effectively for the tasks entrusted to it. On the question of procedure, he argued in favor of the proposal that his delegation had supported, and, while not supporting the British proposal he suggested that the cochairmen should meet informally with the heads of the various delegations to resolve the issue. In short, the United States representative was indicating that some compromise proposal, though he did not specify its terms, would be acceptable to his country. Indeed, he said, "It is impossible for me to believe that any delegate would want to leave the impression that only his delegation's viewpoint is acceptable." [22]

On the same day, Jean Chauvel (France) supported the British proposal. As was to be expected, the two Vietnams aligned themselves on opposite sides. Other speakers too expressed opinions on one side or the other.

In these circumstances a further effort at compromise was necessary. The Indian delegation discussed this matter and Krishna Menon, on July 13, 1961, suggested to the conference that the crux of the matter was agreement that, while all sides—including the President of the United States and the Secretary of State—had spoken of the importance of arranging the international aspects of the Laotian question, which necessarily meant primarily an agreement on the independence and neutrality of Laos, neither this issue nor that relating to peace in Laos and the terms of reference of the International Commission could be finally determined in isolation. Even if one issue was resolved before the other neither solution could have any effect until there was overall agreement on both questions.[23] On that date, and thereby implying his own preference for first priority, Krishna Menon introduced an Indian draft declaration on the neutrality and independence of Laos.

The next morning James Barrington, speaking for Burma, supported the Indian draft text on neutrality and also asked that neutrality be the first subject to be discussed in detail.

But the question of procedure was still unresolved, and after Krishna Menon had presented the second half of the Indian proposals—relating to the functions of the International Commission in Laos—Chang Han-fu made his second contribution on the resolving of the procedural issue. Referring to Averell Harriman's statement of July 11, 1961, Chang Han-fu contended that by asking that attention be paid to the strengthening of the cease-fire "the U.S. delegates show a big step backward from their past stand." [24] This meant, in effect, said Chang Han-fu, that though the United States delegate had previously commented on the detailed proposals submitted by the Soviet and French delegates and had tabled his own extensive amendments to the French proposals, he was now going back to the very first point raised at the conference in May: the maintenance of the cease-fire. He added:

To date, reports from the International Commission have all indicated that the state of the cease-fire in Laos is good, and in the process of becoming better.[25] The U.S. delegates have raised this question not because the situation in Laos is deteriorating but precisely because the three Laotian Princes have reached explicit agreement in their Zurich talks.[26]

Chang Han-fu went on to state that the United States did not want a coalition government in conformity with the Zurich Agreement, and nor did it wish to see the Geneva Conference arrive at an agreement to recognize and respect the neutrality of Laos. These were imputations of bad faith on the part of the United States and indicated once again to the conference that the Chinese delegate would tend, perhaps through suspicion or perhaps because of more reprehensible motives, to paint the other side in the worst possible colors.

Chang Han-fu concluded his remarks on the United states' posture by saying, "The position of the U.S. delegates is entirely untenable." [27] But Chinese tactics in negotiation are not restricted to attacking the opponent's position. Chang Han-fu went on to make several interesting points. First, and this was entirely unexpected at the conference table, he referred to the right-wing delegate from Laos in the following terms: "It is to be welcomed that Mr. Phoui Sananikone, the delegate from Vientiane, has come at last to take part in our conference." [28] The right-wing element in Laos was in close alliance with the United States; both militarily and ideologically it was in strong opposition to the Pathet Lao. And yet the delegate from Peking used language that appeared to most other delegations to be gracious and conciliatory. The reasons for this tactic were numerous. Some of them were obvious and short-term, others had a longer-term significance. In the first category of reasons was Peking's desire to assure Laos that it had no objection to accepting a composite society and government in which feudal elements would continue to play a role, at any rate in the present. Secondly, there was obviously some calculation of the effect of the aforementioned broadness of Peking's outlook on the other Asian states present, particularly Burma and Cambodia, where social and political forms also include varying degrees of traditional elements that had been virtually crushed in Communist China. The third of the short-term reasons for the Chinese statement was to urge the right wing in Laos to think in terms of national self-respect and full assertion of national statehood. Thus, Chang Han-fu went on with his reference to Phoui as follows:

But it is regrettable that he, probably owing to inadequate knowledge of the proceedings of our Conference at the previous stage, repeated yet once again the view that it would do no harm to sacrifice a little the sovereignty of Laos. . . . This position of Mr. Phoui Sananikone thoroughly runs counter to the Zurich agreement among the three Princes.[29]

This gentle berating of the right-wing delegate from Laos was delivered in a soft-spoken tone and with an intonation of brotherly admonition. These characteristics of the appeal could not have been lost on the aristocratic representative of Prince Boun Oum. They certainly had their effect on most of the other delegates in the room. It should be noted that, in general, Chang Han-fu's tone and manner of delivery were always unaggressive and very often contrasted sharply with the import of the words he was using.

The major long-term implication of Chang Han-fu's remarks to and about Phoui Sananikone was that Peking had probably decided that almost any agreement on the Laos issue based on reassertion of national independence and neutrality for Laos would be acceptable. Not all the delegates at the conference table would have read Chang Han-fu's remarks as carrying this implication, but to many of them his words contained an affirmation of direction, if not of position, that helped to make continuation of an already long drawn out negotiation worthwhile.

Another point of interest, as a matter of negotiating tactics, was made when Chang Han-fu directed some of his remarks to the subject of the International Control Commission. One of the side irritants that had developed at the conference related to arrangements for adequately equipping the International Commission and its staff so as to facilitate its visits of inspection and pacification in Laos. A few days before Chang Han-fu came to this question in his remarks on

July 14, 1961, the situation regarding equipment had touched off a minor crisis. Malcolm MacDonald and Giorgi Pushkin, acting on behalf of the Foreign Ministers of the United Kingdom and the Soviet Union, the cochairmen of the conference, had reached full agreement with the delegates of the states representing the members of the commission [30] on the terms of a communication to the International Commission and the authorities in Laos relating to the supply of equipment. A few hours before this agreed communication was to be issued, word was received from Ottawa that Howard Green, then Foreign Minister of Canada, was unable to accept the communication. It was held up. By this time the other major delegations at the conference had become aware of the agreed communication and some of them chose to regard the objection of Ottawa as a deliberate attempt to divert the attention of the conference from the substantive work of trying to reach agreement on the text of a treaty.

It was to this situation that Chang Han-fu next directed his remarks; he described the question of equipment for the commission as "entirely an artifically created problem." Having done so and thereby differentiating his position clearly from that of some of the Western powers, he went on, not to agree with the Polish position regarding equipment, but to show his broadmindedness by agreeing with the Indian position. He said, "As the Indian delegate, Mr. Lall, pointed out in his statement on the 11th of July, a unanimous rational resolution to this problem had already been found. . . . We completely agree with Mr. Lall in his appeal on this question and earnestly hope that the appeal will be responded to as it should be." [31]

Having, both by his reference to the right-wing delegate and to the question of equipment, widened the zone of sympathetic receptivity around the conference table, Chang Han-fu returned to the major issue of procedure that still stood unresolved: whether the conference should first formulate an agreement on the neutrality and independence of Laos and then turn to the Protocol on the functions of the International Commission; or whether the order of priority should be reversed; or whether the two should progress simultaneously as had been suggested by the British cochairman of the conference. The question was still a delicate one. A frontal Chinese attack on the

problem was likely to have the normal effect of such tactics in a negotiation, to harden the opposition of the other side. However, it might
have been thought that Chang Han-fu, by winning a certain degree of
sympathy round the table with his previous remarks, had prepared
the way for such a frontal approach and that he would try now to
isolate the United States from most of the other participants at the
conference. On the whole, Chang Han-fu rejected this tactic. First he
showed that even the drafting of the declaration on neutrality would
not be "a philosophical discussion" as John Steves (who had briefly
stood in for Averell Harriman) had said on July 4, 1961.[32] In reaching the conclusion that the drafting of a declaration on neutrality
would divert the conference from the immediate needs in Laos,
Steves had said that while the United States government had made its
intentions to withdraw its forces quite clear, he had "listened in vain
during the general debate for some indication of *their* intentions from
the men of Hanoi or from the Soviet or the Chinese delegations." [33]
On this question of the withdrawal of forces Chang Han-fu decided to
reveal the intentions of Peking. He said:

Clearly our proposal that the neutrality declaration should be discussed
first, by no means excludes the discussion on the withdrawal of foreign
troops and foreign military personnel. However Mr. Steves has asserted
that our proposal to discuss the neutrality declaration constitutes an
evasion of the discussion on the withdrawal of foreign troops, trying to
make it appear that the Socialist countries were afraid of discussing this
question. This is groundless.[34]

Though he then expressed some doubts that the United States was
sincere in claiming that it would withdraw its forces from Laos,
Chang Han-fu added:

We think that in the process of the discussion on the neutrality declaration an agreement in principle on the question of the withdrawal from
Laos of all foreign troops and military personnel should be reached and
that, as provided in the second Soviet draft, the specific question of the
implementation of the agreement in principle should be discussed.[35]

These statements tended to show that the drafting of the declaration
on neutrality would not remain up in the air. Chang Han-fu was, in a
manner, trying to open the door to agreement on procedures and was

doing so by showing that in fact the proposal his delegation favored would not exclude agreement on the primary issues raised by the United States. This was understandably an approach to which the conference was receptive.

It was in this context that Chang Han-fu came to the crucial procedural issue before the conference. First he touched on the British compromise proposal and he dealt gently with Malcolm MacDonald. He said, "We understand the point of the Bitish delegate in doing so, [i.e., in proposing a compromise] and we also agree that, under certain conditions, compromise is necessary." [36]

While not ruling out compromise on all occasions, he was not able to accept the British proposal, saying it "cannot be considered as a compromise proposal." He went on to say, "A certain delegate echoed the United States point of view and called our proposal dangerous. . . . Our proposal is but to discuss first the question of recognizing and respecting the independence and neutrality of Laos, in accordance with the nature of the question itself. What plot can there be behind this?" [37] He then prepared the way for his own point by citing the statements of V. K. Krishna Menon (India) and James Barrington (Burma), who on July 13 and 14 respectively had supported the view that respect for the independence and neutrality of Laos should be discussed first and the question of control—or the functions of the International Commission—after that. This done, he dealt with the issue as to whether there was indeed a plot to reach agreement on neutrality and to put aside entirely the question of international supervision. On this point he said:

How is it conceivable that there would be no discussion on the question of control once an agreement is reached on the question of neutrality? Again, how is it conceivable that things can be wound up merely upon agreement on the question of neutrality and not on all the questions? *Everyone knows that only when agreement is reached on all the questions shall we sign on these documents.* This is but a question of common sense.[38]

These words of Chang Han-fu's took the sting out of the procedural confrontation. Till he made this statement it had been whispered or asserted in the corridors and in other informal settings that the

Chinese were trying to trick the conference into working only on the neutrality declaration, which they would sign and then pack their bags. Chang Han-fu's statement, on the record in a plenary session of the conference and distributed in cold print in English translation to all the members of the conference, virtually silenced this point of view.

Finally, on the question of procedure, Chang Han-fu lightened the atmosphere by expressing his belief that there "will be a settlement of this question" and by adding with a flourish verging on the poetic that "any small question but the size of a sesame seed can be swelled up into a huge problem as extensive as the skies and thereby preventing our Conference from moving forward a single step." [39] He closed his important remarks, which admittedly had cleared the air at the conference to a significant degree, with an appeal directed to the United States:

From President Kennedy to Senator Humphrey of the United States, they have all repeatedly indicated that the United States would like to see an independent and neutral Laos. But words alone will not suffice, we want to see deeds follow. . . . We believe that given the sincere desire to reach agreement these obstacles can be overcome and we can, and have to, reach an agreement. We sincerely hope that the U.S. delegates will seriously review their position.[40]

The important statement by Chang Han-fu made on July 14, 1961, was thus a combination of some indications of conciliation and readiness to reinterpret the Chinese positions in a manner that would be conducive to the development of constructive negotiation, while at the same time it departed from the tenor of Marshal Ch'en Yi's earliest interventions in that it substituted for offensiveness a calmly delivered challenge to the United States delegation to join with the Chinese and others in getting the conference moving in genuine negotiation on matters of substance.

The tactics employed by Ch'en Yi, and after him Chang Han-fu, seemed analogous to certain aspects of Mao Tse-tung's dictum: "Concentrate a superior force to destroy the enemy forces one by one." [41] Chinese negotiating tactics generally had been to welcome and distinguish the position of the nonaligned states from that of the

Western states, and then among the latter to pinpoint the United States—not crudely to isolate them, as that would have been too blatant a tactic to have succeeded, but to take them up on the major issues at far greater length than they gave to the postures of other participants. A second sense in which these tactics conformed to those recommended by Mao Tse-tung in his article of September 16, 1946, on concentrating a superior force on the enemy was in the isolation of one or two issues instead of trying to carry out an attack across the whole front presented by the complex problem of Laos. *Chieh-fang-chün pao,* the *Liberation Army Daily,* in its editorial of September 17, 1966, written to commemorate the twentieth anniversary of the publication of Mao's article on concentrating a superior force to destroy the enemy, interpreted one aspect of Mao's teaching in that article as follows: "It is necessary to concentrate forces and lay stress on the solving of one or two major issues at a time and have a firm hold on them until they are thoroughly solved." [42] The tactic of clinging tenaciously to one or two issues, of returning to them with wave after wave of interventions, is one that the Chinese employed in dealing with the preliminary issues. The fact that Ch'en Yi made five interventions in the conference on Laos in its early weeks as against one or two by other Foreign Ministers was in a sense a manifestation of this wave-like tactic of returning repeatedly to the selected issues. We shall see in the following chapters whether these Chinese tactics were to succeed.

CHAPTER IX

The Deadlock Breaks

THE STATEMENT made by Chang Han-fu on July 14, 1961, which was the subject of analysis in the previous chapter, was a factor in clearing the way for the next phase of the conference's work. Instead of reconvening immediately after July 14, the cochairmen engaged in a series of informal discussions with the other delegations in a search for agreement on the question of procedure. This course had, indeed, been suggested by Averell Harriman on July 11, when he said,

I would suggest . . . that the two Co-Chairmen arrange, outside the confines of this rather formal plenary session, to have informal discussions among the thirteen heads of delegations and the three representatives from Laos. It is my sincere hope that such discussions . . . will produce . . . a procedural agreement which will permit our substantive work to move toward a successful conclusion.[1]

This process of informal consultation also involved meetings between the major delegations to see whether they could present the cochairmen with an agreed position. The nonaligned delegations discussed the position further with the Soviet and Chinese delegates and assured themselves that it was clearly the intention to prepare both the draft documents relevant to a Laotian settlement—that dealing with the functions of the International Commission as well as that on the neutrality and independence of Laos—before either of them could be regarded as final and ready for signature by the Foreign Ministers. These delegations then met with the Western delegations, and in particular with the United States delegation, to convey to it their understanding of the situation. I laid particular stress on the point that India would insist on completion of all the documents, for, without a clear agreement on the functions of the Control Commission, the role of the chairman of the commission—which India had to perform—would be an impossible one. Indeed, because the commission was already functioning in Laos, there was an element of urgency in completing the document on control and therefore India would press for its completion as soon as possible, though it felt that the declaration on neutrality must necessarily take logical precedence because it would set out the principles that would guide the formulation of the specific measures of control to be exercised by the commission. Intensive informal discussion and probing of these issues took place over a period of several days.

Eventually it came to be accepted unanimously, in private, that helpful guidelines to the working out of effective and appropriate control measures could only be formulated by giving precedence to the preparation of a declaration on the independence and neutrality of Laos, in which document the agreed international postures in regard to Laos would become crystallized and could then direct the conference in its approach to the parameters of control.

These views were put to the cochairmen, who were able to reconvene the conference on July 19, 1961; Malcolm MacDonald, who in accordance with the accepted rotation was in the chair that day, read out: "Proposals of the Co-Chairmen on the Procedure for the Further Work of the Conference." First, the proposals of the cochairmen acknowledged in effect that the resolving of the major procedural issue before it had closed the phase of general discussion at the conference and that henceforth work could be undertaken on a detailed consideration of the drafts presented as a basis of a settlement of the Laotian question.[2]

The next procedural proposal was that detailed work should take place at "restricted meetings" of the conference attended only by heads of delegations and their advisers and experts. This proposal was an ingenious compromise to meet the wishes of both the United States and the Communist delegations. The United States had been pressing for smaller meetings of the important delegates so as to reach agreement quickly on the major issues in contention. The Soviet and Chinese delegations, on the other hand, were strongly in favor of a procedure that would continue to keep the discussions open to all members of the conference. They pressed the argument that the conference in the first place consisted of selected states and a further refinement of that selection would now be invidious. The real reason, however, for insisting on maintaining the forum for discussion as it had thus far existed was that any selection would tend to reduce the Communist voices to the Soviet Union and China. This would leave out North Vietnam, which was vitally interested in the issue, and Poland. Communist states tend to overestimate the influence that world opinion exercises on negotiation. And, in this case, they felt that world opinion would be better represented through a forum of fourteen states rather than one of half a dozen states. The compromise proposal of the cochairmen was to maintain the place of all fourteen states at the conference table but to change the form somewhat by reducing the number of persons present from each delegation. If this looked like a greater success for the Communist point of view than for that advanced by the United States we shall soon see how, when it came to the core of the negotiation, a new forum had to be devised that was constructed in accordance with United States thinking.

The third point in the procedural proposals of the cochairmen recorded what had now come to be accepted by all members of the conference: the documents that were to be formulated would form a single whole. "Any decision reached in regard to particular provisions or articles of these documents will be considered as final only after the Conference has adopted these documents as a whole." [3]

The fourth point in the joint proposals of the cochairmen was simultaneous consideration of the Soviet, French, United States, and Indian drafts and any other proposals that might be introduced. Here, then, Marshal Ch'en Yi's original position that the United States and French proposals—particularly in regard to the functions of the International Commission—could not be taken into account was overruled. All the various proposals submitted to the conference had been placed on an identical footing.

The fifth point in the cochairmen's proposals addressed itself to the crucial question of priority between independence and neutrality on the one hand and control provisions and the functions of the International Commission on the other. The proposal was: "Discussion will begin with the consideration of the drafts of the Neutrality Declaration. Afterwards the Conference will proceed to the consideration of the draft of the Agreement [Protocol] and other connected proposals." [4] Thus, in this important issue, the view pressed by the Soviet and Chinese delegations (more particularly by the latter), as well as by the nonaligned states, had won the day.

However, an element of compromise was contained in the cochairmen's proposals. In order to alleviate the apprehensions of the Western delegations and some of the nonaligned delegations that discussion could become deadlocked again on a particular aspect of the neutrality and independence declaration, the cochairmen's proposal contained the following provision: "If discussion shows such a divergence of views on a particular provision that the Conference cannot reach agreement on this provision, further discussion of it in restricted session will continue for not more than one additional day, after which the Conference will proceed to consider the next provision." [5] This provision was in some respects a mitigation of concentration for an indeterminate period, which might be unending, on the draft declaration on neutrality and independence.

Malcolm MacDonald, in his exposition of the proposals of the cochairmen, after having put them to the conference, returned to cite again the provision giving priority to consideration of the declarations on neutrality and independence and pointed out that the cochairmen had retained in their hands another important function, which was as follows: "The drafts [of the neutrality and independence declarations] will be considered provision by provision in accordance with the schedule which is being prepared by the Co-Chairmen. The order in which the provisions are to be considered will be recommended to the Conference by the Co-Chairmen." [6] The effect of this arrangement was to give both major sides at the negotiation (the Western powers and the Communist states) through their representatives (the British and Soviet cochairmen) an opportunity to influence the details of the scheme of priorities for discussion. This too represented an element of compromise in the crucial procedural decision at the conference.

In spite of the fact that the cochairmen's proposals had been made after extensive discussions with all the delegations, Malcolm Mac-Donald's statement was followed by a series of objections, most of them rather minor, by the delegates of South Vietnam and Thailand. However, these objections were not widely supported and the procedural proposals were accepted by the conference after Malcolm MacDonald had gently rebutted the objections raised.

Though the Peking delegate did not comment at the session on the procedural proposals of the cochairmen, it is relevant that the representative of North Vietnam (S. E. Xuan Thuy) expressed the pleasure of his delegation at seeing that the conference had reached agreement on the order in which its discussions were to proceed. He too verged on the poetic as he expatiated on his happiness: "Whilst hailing the success, we are glad to recall that we will be celebrating shortly the anniversary of the 1954 Agreement on IndoChina seven years ago, here in this lovely hospitable city of Geneva, in this very same Palais." [7]

The proposals of the cochairmen had also mentioned that a drafting committee would be set up, which would put into appropriate language the substantive decisions reached at the restricted sessions. The language of the drafting committee would then be resubmitted to the conference for final approval. The drafting committee consisted of two states from each side and one nonaligned state: China, France, India, the United Kingdom, and the Soviet Union. The omission of the United States from this list was not significant. Since there were to be only two states from the Western side the choice was between the United States and France, the United Kingdom being an essential participant as one of the conference cochairmen. France had presented a major set of proposals and, moreover, was thought to be best placed among the Western powers to understand the needs of the actual situation in Laos. Furthermore, the views of the United States would be presented by France and the United Kingdom. And, finally, it had become part of the accepted procedures of the conference that the Western chairman maintained a close and continuing liaison with the delegations of the United States, France, Canada, Thailand, and

South Vietnam, while the Soviet chairman did likewise with the Communist delegations. This being so, membership of the drafting committee did not really signify an exclusive position. To round out this description of the arrangements, I might add that the nonaligned delegations were in some ways both better and worse off than the aligned delegations. On the one hand, they could not expect the continuous liaison with one or the other chairman that their colleagues enjoyed; on the other hand, they had access to both chairmen and obtained a wider, if not always as intimate, view of the progress of the conference than did the aligned delegations.

But the Chinese negotiators probably suffered little in so far as a full view of the conference was concerned. They were on very friendly terms with the nonaligned delegations and it must be assumed that they shared, generally speaking, in the information some of those delegations obtained from the aligned delegations.

It was noteworthy that the Chinese delegation expressed no overt reaction at the conference table to the "victory" they had won in the procedural battle. This stoical restraint was a wise negotiating tactic. No good negotiator will make much of the successes he achieves while a negotiation is in progress. He knows that what counts is the final result of the negotiation, the terms of the agreement reached. Anything that is achieved on the way to that conclusion is transitory and will be forgotten. Secondly, any display of pleasure over procedural or other passing gains is likely to rouse the competitive spirit of the other protagonists to even up the score, which would, clearly, negate the victory in question.

The Chinese, in their sophisticated demeanor, indicated that they understood those factors. Even in private they made light of the procedural decision: "It was bound to be this way. Who supported the U.S. position? Only Thailand and Phoui! How could they expect to win? The logic of life was against them. *You* helped them lose this" (the "you" being whichever delegate they were talking to). Thus, the Chinese made the nonaligned states feel it was *they,* rather than Peking, who had gained the procedural victory. In this too was a safe negotiating investment.

CHAPTER X

Substantive Negotiation Is Under Way

THE FACT that the Chinese delegation had not crowed over its substantial success in regard to the important procedural problem that had preceded the decision to embark upon substantive negotiations did not mean that the way was now clear for speedy progress. Negotiation, particularly on a problem that has become of global interest, is so complex a process that obstacles to progress will present themselves virtually from moment to moment.

The preliminary issue that faced the first restricted meeting of the Laos Conference on July 20, 1961, was the form in which the declarations of neutrality and independence should be written. The Russian proposal favored one declaration by all the fourteen participants of the conference, including Laos.[1] The French proposal was that there should be a declaration by Laos of its own neutrality and independence, which would be followed by a declaration of the other participating states at the conference in which they would take note of the declaration of the government of Laos and undertake to observe it. The Indian proposal was very similar to that of France except that it spelled out in somewhat more detail the obligations to be accepted by the thirteen other participating states. On July 20, 1961, at the first restricted meeting Averell Harriman supported the French formulation and by implication did not object to the formulation proposed by India.

The Chinese position on this new obstacle to negotiation on substantive issues was not markedly partisan and, in addition, indicated

a possible way of surmounting it. While Chang Han-fu supported the
Soviet formulation of a single declaration on neutrality, he added,
"But we believe this is a question of form only and the final solution of this question will have to depend on the view of the single delegation to be sent from the Government to be formed in Laos." [2] He
concluded his statement by saying, "We also have our view [on the
form of the document]. We feel that if the coalition government of
Laos should make a Declaration on neutrality, it is all up to that government to decide what form it should take. As to what we think that
government should do with regard to this or that point, concerning
this Declaration, it is quite improper." [3]

In his brief statement Chang Han-fu had thus upheld the rights of
little Laos and had revealed willingness on the part of the Chinese
delegation to give a secondary place to its own position—and the Soviet's—on the form of the declaration so as to put first the wishes of
the Laotian delegation. This was both conciliatory as a negotiating
tactic and a reassurance to the other delegations representing small
countries.

As a subsidiary point Chang Han-fu was able in his very brief
statement of no more than three minutes' duration to advert approvingly to a reference I had made in a previous statement to the Zurich
communiqué of the three Laotian Princes.[4] He need not have
brought in this point but presumably did so in order to place the reasonableness of the Chinese posture on as wide a basis as possible.
There were two interesting aftermaths to the Chinese statement. One
was that Giorgi Pushkin, the Soviet Deputy Foreign Minister, who
was chairman of that session of the conference, summarized the views
of his delegation on the form of the declaration on neutrality. In doing so he referred to Poland's support of the Soviet position and he
added that the Soviets were willing "to pay strict heed to the other
proposal that has been moved by India and France to the effect that
the Conference would adopt two documents." [5] He went on to say
that the question of the form would be determined when a government of national unity from Laos could speak in favor of one or the
other alternative: this was Chang Han-fu's point, but Pushkin did not
mention the Chinese delegate at all in his own intervention.

The second interesting aftermath to these interventions was that Averell Harriman closed the discussion by saying, "It seems to me the proposal . . . namely whether there should be a single document or two, may well be set aside until we have the views of the government of national unity." [6] Since the United States delegate had earlier in the meeting supported unequivocally the French proposal for two declarations, he too now was being conciliatory and was, in effect, though of course not explicitly, accepting the point of view first set out by Chang Han-fu. At Averell Harriman's suggestion it was decided to put aside for a time a decision on the question of the form of the declaration or declarations on neutrality.

This seemingly unimportant result grew in significance because of its timing: we were about to enter upon substantive negotiation and the convergence of the views of the major delegations just achieved presaged that the long-delayed move forward from the stage of general discussion to the details of negotiation would, at least to begin with, probably be a forthright one.

The session on July 20, 1961, adjourned in a new mood of unadulterated elation, for the first time since the conference had opened more than two months ago. But this only showed that even seasoned negotiators can fail to apply an adequate measure of caution to the situations in which they are personally involved. Practically the whole of the next session of the conference, on July 21, 1961, was spent in trying unsuccessfully to determine what had been decided on the previous day. The meeting opened with a formal statement by Malcolm MacDonald, on behalf of the cochairmen, setting out the previous day's decision.

There seemed to me to be two errors in the decision as recorded. One was that it was so worded as to convey the impression that Laos was not a participant at the conference. The verbal amendment that I suggested to set this right was readily accepted by the conference. My second amendment related to what Malcolm MacDonald read out as conveying the position of the United States. He read, "The United States delegate accepted this decision [to defer the question till the views of the coalition government of Laos became known] on the understanding that it related to form only and did not preclude discussion of any matter of substance to be contained in any of the declarations." [7]

I pointed out that this formulation made it look as if the United States were entering a reservation, whereas my understanding had been that Averell Harriman had not made a reservation but had simply underlined the fact that we had discussed form and not substance so far as the declaration and/or declarations on neutrality were concerned. The Soviet and Poles responded by saying that they, on the contrary, considered that the United States had made a reservation.

Averell Harriman and Malcolm MacDonald on the other hand agreed with my point of view. At this stage Chang Han-fu intervened in the discussion, which had already gone on for well over an hour, to say that the real trouble was that there was a discrepancy between what Mr. Harriman had said at the conference and the wording that the United States delegation had handed in to the cochairmen after the meeting, to be included in the recorded decision. The second version, said Chang Han-fu, "is actually a reservation by the U.S. delegation. As a reservation I consider it quite proper to have it on the record." [8] The point of this remark was to attribute the reservation clearly to the United States delegation alone, so that its position should stand out in isolation from that of all the other conference participants, including its own Western allies.

William Sullivan,[9] Governor Harriman's aide, who had given the United States version of its position to the cochairmen, explained: "I did not submit anything that should be considered a reservation." [10] He thereby fought back against the Chinese tactic of isolating the United States. However, Averell Harriman himself then judiciously suggested that the matter be left to the cochairmen, who had now heard the views of most delegations, with a view to finding the best way of recording the decision of the conference. This was accepted and the matter was remitted to Malcolm MacDonald and Giorgi Pushkin, but not settled.

To an outsider it might seem difficult to believe, but the fact remains that this counterdevelopment of July 21 resulted in enough discontent with the procedures of the conference—though it had just embarked on what it believed would be the severely workman-like forum of restricted meetings—to get the major delegations thinking again on other possible procedures that might advance the work of the conference. An outsider might have thought that such reconsideration was at least premature, but this view would overlook the reality that the participants in any important international negotiation are in a constant state of tension, pitting themselves against one another not simply as individuals but conscious of the responsibility they bear to their governments, media of public information, and forums of legislation and public debate. Their personalities tend to be keyed up and their antennae inordinately sensitive to all possible developments and misadventures that might interfere with progress in the direction they desire.

However, some of us, including particularly the Chinese, suggested that we should allow the restricted meetings to proceed for some time before taking a decision on setting up other procedures. Moreover, the crisis passed because the cochairmen were able to reach agreement on a formulation relating to the decision on the form of the neutrality documents, and the next restricted meeting addressed itself to questions relating to the preamble of the declaration of neutrality.

Taking the Soviet text as a basis, the Canadian and Indian delegates introduced certain amendments. The United States delegate found acceptable the proposals I introduced [11] but did not find it necessary to accept the Canadian proposal. Chang Han-fu's intervention was in effect similar to that of the United States: he accepted the Indian amendments but did not concur with the changes suggested by Canada. The only substantive point of difference between his statement and that of the United States was that he commented adversely on a suggestion by South Vietnam that countries should agree not to use the resources of Laos to intervene in the internal affairs of other states. Chang Han-fu said, "I think we are discussing the principle to be embodied in the preamble. . . . As to the other concrete undertakings or provisions, all delegates, or any delegate, may propose their suggestions or point of view when we discuss concrete measures." [12] No objection was raised to this Chinese suggestion.

Again it had been demonstrated that there was not necessarily an incompatibility of views between the Western powers and the Chinese when the two sides sat down to discuss the details of a point.

The conference next considered general provisions on the recognition by other states of the independence and neutrality of Laos. This important and basic matter had figured in the discussions between President Kennedy and Chairman Khrushchev at Vienna. They had agreed that Laos should be a neutral state. But this did not settle the issue once and for all, for each of the major power blocs was keen to ensure that the brand of neutrality prescribed for Laos should not be such that the country would "lean" toward the other side. Wariness by the West and the nonaligned on this account was all the greater because of Mao's statements to the effect that no real neutrality was possible.[13]

Chang Han-fu showed the importance that China attached to the issue by being the first delegate to express views on the subject of respect for the sovereignty and neutrality of Laos.

His tactics were interesting. His first point was that the three proposals before the conference, those submitted by France, India, and the Soviet Union, were, to use his own words, "about the same." This led him to the view that "it is not difficult for us to reach agreement in studying the relevant parts of the Soviet, French and the Indian proposals on this point." [14] This statement left the door open for further negotiation on the matter. Though he expressed the view that the Soviet proposal was the best of the three, he did not urge with conviction or emphasis that the conference accept that proposal. His conclusion was stated in moderate enough terms: "The Chinese delegation deems it advisable that we should adopt the Soviet suggestion on this question." [15]

A long discussion followed on appropriate wording to be included in the final documents of the conference on the neutrality and independence of Laos. Chang Han-fu took no further part in the debate and did not demur when the cochairmen announced that the drafting committee (on which the Peking government was represented) was being asked to prepare the appropriate texts, taking into account the views expressed and the proposals presented on the subject. Thus it appeared that the delegates of Mao Tse-tung were not making a special effort to ensure that Laos would lean in their direction.

At the next session of the conference (July 26, 1961) three interesting points were raised at the very outset. One was a suggestion by Phoui Sananikone, the representative of the so-called right-wing Laotian delegation to the conference, that one of the subjects which the conference should formally consider was the composition of the International Commission for Supervision and Control in Laos, which since 1954 had consisted of India as chairman and Canada and Poland as the other members.

The second and third points raised were proposals that came from the delegate of South Vietnam. His first proposal was that there should be a general undertaking by all states not to contribute directly or indirectly to the establishment, maintenance, or development of military or paramilitary force other than those of the government of Laos. His second proposal was that there should be an undertaking by the government of Laos to disarm and dismiss such forces belonging to political parties as could not be integrated with the national army.

The first of these three proposals led to an immediate riposte from Chang Han-fu. Interestingly enough, though by now relations between the governments of China and India were strained as a result of border problems and developments in Tibet, Chang Han-fu rejected out of hand the suggestion that the composition of the Control Commission be reconsidered. "The Chinese delegation thinks that this is no longer a question; and this issue shall not be considered an issue and shall not be in the schedule [of points before the conference]." [16] This was much stronger language than he had used in regard to the more important provision relating to the independence and neutrality of Laos.

Turning to the proposals made by the South Vietnamese delegate, Chang Han-fu rejected them also on the ground that they fell within the domestic jurisdiction of Laos and were therefore matters that the Laotian government, which was about to be formed, would arrange.

CHAPTER XI

The Question of SEATO

AN ESSENTIAL ELEMENT in the current concept of nonalignment is that a nonaligned or neutral state must neither be a participant in, nor be included within the jurisdiction of, any military alliance that binds together the allies of one or another of the great power blocs. This concept was not seriously contested at the conference on Laos. All three proposals before the conference, those of France, India, and the Soviet Union, included wording to cover the point. Countries other than Laos were to "undertake not to involve Laos in any military alliances or other alliances incompatible with her neutrality." [1]

Averell Harriman was the first speaker on these proposals. He expressed the view that the word "involve," which appeared in both the Indian and Soviet proposals, was both ambiguous and vague. He proposed to amend the Indian draft deleting the concept of involving Laos in military alliances and substituting the words "they undertake not to invite or encourage Laos to enter into any military alliances." [2]

Speaking for India, I accepted the United States amendment with the addition of two words. At this point Chang Han-fu intervened. It should always be kept in mind that he was speaking in Chinese, while the texts under consideration were available in English, French, and Russian. However, he reacted immediately to Averell Harriman's suggestion by saying that the Chinese felt that the word "involved" was more precise. In a somewhat clumsy sentence (as translated) he asserted: "It involves direct and indirect involvement." [3] He did not proceed to an attack on the United States suggestion but simply said that its language was less strong than the wording proposed by the Indian and Soviet drafts. No demand was made to reject the United States proposal. The formulation used by Chang Han-fu throughout was, "We feel that . . ."

This discussion was closely related to the question of the SEATO umbrella over Laos. In terms of the Protocol attached to the SEATO Treaty Laos had been included among the countries that might ask the SEATO alliance for military assistance against aggression.

In spite of the firmly held view of the Indian government, and in particular of Prime Minister Nehru himself, that the SEATO concept was not a helpful one in Southeast Asia, the Indian proposal (and this was true of the French proposal too) did not contain any wording specifically on the role of SEATO in Southeast Asia. So far as India was concerned, it was considered that the undertaking not to involve Laos in military alliances was adequate protection against any direct operation of SEATO in the country. Besides, the Indian view was that this was more properly a matter for decision by the government of Laos, and it was known that Prince Souvanna Phouma, the likely Prime Minister of a unified Laotian government, would make it clear that his country and government would reject the protection of SEATO.

The Soviet proposal was the only one of the three before the conference that touched specifically on the SEATO issue. Its relevant part stated: "The countries participating in this Conference agree that all provisions of treaties and agreements relating to Laos and conflicting with the independent and neutral status of Laos, including the provisions of the Treaty on the Collective Defense of Southeast Asia [SEATO] and the Protocol thereto, cease hereby to have effect." [4]

As soon as the cochairmen put this issue to the conference, Chang Han-fu elected to speak. He said that his delegation considered "that this provision is very important and necessary and should be written into our document." [5] The first reason he gave in support of this view was that the Soviet proposal was a logical consequence of the agreement reached that Laos was not to be brought into military alliances. That being so, he said that it was "unthinkable" to "permit the continued existence of present treaties and agreements relating to Laos and conflicting with its neutral status." [6] His second point was that the Zurich communiqué of the three Laotian Princes had specifically stated that Laos would not recognize the protection of any alliance or military coalition. The Soviet draft was, according to Chang Han-fu, in full accord with this demand.

This much said, Chang Han-fu embarked upon a strong attack on the SEATO Treaty. It was "signed under the sole maneuver of the United States, [and] has violated the relevant provisions in the 1954 Geneva Agreements." [7] He then charged that the prolonged instability in Laos over a seven-year period had been caused by "the crude interference in the internal affairs of Laos by the United States making use of this treaty organization." [8] He contended that the purpose of SEATO was "to suppress the Neo Lao Hakxat and the Pathet Lao Fighting Units under its leadership." [9] He said there would be no tranquillity for Laos if the SEATO bloc was not abolished. He declared that the United States had used SEATO to "establish many military bases . . . and put them in a constant state of preparedness for war. . . . This bloc has become one of the principal tools of the United States for waging the cold war and preparing for a hot war." [10] Dismissing the suggestion that SEATO was a defensive arrangement Chang Han-fu asserted "SEATO is a one hundred per cent aggressive military bloc. No matter how one wishes to invert the truth and call black white, it is impossible to say that it is defensive." And even if it were described as defensive, "would anyone venture to say that it is permissible to involve Laos in a so-called defensive military alliance?" [11] Altogether, Chang Han-fu's was a strong statement but it did not contain the element of sheer invective that had characterized the earliest statements at the Laos Conference made by Ch'en Yi.

After I had intervened on behalf of India, Averell Harriman spoke for the United States. Wisely and in order to preserve the possibilities of negotiation, he did not specifically refer to the Chinese statement. Apart from describing SEATO as a defensive arrangement, he stressed two points. The first was that "if all nations respected Lao neutrality, the question of SEATO protection of Laos against aggression or subversion would never arise." [12] The second point made was that the Laos Conference could not take action to remove Laos from SEATO's protection. "Removal of Laos from SEATO's protection would involve an amendment of the treaty requiring agreement among the parties that are member to the treaty." [13] He pointed out that such an amendment could only be adopted in accordance with the constitutional processes of the eight parties to the treaty, only four of whom were members of the Laos Conference.

Both the United States and the Chinese statements had been delivered in permissible negotiating styles but both were so forthright in the positions enunciated that it was clear that the conference had touched upon an issue on which agreement could not be reached through debate across the table, in the presence of all fourteen participants.

For three days the debate continued on the SEATO issue. The Western powers and their allies supported SEATO. James Barrington added the voice of Burma to those who opposed SEATO, and on July 28 Chang Han-fu made his second statement on the subject. His first assertion was that Averell Harriman had not answered a basic question, which was "that the Laotian people have not asked for your protection, therefore why, you gentlemen of SEATO, are you pressing this protection on the Laotian people?" [14] Later he again repeated this point: "The Laotians say 'We do not want to have your protection.' However there are some here from thirteen other countries who say 'we insist on protecting you.' " [15]

To Chang Han-fu the position was crystal clear. He saw it through the Maoist lens of forthright distinction between truth and falsehood: "Black is black and white is white. How can anyone claim black to be white or vice versa? . . . With respect to civil war in Laos, this is a blatant act of interference in the internal affairs of Laos. It is black and can never be claimed to be white." [16] Such was the conclusion to which Chang Han-fu had been driven by his Maoist search for the truth. He had, in fact, reached a mystical and incomprehensible abstraction in his urge for clarity. His last few words confirmed that on this issue the conference had reached a deadlock:

The Chinese delegation is of the view that the abolition of SEATO and its so-called protection over Laos is a key question of our present Conference. We cannot tolerate the continuation of the tragedy which has been continuing since 1954, with the SEATO bloc interfering in the internal affairs of Laos. We cannot permit our Conference to show duplicity with respect to word and motive. . . . We must not allow ourselves to fall into self-deception, while keeping our eyes wide open. The Southeast Asia Collective Defense Treaty must be abrogated and the Chinese delegation is firm on this.[17]

The United States delegation remained silent, which was a wise negotiating decision. It was clear that no resolution of the issue could be achieved by prolonging the process of debate at the conference table. Harriman's silence was interpreted differently in the *Peking Review,* the Chinese government's voice to the world. It asserted that the three days spent at the conference table on the SEATO issue "were in fact a court trial of the U.S. policy of using SEATO for intervening in Laos" [18] and it chided the United States for having made but one speech in the course of the three-day debate. It asserted that Harriman's "way out at this international hearing" was to try and keep the subject out of the conference: " 'No discussion' is the magic panacea he used: asserting that the matter could not be discussed at the Geneva Conference." [19] The Chinese publication continued: " 'No signature' is another trick of his: getting the Thai delegate to indicate that he would not put on his signature to the declaration of Laotian neutrality if the above-mentioned provision in the Soviet draft [dealing with SEATO] was included in it." [20] Written by "Our Correspondent" the *Peking Review* article was clearly the work of a member of the Chinese delegation who had been present at all the restricted sessions. In brief, China had decided to make SEATO a major issue by pressing for its abolition, which was a more radical alteration of the status quo than the Soviet proposal aimed at.

Again we should note that an interesting aspect of Chinese tactics was to refrain from making any proposals or presenting any amendments to proposals and to depend entirely upon their influence at the conference to get movement in their own direction. It must not be concluded, however, that the Chinese would always refrain from making their own proposals at an international negotiation. At the Laos Conference the Soviet Union was more fully involved than the

Chinese, both diplomatically as cochairman of the Geneva Conference and as the major supplier of military assistance to the Pathet Lao. Furthermore the Soviets had preempted the field of proposals by being the first to present a comprehensive scheme to cover all the problems to be dealt with at the conference. Since the Soviets had covered all the problems, any new proposals or amendments by the Chinese would have appeared as splitting the solidarity of the Socialist states. While later revelations showed that already the ideological and other differences between the Chinese and the Soviets were great, neither the Chinese nor the Soviets, by their words or actions, gave the slightest indication of any divergence of views in regard to the problems before the conference. If the Chinese took, in general, a more forthright and extreme position than the Soviets, the latter backed them up, or at any rate never uttered a word in opposition to the Peking government.

The sharp difference over SEATO activated once again discussions behind the scenes between the heads of a few delegations—the "inner six" as they later came to be known in their own gatherings—about conference procedures. The Chinese, however, continued to oppose the setting up of small negotiating groups. World opinion is one of the tools the Chinese feel entitled to use, and being denied this tool would put them in a strategic position not to their liking. However, since they demanded action in regard to SEATO and the United States appeared unwilling to discuss this issue further at the conference table, another forum for negotiation was becoming inevitable.

To Giorgi Pushkin, the Soviet Deputy Foreign Minister, fell the difficult task of maintaining a unity of front with the Chinese—which he did—and yet of focusing attention on the issue of SEATO in relation to the independence and neutrality of Laos. His task was all the more difficult in that it was the Soviet proposal alone that had raised the issue of SEATO. However, and this made it possible for him consistently to focus his remarks on a restricted aspect of the SEATO issue, the Soviet proposal had not asked for the abolition of SEATO but simply that its provisions should cease to have effect in regard to Laos.[21]

The pressure maintained by the Peking representatives and by the

Soviets to the extent of the restricted objective indicated above was
strong. Moreover there was the Zurich communiqué of the three
Princes of Laos "not to recognize the protection of any military alliance or coalition"; [22] and, again, there was the known opposition of
the nonaligned members of the Laos Conference, as well as all nonaligned states outside the conference, to the whole concept of SEATO
and in particular to the permissive extension of its range of operations to such countries as Laos.

From time to time Chang Han-fu would clamor for an unambig-
uous statement by Averell Harriman and Malcolm MacDonald that
Laos' full release from SEATO was being effected. Off the record,
Malcolm MacDonald would respond with great diplomatic tact that
the issue was being considered in appropriate ways by the states concerned and that he was sure that an acceptable arrangement would be
arrived at.

At the end of September 1961, at the thirty-ninth restricted meeting, Chang Han-fu returned to the attack: "The United States up to
now is still insisting on giving protection to Laos through SEATO,
while at the same time it is interfering in the formation of a Laotian
coalition government." [23]

Averell Harriman responded to these remarks, not with any re-
sentment, but with an appeal to reason and to the need to keep the
conference at a pitch of negotiation instead of invective. Harriman
had just returned from a visit to Laos, where it was known that he
had exerted his own influence and that of the United States to curb
the overly ambitious right-wing General Phoumi Nosavan. He referred to this visit, but in a manner that would not give offense to the
faction the United States had been supporting in Laos: "I think you
know where I have been, in order to further the objectives which we
have in mind here, namely, that we should get agreement on the spot,
as well as here, as rapidly as possible." [24] Then he made a very conciliatory appeal to both the Chinese and the Soviet delegations:

I understand that there are press conferences called immediately after
this meeting, at 4:45 by both the Chinese and the Soviet delegations. I
hope that both of them will not spread distrust throughout the world. If
you sincerely wish, my good colleagues, to come to an agreement you

will tell the world that we are making progress. Perhaps you can express your view that we are not making it as fast as you would like, but in any event, you are going to continue to persevere, as my Delegation will, and I believe the other delegations sitting at this table will, in finding a solution.[25]

In the month of October intensive discussions were held, outside the formal conference sessions, in order to attempt to break the deadlock. We learned that the Western powers had made suggestions to their SEATO allies and were awaiting responses. For five weeks, from September 26 to November 1, even the restricted meetings of the conference remained suspended: it would have served no purpose—other than giving opportunities to trade charges and countercharges—to gather at the conference table. During this period the conference could have broken up had it not been for the steady counsel of hope and patience given by both MacDonald and Pushkin. Chang Han-fu and his men were restive. He told me that their continued presence could not be taken for granted and that if the Americans refused to alter their position on SEATO he might as well return to Peking.

The situation was not helped by Phoumi Nosavan. On October 27 and 30 his forces attacked Xieng Khouang, and on the latter date the resulting casualties included a number of children and their mothers.

The Chinese asked for a session of the conference. The cochairmen agreed, and in his statement at the restricted meeting on November 1 Chang Han-fu attributed these events to SEATO: "What causes us particular anxiety is the fact that during this period, as a result of the stepped-up intervention of certain members of the SEATO bloc, the situation in Laos, Indo-China and Southeast Asia, as a whole, has further deteriorated." [26] Chang Han-fu went on to make an ominous prediction about South Vietnam in the following words:

The American press is now clamoring that the United States would send combat units to South Vietnam to take part directly in the fighting there. Developments in South Vietnam are bound to affect Laos. As everybody knows, with regard to South Vietnam, there are the 1954 Geneva Agreements on the Vietnamese question as well, and in South Vietnam there is likewise an International Commission similar to that in Laos. Should the United States be allowed to ignore these solemn international agreements and international machinery and send combat units to South Vietnam, then how much sense will there be for us here to reach another international agreement on the Laotian question? . . . As a result of the provocations carried out against countries which firmly adhere to a policy of peace and neutrality by members of SEATO, the situation in Southeast Asia, as a whole, is on the verge of a flare-up.[27]

Inevitably Averell Harriman reacted. He informed the conference that the information received by his government was that the Xieng Khouang incident had been started by the neutral forces there with the support of nearby Pathet Lao elements. As to Chang Han-fu's statement, he said:

I was surprised to hear the distinguished delegate from the People's Republic of China put together a lot of rumors and misinformation about what has gone on in Laos, and then to assert them as facts. I think he was out of order when he talked about events in South Vietnam. But since he has brought that subject up, I am compelled to say that it is well known that the guerrillas who are fighting the government in South Vietnam, causing a great deal of human misery, have been supported by, built up by, if not directed by, North Vietnam.[28]

After expounding his defense of the United States position, Harriman returned to a most conciliatory note, saying, "I for one am ready to forget what has been said. I would like to hear from the other speakers whether they would be willing to strike their words from the record." [29] There was no response to this suggestion and the speeches on all sides remained in the record.

Malcolm MacDonald, always striving to be the peacemaker between the United States and the Chinese, who were clearly at the two extremes of the gamut of positions held on contentious points, very privately whispered to some of us that the SEATO issue would soon be resolved: Australia had agreed to respect Laos' wish to be excluded from the protective wing of SEATO, and replies of a similar character would soon be forthcoming from Pakistan and Thailand. Harriman too impressed on the other delegates the determination of President Kennedy to arrive at generally acceptable provisions for a Laotian agreement.

A month passed in informal meetings of individual delegates with each other and with either of the two cochairmen. These activities resulted in the resolving of differences of nuance in regard to a number of issues such as consultation with the government of Laos in the event of violation or threat of violation of Laotian neutrality, unity, or integrity, and agreement not to establish military bases in Laos. When the next restricted meeting was convened on December 4, 1961, Chang Han-fu made one of his most mildly worded statements on behalf of the Peking government. He continued to maintain that the United States was fomenting war in Laos but his tone was different:

A few days ago U.S. President Kennedy said, "If we can conclude our efforts in Laos and insure a government and country which are neutral and independent, then we would be able to move into other areas of tension." These words sound quite plausible. However facts of the seven months since the cease-fire in Laos show that what the United States has been seeking is not an independent Laos. . . . We have remaining here only three questions not yet resolved, namely the abolition of SEATO protection over Laos, foreign interests in Laos, and the time limit for the withdrawal of foreign military personnel.[30]

On the whole the American reaction was correspondingly pitched. William Sullivan, speaking for the United States, simply said that the work that had been accomplished by the conference was totally inconsistent with "the tendentious and fallacious statements that have been delivered here this morning by the Chinese delegation and Mr. Vong Vichet [the representative of the Pathet Lao] . . . I can assure you that my delegation will have absolutely no difficulty in ignoring them altogether." [31]

By now it was clear that some hitherto untried effort would have to be made to resolve such issues as those pertaining to SEATO, the use of Laotian territory by outside powers, the voting procedures applicable to the decisions of the International Commission for Control and Supervision in Laos, the circumstances in which the commission could initiate investigations and prescriptions that would govern its reporting to the cochairmen. None of these essential aspects of a Laotian settlement had been fully resolved, though on some of them various formulations that had been tried on the United States and China by the cochairmen and by me had appeared to narrow the initial wide differences.

Three methods had so far been tried: plenary sessions of the conference, restricted sessions, and informal discussions in which either
one of the cochairmen (generally Malcolm MacDonald) or I acted as
the link between the United States and the Chinese delegations. Those
delegations had no private, purely bilateral, contacts.

One possibility now was to persuade the United States and the Chinese delegations to meet with each other. This was attempted, but
without success. It was not even possible for a third delegation to get
just these two delegations together at an informal social occasion.

But the need to add another dimension of effort was by now per-
sistent and urgent. It was in this situation that informal discussions
with the cochairmen led to an ingenious, if somewhat risky, suggestion. This was that the heads af the six delegations who were internationally most involved should meet together in strict privacy, without
their advisers and without any records being kept of statements made,
in order that as direct a negotiating confrontation as possible should
be created between the Americans and the Chinese. At the same time,
in a forum of as many as six delegates, neither of those two delegates
could complain that it was being brought into a purely bilateral discussion.

There were additional plausible reasons for picking delegates other
than those of the United States and China for these meetings. The
issues remaining unresolved concerned other states at the conference:
those relating to the International Commission were of special concern to India; those relating to SEATO and the use of Laotian territory were of great concern to the Soviet Union; and the issue of the
French installations in Laos also remained unresolved.

But how would the other eight delegations react to meetings of six
delegates? Clearly, they would not have favored forums that excluded
them: all fourteen states had been invited to the conference and it
had been agreed that decisions of the conference would require the
assent of all participants. This rule could not be ignored or bypassed.
These were valid objections, yet the need to intensify the effort to
reach agreement remained.

The solution finally was that the six heads of the delegations of the
United Kingdom and the Soviet Union (the two presiding states), the

United States, China, France, and India would meet elsewhere than at the Palais des Nations and not use any of the interpretation or other conference facilities provided by the United Nations. The format of their meetings would be social. They would meet for cocktails or elevenses alternately at the British and the Russian villas at Geneva. They would all maintain the strictest secrecy about these meetings, but if it did get known that they had met it could, after all, be not entirely unfairly be given out that the meeting had been a social one. In point of fact, though some twenty meetings were held, their existence did not become known to any delegation that might have taken exception to them. Toward the end of the series, late in February 1962, there were some indications of discontent, but steps were taken to satisfy the other delegations: the cochairmen met with them from time to time and explained the progress they had made in the consultations with each other and with individual delegations on specific issues on the agreed agenda of the conference. This procedure was, in fact, permissible in terms of the approval given by the conference, on September 14, 1961, to certain procedural proposals of the cochairmen, one of which read as follows: "They [the cochairmen] will hold discussions with heads of other delegations as appropriate, with a view to narrowing differences and reaching provisional agreements. All delegations will be kept in touch with those consultations." [32]

The previous (and occasionally continued) meetings of the cochairmen with individual heads of delegations too fell within the purview of the above-cited sanction, but regular assemblages of six delegates while permissible were another matter. However, this was the device that was used for the negotiation of the hard-core issues of the Laotian question. Of course, all agreements reached by the "inner six" would have to be submitted to the conference and then be remitted to the drafting committee for the formulation of appropriate refined phraseology. This new system was to yield important results, though not at once.

After the heads of the six delegations had met a half dozen times, on December 18, 1961, both restricted and plenary sessions of the conference were convened. The SEATO issue still remained unresolved though Malcolm MacDonald continued, behind the scenes, to urge patience while he predicted that an acceptable solution would be found. At the plenary in the afternoon Chang Han-fu made a long statement to which we will refer also in other contexts. A considerable part of his statement dealt with the alleged misdeeds of SEATO; his language was stronger than before:

SEATO is totally incompatible with the Declaration on the Neutrality of Laos. . . . Article 4 of this Treaty presumptuously stipulates that the parties to the Treaty have the right, under the pretext of preventing aggression, to designate any state or territory as within their so-called treaty area. It is precisely in accordance with this Article that the Protocol to this Treaty presumptuously places the states of Cambodia and Laos and the free territory under the jurisdiction of the State of Vietnam, under SEATO protection.[33]

In his view all this amounted to "a most brutal trampling on the sovereignty of the states concerned," and it was "absolutely impermissible" to let this state of affairs continue. He further stated that if the Western countries were "genuinely desirous of a peaceful settlement of the Laotian question, even such an important issue as the abrogation of SEATO protection over Laos can be solved. However, the good faith of the Americans is questionable." [34]

Thus, as late as the end of 1961 the unresolved SEATO issue was a factor that could have wrecked the negotiations and nullified the large area of agreement already reached among all the conference participants. In his statement of December 18, Chang Han-fu also said that he fervently hoped the conference would "speedily settle the sole remaining question, that is, the abrogation of SEATO protection over Laos, and finally conclude our work." [35]

Chang Han-fu was followed by the representatives of the three factions of Laos and by the representative of the Democratic Republic of Vietnam. Most of them continued in the vein of strong diatribes against United States actions in Laos. Again, the result was that William Sullivan, acting for Averell Harriman, decided not to reply: "I consider," he said, "that the provocations we have heard today are of such a low level of impertinence that they should not, in any measure, sway us from our primary purpose. I therefore have no intention of dignifying them with an answer." [36]

Malcolm MacDonald, the day's chairman, made a conciliatory statement appealing to the delegates to let the spirit of Christmas prevail; "let us recognize and not be ashamed," he said, "to confess that we here have been striving and, to some extent, have been succeeding in making a small contribution toward peace on earth and good will amongst men." [37] However, the problem of SEATO remained unresolved and the year 1961 closed more in distrust and anger than in reconciliation at the conference on Laos.

Early in January the meetings of the heads of the six inner delegations resumed. There was still no breakthrough on the question of SEATO. Chang Han-fu directed his attention to what he said was a connected issue—the French military establishments in Laos; he insisted that they be liquidated since they might be used by SEATO. Jacques Roux, the French representative, replied that France would be willing to discuss this matter with the government of national union in Laos as soon as it was set up. This was satisfactory as far as it went, but it did not meet the demands of the Chinese. Finally, the suggestion that the French should accept in principle the transfer of their establishments to the government of Laos, the modalities of transfer being worked out later with the Laotian government when formed, was generally approved. It was also agreed that Laos could ask for a few French military personnel to stay for a limited period of time. It was on this basis that Article 5 of the Protocol to the Declaration on the Neutrality of Laos was drawn up.

On January 23, 1962, Chang Han-fu made one of his longest statements at the conference, in which he expressed surprise and indignation regarding the still incomplete agreement regarding SEATO. He read sinister designs into President Kennedy's reference in his State of the Union Message on January 11, 1962, to the Laos Conference: "A workable formula for supervising Laotian independence is still to be achieved." [38] Remarking on the President's statement Chang Han-fu said:

This is indeed strange. Can it be that Mr. Harriman had not briefed the United States President? Can it be that the United States President did not know that our Conference had already basically reached agreement? . . . No, there is no doubt that the United States President knew per-

fectly well all that had transpired here among us. He said this only because their proposal for the control of the reintegration of Laotian
armed forces and their refusal to abrogate SEATO bloc protection over
Laos were not accepted. . . . SEATO bloc protection over Laos must
be abrogated, the agreements we have already reached here must not be
changed by a single sentence, a single word or a single punctuation mark
to meet the absurd proposal put forward by the United States on the so-
called control of the reintegration of the Laotian armed forces.[39]

These were strong words and they called forth a rebuke from William
Sullivan:

I will address myself directly to our Chinese colleague Mr. Chang Han-
fu. When you go back to China, please tell your leaders that, despite
their desires and despite their dogma, the United States and the Soviet
Union have no intention of fighting a war, on your behalf in Laos. What
we intend to do is practice peaceful co-existence there. . . . I think that
your leaders should be informed of the truth and they should come from
the dreamland of their ideological imagery into the reality of the circumstances which will prevail in Southeast Asia. There will be a unified,
peaceful, independent and neutral Laos.[40]

Chang Han-fu did not respond to Bill Sullivan's brilliant Irish rheto-
ric. The speaker of these words, as the present (1967) Ambassador
of the United States in Laos, continues his struggle for a unified neutral and independent Laos.

That sharp midwinter encounter between Chang Han-fu and William Sullivan did not resolve the long drawn out issue. Malcolm Mac-
Donald continued to hope that the members of SEATO would find a
way of excluding Laos from their jurisdiction but there was no clear
evidence that this was about to happen. Was there another way
around? Though Chang Han-fu had repeatedly said at the private
meetings of the six delegates that China would never lose its patience,
not long after the January meeting he and many of his colleagues
left for Peking. The Russian cochairman stayed on at Geneva but
Malcolm MacDonald, as if to explore the possibilities of settlement,
went briefly to Laos.

For the next five months the conference met sporadically in informal sectional meetings. The British cochairman would call in the
Western delegations and allies to tell them of such developments as

were taking place, and the two cochairmen together would, every two weeks or so, hold a formal meeting with the nonaligned delegates of Burma, Cambodia, Laos, and India and inform us of what was happening. For part of this time the Chinese delegation functioned under Ambassador Li Ch'ing-ch'üan, a bureaucratic diplomat, who started by maintaining the pretense that he could speak no European language. I was soon able to break through this barrier and converse with him in French, however.[41] Li Ch'ing-ch'üan and I established the custom of meeting once a week to review developments, but these meetings yielded few results. I essayed the view that if the government of Laos itself were to put into its statement on neutrality that it would not recognize the protection of any military alliance including SEATO then it would not really matter whether or not the SEATO powers took steps formally to exclude Laos from the theoretical jurisdiction of the alliance: that jurisdiction could only become an actuality at the bidding of the government of Laos. But this view was totally unacceptable to Li. It left intact the "overlordship" of the Western world in the Southeast Asian region.

I had first pressed the above view also at the meetings of the six heads of delegations, but in view of the recalcitrance of the Chinese delegation I had suggested the alternative course of the SEATO countries' opting out of their proclaimed Laotian jurisdiction. To my surprise it was this suggestion that was for some time espoused by some of the SEATO powers at the conference. The long drama of events in Laos itself reached a more favorable point when on June 12, 1962, the three Princes were able to complete their negotiations and form a coalition government of national unity under Prince Souvanna Phouma.

This development brought Chang Han-fu back to Geneva and, after a lapse of more than five months, the conference met in its fortieth plenary session on July 2, 1962. The clause on SEATO was now virtually the only one that had not been written into the agreed documents in a final form. Chang Han-fu, on July 2, acknowledged that this was the only remaining question,[42] and then demanded an answer from the Western powers to the by now familiar Chinese question:

Since the Provisional Laotian Government of National Union has already declared in its political program that it does not want the protection of any military alliance or bloc, that it does not want the protection of the Southeast Asia Treaty Organization, then why should there still be the desire to continue to impose such "protection" over Laos? [43]

A little later he added, "The totally unreasonable 'protection' of Laos by SEATO must be abolished." [44]

Apparently the Western powers had run into difficulties in trying to persuade their colleagues to exclude Laos from SEATO's jurisdiction. Malcolm MacDonald did not even mention the possibility of resolving the issue,[45] nor did Averell Harriman. By now the situation had become extremely tense. Chang Han-fu had said that he would not stay in Geneva for more than a week. By then he must have an answer one way or the other so as to be able to advise Foreign Minister Ch'en Yi whether the latter should come to Geneva for the signing of the final agreement or whether the Chinese must conclude that the Laotian situation was to become part of the maelstrom of Southeast Asia. He had referred in his statement on July 2 to the sending of United States troops to Thailand, and privately he expatiated on this move, claiming that it showed clearly that the United States had adopted a far-flung military strategy to hold Southeast Asia in its grip.[46]

The situation was saved by Prince Souvanna Phouma, who arrived in Geneva with the text of a declaration of Laotian neutrality that had been approved by the new Laotian government. The cochairmen convened a meeting of the full conference on July 9, 1962, at which Quinim Pholsena, the new Foreign Minister (throughout the conference he had been present as the representative of the neutralist faction) read out the Laotian declaration of neutrality. The part dealing with foreign alliances and SEATO stated that the government of Laos would

not allow the establishment of any foreign military base on Laotian territory, nor allow any country to use Laotian territory for military purposes or for purposes of interference in the internal affairs of other countries nor recognize the protection of any alliance or military coalition including SEATO.[47]

Quinim Pholsena explained that if the SEATO powers themselves were to exclude Laos from their jurisdiction then the words "including SEATO" would not remain in the Laotian Declaration.

Malcolm MacDonald, who was in the chair, said, "Today is certainly one of those brighter, happier days" for the conference. He was at once optimistic and yet, for some of the members of the conference, a prognosticator of further and by now unbearable delays in regard to SEATO. He officially told the conference that the proposal that the SEATO governments should declare formally that they would respect the wish of Laos not to receive any protection was being considered by all the SEATO governments. This we already knew, but at least it was a confirmation and the fact that it was made in a plenary session of the conference was taken at first to indicate that the SEATO powers were about to release Laos from their jurisdiction. However Malcolm MacDonald added:

As four of those governments are not represented at this Conference, it will unavoidably take a little time to receive and coordinate opinions and answers, but I assure our friends in other delegations that we shall conduct these consultations with the SEATO governments with the utmost speed.[48]

Any seasoned diplomat knew that this language gave no assurance the issue would be resolved in the next few days.

Fortunately, however, the Laotian Declaration itself contained what amounted to an alternative solution to the problem of SEATO. The Laotians had been able to accept the view that some of us had pressed: that if the SEATO powers did not exclude Laos from the potential jurisdiction of their treaty, the government of Laos itself could declare that it did not recognize the protective wing of SEATO. The Laotian Declaration did precisely this. However, Chang Han-fu in his speech on July 9, 1962, while welcoming the Laotian Declaration on neutrality, stuck to Peking's position for an explicit abolition, by the SEATO powers, of any protection over Laos. He said:

Since all the countries participating in our Conference have expressed their willingness to respect the independence and sovereignty of Laos and to respect the will of the Laotian people, they should explicitly declare the abolition of the "protection" SEATO has imposed upon Laos.[49]

And before closing his remarks he stated that "on questions of principle we absolutely will not compromise." [50]

The next few days were given to intensive private discussion and negotiation. What closed the matter was the wide realization that in a very real sense the SEATO issue was now an artificial one. This was so because the terms of the SEATO Treaty and Protocol did not give the alliance the right to enter any area of Southeast Asia without a prior request for assistance by the government of the country to be entered. Therefore the SEATO geographical limits could be looked upon as merely a cartographic delimitation beyond which the member states gave themselves no responsibility and within which their operations were contingent upon the sovereign actions of other states. In this view it did not really matter whether or not the final documents of the Laos Conference contained any mention of SEATO. It equally did not matter if they did not mention that SEATO protection was inoperative in Laos. Even if the latter were to be mentioned, it would still be open to a government of Laos, if the country were attacked, to call for the assistance of friendly governments in accordance with Article 51 of the Charter of the United Nations.

It followed that if Chinese persistence about abolishing SEATO "protection" were to be rewarded by appropriate wording of the documents, the reward would be purely symbolic and would leave the practicalities of the situation unchanged. In short, the SEATO issue, whichever way it was resolved, was really in the final analysis not a substantive matter.

Some of us pressed this view to the fullest in the next few days and nights in an intensified round of private negotiations. It was finally agreed that the Laotian Declaration of neutrality cited above would contain the words "including SEATO" and that the declaration of the other thirteen governments at the conference would also state the following: "They will respect the will of the Royal Government of Laos not to recognize protection on the part of any alliance or military coalition including SEATO." [51] At the behest of Malcolm Mac-Donald the record of the meeting also contained the following statement:

The representative of the United Kingdom [Mr. MacDonald] informed the Conference that agreement of the four SEATO members represented at the Conference, the agreement to have the reference to SEATO in the text, is the result of consultations between all governments of SEATO members.[52]

That closed the wearing debate of some ten months on the role of SEATO in Laos. Formally, Chinese persistence had been rewarded, but in substance this reward changed nothing that had existed before and continues to exist today.

Much more significant was the fact that though Chang Han-fu had previously asserted that the Chinese would not yield on the abolition or abrogation of SEATO,[53] they had, while continuing to concentrate a great deal of fire on the organization, unobtrusively dropped this firm insistence. Once again it had been demonstrated that even strongly avowed convictions of the Peking government could be whittled down in the course of patient negotiation. In short, like any other state involved in international life, the People's Republic of China is subject to the general principle that in negotiation there is almost invariably a difference between the stated objectives of a party and its irreducible minimum objectives.[54]

CHAPTER XII

The Withdrawal from Laos of Foreign Forces and Military Personnel

WHILE THE SEATO ISSUE was a largely artificial one—a fact soon to be confirmed by the Peking government's development of very close relations with a member of SEATO though at the Laos Conference it had clamored for complete abrogation of the alliance—the involvement of foreign forces, and other forms of foreign military intervention in Laos undoubtedly raised a crucial issue of a substantive character.

The major expression of this tangible factor was the presence of foreign military personnel. It was widely suspected, although the difficulties of confirming the suspicion were obvious, that mixed in with the Pathet Lao forces were military personnel from North Vietnam. Informally the Western estimates were that around 6,000 North Vietnamese uniformed men were in Laos, many of them being in the region of the Ho Chi Minh Trail whereby North Vietnam was supplying and assisting the Vietcong in South Vietnam. On the Western side, the French still had two small military establishments in the country, the facilities of which were said to have been placed at the disposal of the United States. (In Chapter XI we indicated the solution that was found for this issue.) Some remnants of Kuomintang forces were also operating in Laos.

The United States itself had a military mission in Laos that had grown from a strength of several hundred men to perhaps a thousand or more. In addition, the United States, North Vietnam, and the

Soviet Union were supplying military hardware to the factions of their choosing in the country. It was clearly a primary task of the Laos Conference to reach agreement on the withdrawal of armed forces and on the cessation of the practice of sending military supplies to one or another faction in the country.

In previous chapters we took note of the elements of the general Chinese position in regard to these matters. First, the Americans and their allies were to withdraw.[1] However, the Chinese had not disavowed general formulations calling for the withdrawal of all foreign forces; they had simply not admitted that any foreign military personnel from Communist states were present in Laos. Secondly, the Chinese had asserted that the size of the Laotian army and the supplies it should receive were matters within the domestic jurisdiction of the Laotian government and were not for the conference to determine. In this connection they placed themselves on record as firmly supporting the joint communiqué issued by the three Laotian Princes at Zurich on June 22, 1961. That communiqué had stated that a provisional government of national union would "realize the unification of the armed forces of the three parties in a single national army according to a program agreed by the parties." [2]

The conference had before it proposals by India, the Soviet Union, and the United States on the withdrawal of foreign forces. The Indian and United States proposals did not state the exact period within which the forces were to be withdrawn; however, the Indian proposal was for immediate withdrawal to be completed within X days after the agreement became effective. Whether it should be thirty or sixty days, or more, would be decided by the conference. The United States too had the X-day formula but the days were to be counted from the time the International Control Commission certified that it was fully in position and could monitor all withdrawals. The Soviet proposal was that all withdrawals should be completed within thirty days after the agreement came into force.[3]

Averell Harriman opened the discussion on the issue:

The largest group [of foreign military personnel in Laos], according to our information, who remain are the forces of the Viet Minh who are associated with the Pathet Lao fighting units. In addition to which there are a certain number of foreign nationals such as the Soviet personnel who are engaged in the airlifts from Hanoi to Xieng Khoung and to Vang Vieng. These personnel have been engaged in transporting weapons and other military supplies to the Pathet Lao and their fighting units.

My government and my delegation have made no mystery about the presence of the United States military personnel. . . . Time and again, I have indicated our willingness to withdraw these military personnel under appropriate conditions to be established at this Conference.[4]

It is to be noted that the United States delegate did not contend that Chinese military personnel were present in Laos, a significant fact taking into account the embroiled Laotian situation and the common frontier that Laos has with China.[5]

Had the Chinese introduced any military units or personnel into Laos it is obvious that the Laotian right wing and the United States' own channels of information would have made the presence of the Chinese Communists a major factor at the conference. Indeed, the whole negotiation at Geneva, already complex, would have been still further complicated if Chinese fighting elements had been in Laos. Whatever other reasons might be advanced for the absence of Chinese forces, my impression as a result of a number of informal conversations with the Laotian delegates and the Chinese was that the latter realized that the primary urge among the Laotians was a desire to reassert their independence. To send in Chinese military personnel, particularly with the background of periods in history when previous Chinese regimes had taken more than a benign interest in Southeast Asia, could only result in a loss of face and influence for China in Laos.

As it was, both the Pathet Lao and the Centrists under Souvanna Phouma, seemed, at that time, to be convinced of the sympathetic attitude of China toward the reassertion of full Laotian independence. It was relevant that the Pathet Lao and the Centrists together commanded the loyalty and support of a majority of the population. One striking result of this factor was that though right-wing forces were very much better equipped for combat and were better supplied than the opposing elements, they rarely won a battle or a skirmish. Thus the Chinese felt they could claim that the elements they were supporting could be regarded as "the People" (though this is of course not to say that there were no Laotians who were not opposed to the Pathet Lao and the Centrists).

In these circumstances it was clearly wiser for the Chinese not to introduce any of their own armed personnel into Laos. It does not necessarily follow that Peking would have been equally restrained if the Pathet Lao and the Centrists had not appeared to be in increasing command of the national situation. This is not to suggest that we can draw the conclusion that if their friends had been weaker China would have intervened militarily. There would still have remained the important consideration, repeatedly stressed to me by the Laotians, that all foreign forces, and perhaps Chinese forces more than any other, were anything but welcome in Laos.

Averell Harriman, before he concluded his speech, made it clear that the removal of United States forces

must be phased and coordinated under the supervision of the ICC, with the removal from Laos of other foreign forces that have been supporting the Pathet Lao. . . . The ICC supervision is essential to the establishment of mutual confidence so necessary for the permanent carrying out of the engagement that we make here and confidence in the effective execution of the actual withdrawal.[6]

When Giorgi Pushkin contended that it would interfere with the rapid withdrawal of foreign forces to wait till the ICC could count all foreign personnel present and then in detail monitor their departure, Averell Harriman replied as follows:

The ICC is the organ of this Conference to carry out the responsibility for supervising the withdrawal. My government is going to insist, my good friend, Mr. Pushkin, and we will do it tomorrow and as long as this Conference lasts, that the ICC has the authority and the means to assure all of us that withdrawals of all foreign personnel have been completed.[7]

After the Polish delegate had made a brief statement, Chang Han-fu spoke on this issue. In spite of the fact that Averell Harriman had spoken twice and insistently, Chang Han-fu made a rather mild statement: he did not refer directly to the American delegate's interventions though, of course, he dealt with the American proposals that were already before the conference.

First he expressed his satisfaction with the Soviet and the Indian proposals. This itself was an interesting tactical step. Chang Han-fu contended that "the setting of a definite deadline [for withdrawals] is absolutely indispensable." [8] While the Soviet proposal did contain a deadline—thirty days after the agreement had come into force—the Indian draft had, as we have seen, used a formula that in several respects was closer to that of the United States. However, it had stated that the withdrawal was to take place immediately and to be completed in X days. Chang Han-fu fastened on the word "immediately" as the basis of his acceptance of the Indian proposal. Again he was adopting tactics of isolating the United States (together with its close allies) from as many as possible of the participants at the conference. Of the United States proposal he said:

We are categorically opposed to the United States' variant. We consider that it is necessary to set a definite deadline for the withdrawal of this personnel. And we consider that the withdrawal should be accompanied by no conditions. It should be unconditional; it should be categorical; whereas, the United States' alternative does the opposite: it accompanies the proposal with all sorts of conditions.[9]

According to Chang Han-fu the purpose of the United States was clearly "to postpone as long as possible the withdrawal of foreign troops and personnel." [10]

Chang Han-fu's second objection was that by insisting on the prior establishment of the Control Commission in position in Laos, and in stipulating that the commission should monitor withdrawals, the United States proposal "constitutes a gross violation of the sovereignty and independence of Laos." [11] This argument was one to which he could expect a sympathetic response from many countries at the conference. He accordingly made much of the point. If, in spite of the delaying tactics of the United States, their troops were finally withdrawn, and if the United States proposals were implemented, Chang Han-fu said, "you would, nevertheless, have a control body which would apparently be the prime purpose of the United States' proposal. I repeat: all this runs counter to the independence of Laos." [12]

Chang Han-fu ended his statement on a milder note: "We hope that the United States representative will ponder very carefully these views. They themselves admit that they are devoting much attention to this. Well, they should consider very seriously the views that have just been stated by the Chinese delegation." [13]

It was clear by now that there was a considerable gulf between the United States, broadly supported by the United Kingdom, on the one hand, and the Communist countries and more particularly China, on the other hand. The gulf was to become wider as a result of further statements by the two sides.

Chang Han-fu took the floor and accused the Western powers of insisting, as a precondition to the withdrawal of foreign troops, on the establishment of an international trusteeship over Laos. He said the United States had evaded the question as to whether it was "ready to withdraw unconditionally its armed units and military personnel from Laos." [14] He charged that while evading this question Averell Harriman had raised the question of control over the withdrawal of foreign troops and military personnel. But, said Chang Han-fu, "this was not to the point."

At this stage Chang Han-fu led the discussion into a possibly constructive channel in order to obtain his own immediate purpose, which was a firm agreement in principle that all foreign troops and military personnel would be withdrawn from Laos. He asked a number of straight questions and demanded answers. First, "Are you or are you not prepared to withdraw your armed units and military personnel from Laos?" [15] His second question referred to the Chiang Kai-shek troops. He said he was glad to have heard a statement from the British delegate on this matter but it was not enough. Of the United States he asked, "What, after all, is your attitude? Why not one single word on this question up till now?" [16] He then referred to a statement of the Centrist Laotian delegate to the effect that armed units and military personnel of South Vietnam, Thailand, and the Philippines were also in Laos. Regarding them he asked of the United States, "Are you in favor of their withdrawal or are you going to continue covertly to back their stay in Laos? Yes or no." [17]

Having thrown out these challenges he tempered their impact by indicating that the Chinese delegation was perfectly willing to discuss the question of supervision and control over the withdrawal of foreign forces and military personnel:

Supervision and control over the withdrawal of foreign troops and military personnel is precisely a question we shall discuss later. The question now is the withdrawal of all foreign troops and military personnel from Laos within a specified period of time. . . . While putting in abeyance the provisions concerning control in the United States draft, we are not however against necessary and proper supervision and control over the withdrawal of all foreign troops and military personnel.[18]

Thus the Chinese conceded in principle the need to supervise withdrawals, but required as a *quid pro quo* a clear enunciation by the conference of agreement on the principle that all foreign military elements were to be withdrawn.

From the Chinese point of view this was a concession. Ordinarily negotiators do not follow up immediately by making a second concession; they wait to see whether one concession alone will achieve their purpose. However, somewhat to the surprise of some of the other delegates to the conference, Chang Han-fu turned approvingly to remarks Malcolm MacDonald had made on the question of withdrawal and asked, "Why not put this sentence of approval of the principle of withdrawal in the agreement and leave the question of a time limit for decision later on?" [19] In other words Peking was willing to put in abeyance for the present an integral part of the Soviet proposal: that withdrawals take place within thirty days of an agreement's enactment.

Before he closed, he again said that the withdrawal "does call for, in a way, necessary and appropriate control by the International Commission." [20] This was calculated to make it quite clear that the Chinese were not against controls as such.

A statement containing two "concessions" by Chang Han-fu was naturally well received by most members of the conference. It indicated again that there would not be total inflexibility in the Chinese position.

Chang Han-fu made some significant remarks in the course of his speech in regard to China's attitude toward a neighboring state, and since they were relevant also in regard to the issue of the withdrawal of foreign forces it is appropriate to give some attention to them:

Laos is a close neighbor of China. United States troops have entered Laos; the United States is supporting remnant Chiang Kai-shek troops in their interventionist activities in Laos; and, furthermore, has brought armed units of some SEATO bloc countries into Laos. All this inevitably threatens China's security. But China has never sent a single soldier to Laos. We sincerely hope that our Conference will be able to settle the question of the withdrawal of all foreign troops and military personnel from Laos.[21]

This was a dramatic way of asserting China's disengaged position vis-à-vis Laos; and, as we have noted, this assertion was not challenged at the conference. Secondly, the statement made it clear that the close proximity of the military positions of an inimical superpower—and perhaps even of a friendly one!—created a sense of discomfort in China, of insecurity; and this was a line of thinking that was readily understood by the other states at the conference table.

However, agreement was not immediately reached on the issue of withdrawal. Understandably, Averell Harriman responded to Chang Han-fu's direct questions by saying that he would study the record and see if they needed to be answered. He was not yet prepared to authorize the drafting committee to formulate language on the withdrawal of all foreign personnel within an agreed (but still unspecified) period.

Giorgi Pushkin, the Soviet cochairman, known as a delegate who rarely became heated or rhetorical in his statements, was forthright on this issue however. He said:

I think they [the United States] are over-bidding themselves. I think whether the United States wishes it or not, they are, in fact, obstructing the solution of the problem of withdrawal of troops from Laos and that is the only way we can interpret the situation that has arisen. . . . Well we will not participate in this. Those who speak against the withdrawal of troops from Laos, or make this basic provision contingent upon all sorts of conditions and qualifications and reservations shall have to assume responsibility for disagreement on this subject.[22]

However, matters were not really as bad as this statement sounded. All the conference participants were basically agreed on the withdrawal of foreign military personnel. And almost all of them, particularly the nonaligned, regarded it to be of prime importance. Moreover, the Chinese concessions had had a beneficial effect on the possibilities of movement forward. The next morning the cochairmen had consultations with some of the delegates. In spite of the stated reluctance of the United States to put an agreed text to the drafting committee, the cochairmen were examining whether there was not sufficient agreement for part of the provision on withdrawal, if not the whole of it, to go to the drafting committee. The cochairmen and some of the delegates worked out a formula that covered the withdrawal of all military personnel as well as the phrases in the United States and Indian drafts which said that this withdrawal should take place "in any case not later than X days after . . ." The Soviet text was also sent to the drafting committee with a blank instead of the thirty day period previously insisted upon. All that was not remitted to the drafting committee was agreement on the precise point in time when the still to be agreed period for withdrawals would begin. In other words, the Soviets and the Chinese both dropped their insistence on immediate agreement on a specified period; and secondly, they implicitly agreed that the commencement of the period would be subject to further negotiation, which, in its turn, would obviously raise the question of appropriate supervision and control—an element they had so far denounced as an American precondition.

Averell Harriman, who had been consulted, as had some others among us, on the terms of the proposed compromise and had contributed to its formulation, at the next meeting of the conference warmly accepted the proposal. He described it as "an eminently fair and appropriate decision which I hope will be satisfactory to all. It is satisfactory to my delegation." [23]

Chang Han-fu said nothing: apparently it was embarrassing to him to acknowledge so swiftly after his criticisms that he was now in agreement with the United States. However, he raised no objection and the agreement on a major aspect of the withdrawal issue was reached and passed to the small technical committee that would provide the appropriate wording.

In this crucial question as a whole, the major shifts in position had to be made by the Chinese in order to take the negotiation to a point of consensus among the participants at the conference. The biggest movement met the major requirement of the United States: that the withdrawal of military personnel would have to be supervised by the International Control Commission. On the other hand, a control of the withdrawal of the North Vietnamese forces would be virtually unworkable. If the North Vietnamese were in Northern Laos in any significant numbers, it was clear to most of the participants at the conference that they would in fact withdraw before any control measures could be initiated or would find other ways of evading the agreed controls. The ICC would hunt for them in vain, for they would be back in their homeland across the border, or lost in impenetrable jungles. But the very fact that the principle of control had been conceded was certainly a negotiating victory against the Chinese.

The questions of the timing of the withdrawal and the time schedule for its completion remained to be resolved. These were important questions, for on their resolution largely depended the success or failure of the now agreed application of the control activities of the International Commission.

Discussion on these questions occurred at several sessions of the inner six. At first the Chinese were adamant in the view that the controllers would find that their only work was to see that the United States and its allies left Laos. They would not find other armed foreigners in Laos. I pointed out to Chang Han-fu that if this was really so it made no sense for China to oppose withdrawal beginning only after the ICC had got itself in position: it would not supervise the Vietminh anyway (if the Chinese were right in their assertion that no North Vietnamese were present). "True, but the Americans will delay their own withdrawal on the ground that the inspection teams are not present at all the check points. They will stay on and on. We know that this is their plan!"

I assured him that I did not believe that was the American plan. "Then they should agree to withdraw within thirty days of the entry into effect of the protocol," he rejoined.

"But that means you are sticking to your original position. You know very well that that is too much for the Americans to accept."

"No, we are not sticking to our original position. We are willing to have all the withdrawals take place along controlled routes. We have moved."

I went back to the Western members of the conference. It was agreed that there had been some movement on the part of the Chinese. Meanwhile, it was becoming increasingly clear that there would be a good working relationship between the Centrists under Souvanna Phouma and the International Commission. This being so, it could be reasonably expected that the commission and the Laos government could work out a timetable for establishing all withdrawal points and for posting commission personnel at those points. It was agreed that forty-five days should be allowed for the completion of these two stages of the control arrangements. After that there would be a stated period during which the withdrawal of foreign military personnel of all categories would have to be completed.

The Western powers suggested three months. The Communists rejoined that by agreeing to forty-five days they had conceded a month and a half to the West, and if the withdrawal were to take another thirty days the total period would be two and a half months from the date on which the Protocol would come into effect. This, they said, was a considerable concession.

It certainly was a movement from the original thirty days in the Soviet draft, and finally, by mid-December 1961 (four months after the principle of control had been agreed in the restricted meetings of the full conference), agreement was reached on this basis by the inner six delegates. Article 2 of the finally agreed Protocol reflected this agreement.[24]

On balance it would be fair to say that the final provisions in the Protocol governing the withdrawal of foreign forces illustrated the give and take that go toward the making of a successful conclusion to a process of negotiation. In such a process both sides have to be willing to make movements if a point of agreed coincidence is to be found. This is precisely what occurred in regard to the withdrawal provisions. The article of the Protocol that we have cited was followed by Article 3, which reads as follows:

The withdrawal of foreign regular and irregular troops, foreign para-military formations and foreign military personnel shall take place only along such routes and through such points as shall be determined by the Royal Government of Laos in consultations with the Commission. The

Commission shall be notified in advance of the point and time of all such withdrawals.[25]

This formulation, read together with Article 2, differs from the original proposals by strengthening the substantive functions to be performed by the government of Laos. Neither the original Soviet proposal nor that of France had stipulated that the government of Laos would determine the points through which withdrawal would take place and at which the commission would check them off. The Indian proposal had come nearest the final position by stipulating that "withdrawal shall take place along routes and through points to be agreed and indicated by the parties to hostilities in Laos, or the Government of Laos after its formation, to the International Commission for Supervision and Control." [26] It assisted the process of compromise between the United States and China to inject into the relevant articles of the Protocol agreed functions for the government of Laos. By doing this it became possible for the two negotiators originally holding positions at the two ends of the spectrum to claim the satisfaction of making concessions not to each other but to a third party, in this case the government of Laos, whose interests they were both willing and even anxious to espouse.

In negotiation it is frequently possible for a third party to take the edge off a direct confrontation between two strongly antagonistic powers. This is so because the confrontation between the world powers tends at times to express itself in rival interests in the affairs or postures of other states, be those states in the Caribbean, the Middle East, or Southeast Asia. These other states become the relevant third parties in negotiations, and by adjusting positions to meet their equitable requirements the great powers on occasion succeed in tempering the sharpness of their own confrontation.

CHAPTER XIII

Control "over" or "in" Laos

THE CORNERSTONE of a settlement for Laos would have to be a firmly fixed neutral status for the country. On this point, and virtually on it alone, Kennedy and Khrushchev had agreed at Vienna. The Laotian government-to-be, first through Souvanna Phouma and then through the Zurich agreement among the three leading Laotian Princes, had affirmed its adherence to neutrality.

However, for most of the great powers involved or interested in Laotian affairs and willing to accept the neutrality of Laos as a condition in which they could disengage themselves, a mere enunciation of this status would not be enough. Its initiation would have to be observed, assisted, and confirmed, and its continuance effectively guarded, by viable international arrangements. It had been agreed, despite a brief flutter of murmured discontent from the delegates of Thailand and the Boun Oum Laotian group, that the executive international agency of the conference for this purpose would continue to be the International Commission for Supervision and Control, composed of India (chairman), Canada, and Poland, and first constituted in 1954.

It was clear from the very beginning that the commission would have to undertake a wide range of functions including supervision or control of the withdrawal of foreign forces, of the cease-fire, and of measures to ensure that there was no breach of the neutrality or territorial integrity of Laos by infiltration, invasion, or other means. The problem was to agree on the powers the commission should have in order to be able to exercise these functions effectively. The opposing views held on this matter created a major negotiating obstacle. In the background there was the general attitude of the Communist states toward international or foreign control. Most of the members of the conference were aware of the strong reluctance of the Soviet Union to submit to control measures in connection with possible steps of disarmament.

So contentious was the question of controls, in its various aspects, that it took more of the time of the six heads of delegations in their secret sessions than did any other matter. The Chinese were insistent that international control measures would be tantamount to instituting a colonial regime for the country and would be totally unacceptable to them. This view was supported, though in more moderate terms, by the Soviet Union. The Western position was, broadly speaking, that controls would have to be effective and in particular would have to ensure that not only surrounding states and the great powers but also the government of Laos was living up to its commitments.

The only representative of a nonaligned country among the six who met in secret was the Indian delegate.[1] The view of the Indian delegation was that it was primarily for the government of Laos to determine what assistance it would require from the International Commission to ensure its own neutrality; and since that neutrality would be an important provision in the declaration of the Laotian government the international community should rely mainly on that government to take steps to guarantee the maintenance of the neutral status it was electing for itself.

The stage for efforts to resolve the issues of control was first set in restricted sessions of the full conference. The issue that initially raised questions about the functions of the Control Commission at the conference table was the maintenance of the cease-fire in Laos.

Chang Han-fu was the first speaker on this matter and he immediately set out three principles on which he thought the conference should base its discussion. These were:

First, the independence and sovereignty of Laos must be respected.[2]
Secondly, one must proceed from the actual situation in Laos and distinguish between the situation of today and that in 1954.[3]

Thirdly, a distinction must be drawn between what has already happened and what might happen in Laos, and different methods of control should be adopted to meet different situations.[4]

In explaining his first point he reiterated previous statements stressing that the United States–French draft would make the International Commission "into a super-government in Laos, and Laos a country under occupation." [5] He stated also that the terms of the commission should not be "inexplicit, general and equivocal" and that its operations should not be automatic, meaning thereby that they should not be based on procedures that would be self-generating without the concurrence of the government of Laos. This last point was, to some extent, a reflection of considerations that had been advanced by the nonaligned countries, and particularly India.

Chang Han-fu's second point was, in fact, a crystallization of the above view. He explained this point by saying that the Laotian war of 1954 had been an international war, whereas the new situation in Laos amounted to a civil war. This being so, "the International Commission's terms of reference, as befitting the present-day situation in Laos, can only consist of supervision and control, upon the request of the Laotian government." [6] He added that there was to be no supervision of Laos' neutrality, which "only requires recognition and respect by all, but in no way admits of supervision and control." [7] In a sense this last point was a matter of splitting hairs. The Control Commission's functions in regard to the withdrawal of foreign forces and its continuing presence in Laos to deal with complaints of actions by other states inimical to the neutrality of the country would in fact amount to a degree of supervision and control of neutrality. At the same time, in having its delegate say that, "like that of many other neutral countries, its neutrality only requires recognition and respect by all," [8] the Peking government was paying a tribute to the capacities of the government of Laos and the independence of the country, and this tribute would undoubtedly be well received by all nationalistic elements in Laos. Therefore, from the point of view of China's relations with a small neighboring state, Chang Han-fu's negotiating stand was a well-considered one.

His third principle, which was to distinguish between what had been and what might be, was a more doubtful one though he tried to make it palatable to a future Laotian government. The substance of this point was that though it had been agreed that there should be control over the withdrawal of foreign troops and military personnel from Laos there could not be similar control to prevent the introduction of foreign troops in the future. "Prevention of the introduction of foreign troops and military personnel into Laos is a matter entirely within the realm of Laotian sovereignty; nobody else shall be allowed to have a hand in it." [9] What precisely did this mean? He did not make himself entirely clear but it seemed that the Peking government was unwilling to vest the commission with preventive powers as distinct from powers of control and supervision. In a sense this was a truism. Clearly, if a neighboring or other state were to intervene militarily in force, the International Control Commission would be powerless to prevent such action: the best it could do would be immediately to report the action to the cochairmen and thus to focus international concern on the situation. On the other hand, by seeming to deprive the commission of any function in relation to the introduction of foreign forces into Laos it seemed that Peking might be ensuring that a door remained open to foreign intervention in the affairs of Laos. However, Chang Han-fu added the following sentence immediately after his statement of the three principles quoted above: "The question of the International Commission carrying out some sort of supervision and control can arise only if such a situation [foreign troops, etc., in Laos] actually occurs." [10]

In private Chang Han-fu maintained that his insistence on this principle was necessary because any claim by the commission to exercise preventive powers would amount to the introduction of an autonomous police institution within Laos, which would be completely incompatible with Laos' independence. It is not irrelevant to point out that Chang Han-fu was of course old enough, as were all the top Peking leaders, to remember that regimes set up in the foreign concessions in China had, by the exercise of their powers, curtailed the sovereignty of the Chinese government. For a Chinese representative, then, there was a crucial difference between preventive powers and powers of supervision or control.

On the specific question of supervising the cease-fire Chang Han-fu preferred the Soviet draft because it stipulated that the International Commission would exercise its functions "in accordance with the request of the Laotian authorities . . . [and] it shall conduct its work strictly within the limits of the cease-fire agreement entered into by the three political forces of Laos and in close cooperation with the Laotian authorities." [11]

William Sullivan, speaking for the United States, frankly admitted that "we have reached the point in our deliberations where there will emerge the greatest number of differences among the delegations." [12] As to the Control Commission, the United States' general approach was that it should constitute an instrument that would "work in Laos on behalf of this Conference and its several members, filling the gap, so to speak, between the hopes which we hold for peace in Laos and the reality which constitutes the threat to that peace." [13] Though he preferred the United States–French draft on the functions of the commission relating to the cease-fire, William Sullivan was agreeable to all four texts—the French, the American, the Indian, and the Soviet—being sent to the drafting committee for the development of a suitable provisional article. This meant in effect that the United States was willing to take a fairly relaxed view about the differences in wording among the four proposals before the conference. In substance, although it felt that the Indian and Soviet texts were too restrictive, it did not feel that the differences were so significant that they need be regarded as much more than matters of drafting. In defending "the draft which has been submitted by France and supplemented by the United States," William Sullivan said, "I think it would be appropriate for me to state quite frankly that it has been composed with an explicit recognition of the distrusts and the lack of confidence which beset us." [14]

Although the United States and China had arrived at conclusions regarding the next step at the conference that were not greatly dissimilar, the approaches of the two countries were clearly distinguishable. We have referred to the three basic principles enunciated by Chang Han-fu as being relevant to the exercise of functions of control in Laos. On the other hand, Sullivan started from the distrusts he had frankly brought to the surface. He mentioned three such areas of distrust and said that in doing so he was citing just a few of the total number of distrusts. First, he said, there was the inaction of the International Commission in Laos. He claimed that the commission had admitted its frustration and impotence and had warned that the opposing forces were undertaking a military build-up that could lead to an explosive conflict.[15] He added that the frustration and impotence resulted from a "deliberate attempt to prevent the International Control Commission from being able to do anything effective at this time." [16] A second major area of distrust Sullivan mentioned was the attitude of North Vietnam:

Their refusal to admit the presence of Viet Minh in Laos, despite our specific knowledge to the contrary, does not constitute a basis for confidence. How can we be expected to assume that these authorities will any more respect the competence and integrity of the International Control Commission than they have this Conference? [17]

In this same area of distrust he then touched upon a crucial element in the situation:

Their Viet Cong units use Laos and Lao territory as an avenue of transit for their guerrilla and subversive attacks on the Republic of Vietnam. Mr. Chairman, unless we define the tasks of the International Control Commission in such a manner that they address themselves to this particular threat to the peace of Southeast Asia, our work here will have been in vain.[18]

The third and last cause for the United States' distrust that William Sullivan mentioned concerned the Pathet Lao. Referring to Phoumy Vong Vichit, the representative of the Pathet Lao at the conference, he said, "Neither he nor his associates in Laos have displayed any readiness or willingness to dissolve the Pathet Lao armed forces." [19] He then paid back the Chinese in their own coin saying, "We know, from the experience of the last decade, that this private army was repeatedly used as the instrument of 'a state within a state.' " [20]

In spite of these serious concerns Sullivan was able to describe the United States concept of the International Commission in terms that placed it in the same general area as Chang Han-fu's three principles. He said:

In the first place, the International Commission as we envisage it, would not be a superstate. . . . It would exercise no sovereignty over any person or place in Laos. Second, it would not be an infringement on Lao sovereignty and would have no punitive powers. . . . Finally, it would not exercise trusteeship over Laos.[21]

This being so, Sullivan was willing to have the drafting committee prepare an agreed text on the functions of the International Commission in regard to the cease-fire in Laos. This was among the first striking manifestations at the conference of the prevailing desire to reach agreement and it was, on the United States side, a reflection of the fact that the Chinese had made movements in regard to the principle of controls and had enunciated postulates that in themselves were not unacceptable.

However, the exposure by Sullivan of such crucial matters as the presence of the Vietminh, their use of Lao territory, and the separate military units of the Pathet Lao touched the Chinese to the quick. Although no delegate raised any objection when Giorgi Pushkin formally proposed the next day that the conference decide to refer the relevant excerpts from the Soviet, French (as amended by the United States), and Indian proposals to the drafting committee to prepare "an agreed text, taking into account the views expressed and the proposals made at the meeting," [22] all the Communist members of the conference proceeded ex post facto to react strongly to the points made by the American delegate the previous day.

Chang Han-fu directed his remarks first to the United States claim that its approach did not involve an infringement on Laotian sovereignty and that there was no concept of a superstate. He said that, on the other hand, the United States–French draft proposals [23] did in fact have these characteristics and that Sullivan's mere denial was not sufficient assurance to the contrary. His words were:

When an international commission is to control the troops of a country, possess all its state secrets and lord it over the country without any restraint, then what is it if not a super-state? . . . The U.S. delegate put it quite charmingly, asserting that this was a kind of so-called "temporary supplement" to Laotian sovereignty. So the sovereignty of a country requires to be "supplemented" by an international organ! This is indeed a fairy tale. The imperialist absurdity of so-called "protection of sovereignty" has already gone bankrupt, and the development of this absurdity into the nonsense of so-called "supplement to sovereignty" can only make this imperialist theory all the more stinking and repulsive.[24]

After these strong words, Chang Han-fu turned next to Sullivan's areas of distrust and asserted that "the United States does not have any complimentary record in this connection." [25] He referred to the following matters: the United States' refusal to accept the accords arrived at during the Geneva Conference of 1954, its creation of SEATO and extension of its protection over Laos, seven years of alleged interference in the internal affairs of Laos, and the sending of its military personnel into the country. Having listed his version of United States activities in regard to Laos, Chang Han-fu claimed that the question was not one of trust or mistrust; this issue was being raised as "a smoke-screen behind which the United States attempts to continue to interfere in the internal affairs of Laos, and to wipe out the patriotic forces in Laos." [26] This led him to one of the most sensitive areas for the Communist delegates. He referred to Sullivan's remark about the unwillingness to dissolve the Pathet Lao armed forces and then strongly attacked the United States position:

The three Princes of Laos have already agreed to unify the armed forces of the three political forces. Why does the U.S. delegate ask for the dissolution of the Pathet Lao Fighting Units? Could it be that the U.S. delegate is another Laotian prince? Why should the United States interfere in the internal affairs of Laos? Who has bestowed such a right on the United States? Mr. Chairman, fellow delegates, this is an out-and-out undisguised act of interference in the internal affairs of Laos! [27]

Chang Han-fu then thanked William Sullivan for having so frankly spoken his mind and thereby revealed that the attitude of the United States was "to wipe out the patriotic movement of the Laotian people." But this would not work, he asserted:

I would like to give in all sincerity my U.S. colleague a piece of advice: the Laotian question will not be settled as long as you do not abandon such attempts. You have already tried for seven years and what has come out of your seven years' effort to put down the patriotic movement in Laos? Instead of being weakened, the patriotic movement of the Laotian people has grown even stronger. If you have any doubts, you may very well try another seven years. But I can point out to you even now that should you try for another seven years, the outcome would decidedly not be better, but worse for you than what it is today.[28]

Here then Chang Han-fu revealed certain basic positions of his government. First, there was the identification of the left-wing pro-Communist movement of the Pathet Lao with patriotism. It is axiomatic to the Chinese that attitudes, political or social, that do not fall in step with the movement toward a Socialist revolution are anti-patriotic.

Secondly, Chang Han-fu reiterated the Chinese view of the inevitability of history: in seven years the Pathet Lao had grown in power (this was broadly correct), and in another seven years they would achieve further successes (this is not turning out to be the case). In brief, according to the Chinese, and whatever the facts might be, inevitably the radical left wing would succeed in its march toward a revolution. It should also be noted that the time spans mentioned by Chang Han-fu were fairly long, thus indicating another Chinese propensity: dogged perseverance and patience.

Thus the necessity that both the United States and the Chinese delegates seemed to feel to nail down their respective theoretical approaches to control "over" or "in" Laos was giving rise to serious obstacles to the success of the negotiation. Fortunately there was at the same time a broad measure of agreement on the pragmatic aspects of the issue and neither side was willing to forfeit the possibilities of useful practical developments simply in order to satisfy its own preferred theoretical approach.

Accordingly, immediately after the remarks we have just cited, Chang Han-fu said:

The U.S. delegate said that while we have a number of disagreements we also have a number of points in common; and that in looking upon our disagreements we should proceed from the agreements already expressed and not measure these disagreements in absolute terms. We fully agree to this approach.[29]

This was, in a sense, an avowal of the precedence that the Chinese mind was prepared to accord to pragmatic realities over questions of principle. Chang Han-fu finally invited the United States to follow a similar course.[30]

North Vietnam and the Pathet Lao representative had also reacted to William Sullivan's speech of the previous day; Phoumy Vong Vichit had said:

The Neo Lao Hak Zat intends scrupulously to comply by the three Princes' agreement in Zurich, as it has scrupulously executed the Geneva Agreement and the Vientiane Agreement. Our armed forces will not be disbanded in accordance with the Americans' wishes. They will be an integral part of the Lao national armed forces and will contribute, as such, to the birth of the independence, sovereignty and neutrality of Laos.[31]

William Sullivan's immediate response to the statements of the Chinese, the North Vietnamese, and Phoumy Vong Vichit was to say that the three interventions had

demonstrated most graphically the existence of that undertone of mutual distrust and suspicion to which I alluded yesterday and that indeed they buttressed the reasons why the terms of reference for the ICC, as drawn by this Conference should take those suspicions and distrusts into account.[32]

This was Sullivan's way of saying that he would prefer the conference to get on with the practical tasks before it and, of course, do so realistically.

This debate on the problem of controls sufficiently exercised the Chinese mind to result in a scornful article in the *Peking Review* by Liu Ke-lin. He repeated that all control that the United States wished to exercise was "designed to contain and wipe out the Neo Lao Haksat and the patriotic armed forces it leads. That is no secret to the people of the world, but this is the first time that the U.S. delegate has 'come clean.' "[33] The article claimed that the Laotian patriotic forces, instead of being destroyed in the last seven years, had grown several times stronger. It predicted failure for the United States' scheme for a "powerful" ICC to protect "its policy of aggression and its lackeys."[34]

However, the pragmatic tendencies at the conference gained the upper hand. On August 24 the delegates sent to the drafting committee the proposals dealing with control over the withdrawal of foreign forces and personnel. In that connection Giorgi Pushkin stated that the Soviet delegation considered that the provisions for "supervision

and control over the withdrawal of foreign troops and military personnel from Laos should not mean that the withdrawal from Laos of
foreign troops and military personnel is prohibited, without a prior
approval of such an action by the ICC." [35] Chang Han-fu made his
briefest statement at the conference: "The Chinese delegate agrees to
the views expressed and the reservation made by Comrade Pushkin,
the Soviet delegate." [36]

The effect of the statements of the Soviet and Chinese delegates
was to make it clear that any foreign troops could leave before the
control activities of the commission began. This is precisely what the
North Vietnamese intended to do, if necessary, so that if the commission moved toward the northern borders of Laos it would find no Viet
Minh personnel—which would be consistent with the continuing absence of any admission by the Communist state that the Viet Minh
were in fact in Laos.

To the reservation of the Soviet and the Chinese delegations William Sullivan answered that the United States military personnel in
Laos would go through the ritual that would be established by the
Control Commission. He added, "We would also expect any foreign
forces whose presence in Laos would be inconsistent with the terms
of this agreement, once it comes into effect, also to go through that
ritual, so that we could be, and others could be, similarly assured of
their departure." [37]

However, it would clearly be impossible to insist that all foreign
forces in Laos should necessarily remain there till the commission
was able to monitor their withdrawal. Sullivan admitted this: "Naturally, there is nothing to be intended to prohibit the execution of that
withdrawal, as far as the principle is concerned." [38]

On this basis it proved possible to remit to the drafting committee
the broadly similar provisions contained in the various proposals for
the withdrawal of foreign forces and military personnel from Laos.

Immediately thereafter the conference became virtually bogged
down in trying to resolve the further functions of the International
Control Commission in regard to such matters as its assistance to the
government of Laos to ensure prevention of the reintroduction of foreign forces, its powers of investigation, the provisions governing the

preparation of its reports, and the continuing functions of the co-chairmen of the Laos Conference in relation to the commission. In all these matters the concern of the Peking government was expressed as an insistence on preserving intact the full sovereignty of Laos.

For example, Chang Han-fu strongly preferred the Soviet formulation that the commission, on instruction from the two cochairmen, would investigate cases of violation of the prohibition on the introduction of foreign military units and personnel into Laos. He rejected the Indian proposal, which stated that the commission would, in agreement with the government of Laos, exercise vigilance to guarantee observance of this prohibition. The grounds for rejection were that though the Indian proposal brought in the government of Laos, it vested the commission with a preventive function that would diminish the sovereign responsibility of the Laotian government. The Soviet proposal on the other hand only gave the commission the right to investigate. This, according to Chang Han-fu, was more consistent with maintenance of the sovereignty of the government of Laos in its own territory. [39]

It took four sessions of the conference, from August 24 to August 29, to reach agreement on a formulation that could be sent to the drafting committee. That formulation laid down three principles: an investigatory role by the ICC, the carrying out of this role in full accord with the government of Laos, and an appropriate role (they would be able to ask for investigations) for the cochairmen. Chang Han-fu, in spite of his early strong objection to the kind of cooperation India had proposed between the commission and the government of Laos did not object to the drafting committee's entering upon its task on the basis of these three agreed principles.

The conference went on to consider a United States proposal that the various factions in Laos should notify the International Commission of the position and number of all Laotian forces, of foreign military personnel, and of armaments, munitions, and military equipment.

It was normal practice at the conference for the representative of the proposer delegation to introduce the proposal that had been laid on the table by the chairman for the day. However, on this occasion,

before William Sullivan could speak for the United States, Chang
Han-fu intervened, unable to restrain his forthright disapproval of the
United States proposal. His statement contained two points. First,
"information about the armed forces and military equipment of the
belligerent parties in Laos is the national defense secret of Laos and a
matter wholly and entirely within Laotian sovereignty." [40] This was
the familiar posture of championing the rights of China's small neighbor, Laos. But, at any rate in this instance, its substantive significance
was deleterious to the real interests of Laos. The American proposal
was not that "the defense secrets" of Laos should be exposed but
that Laotians, for their own security, should inform the Control
Commission of the military facts pertaining to each warring faction.
Such information would help further steps in the process of pacification of the country and the unification of the armed forces.

Chang Han-fu's second point was that in fact the issue did not
arise: everyone had agreed that all foreign troops and military personnel should leave Laos and there was agreement on the question of
supervision and control of such withdrawal. In these circumstances it
was unnecessary to ask Laos to assume undertakings over and above
those that should be demanded of any other sovereign state.

William Sullivan's reply was brief. On the question of secrecy he
remarked that he realized that there were delegations at the table
"who place a much greater premium on secrecy and furtiveness in international relations than does my Government and my Delegation." [41] He added that this was, in fact, one of the factors that had
caused the suspicions and distrusts to which he had previously drawn
attention. He did not press for a decision on the United States proposal, saying that it should wait till a unified Laotian government had
been formed so that it could decide on the matter.

Ultimately, neither the Declaration nor the Protocol that were
signed at the conclusion of the conference contained clauses reflecting
the American proposal.

When the conference turned to the manner of decision-making in
the International Commission, several important aspects of Peking's
general position, as well as its negotiating tactics, were clarified.

There were three proposals before the conference as to the manner in which the commission should reach decisions. The Soviet proposal was that on all questions, except purely procedural matters, the decisions of the commission should be unanimous. The French proposal was that all decisions would be taken by majority vote, and the Indian proposal was that all major questions would be decided by agreement among the members of the commission.

After Pushkin had defended the Soviet proposal, Averell Harriman spoke for the United States and made two main points. First, "When parties are set up to obtain action it is of vital importance to have a majority rule, or else, as our Canadian friend has said, a body becomes completely impotent or frustrated, and no action is taken." [42] His second point was that there was a neutral chairman of the commission (India) and it would be sensible for the chairman to have the casting vote when differences existed between the other two members (Canada and Poland).[43]

Chang Han-fu spoke immediately after Averell Harriman. His statement was most interesting in point of substance, but it was also noteworthy in tone and form. Chang Han-fu spoke gently; there was no attack on the United States or France, and there was even a friendly and pleading tone when he said:

Dear Colleagues, please consider the matter coolly and you will see that the Soviet draft is very fair. To tell the plain truth, what is envisaged in the Soviet draft is that we socialist countries have no intention of imposing our will upon the western countries, nor should the western countries impose their will upon us.[44]

On the substance of the matter he rejected the assertion that the commission could operate effectively only on the basis of taking its decisions by majority vote. Chang Han-fu asked, "Could the International Commission have returned to Laos,[45] had it not been for the principle of unanimity? Could our Conference have been convened and have made progress had it not been for the principle of unanimity?" [46] Chang Han-fu was thus drawing attention to the fact that certain unanimous decisions had made it possible for the international community to take valuable decisions that could not have been taken by a majority vote: a majority decision would have been unimplementable and therefore no decision at all.

He next tried to explain the essence of the principle of unanimity as Peking saw it. He said:

In a wider context it means the cooperation among the three types of countries in the world, and in a narrower context, it means the cooperation among the three member states of the International Commission. Without such cooperation nothing can be accomplished. Such is the characteristic of our time.[47]

Here Chang Han-fu was explaining that there was nothing sacrosanct about the principle of unanimity, rather that it was a practical necessity of the situation.

Equally he asked that the principle of the majority vote should not be looked upon as sacred or inviolable:

Some people look upon majority vote as a sacred and inviolable principle. But then I would like to ask: if the International Commission were not composed of such member states as it is now, but of two socialist countries and one capitalist country, would you still advocate the procedure of majority vote? [48]

He agreed that a majority vote was both democratic and convenient. Thus he said, "True, taken superficially, the procedure of majority vote is quite convenient and as one might say, also quite efficient. . . . Naturally under ordinary circumstances and in popular organizations in a country, a majority vote is a normal democratic procedure." [49]

He contended, however, that in fact the majority principle *in this case* would not be efficient; it would "impose the will of one type of country on another," and that such imposition would "not only paralyze the operation of the International Commission, but will also lead to the extinction of the International Commission itself." [50]

Turning to the Soviet proposal he asked what was unfair about it, adding:

Not to impose anything on each other but to secure unanimity would mean peace. . . . In the interest of peace, we socialist countries are willing to cooperate with the western countries on the basis of the principle of unanimity. But it is up to the western countries to decide whether they want agreement, whether they want cooperation and whether they want peace.[51]

Chang Han-fu's statement was not without some effect. First, when the final Declaration and Protocol of the conference were drawn, the decision on voting was more on the basis of the Indian proposal, which he had told me was "all right," than it was on the basis of the French proposal. Article 14 of the Protocol spells out the important decisions on which the commission would have to reach unanimity. On other questions, "including procedural questions and questions relating to the initiation and carrying out of investigations, decisions of the Commission shall be adopted by majority vote." [52]

Secondly, Chang Han-fu's reasonably delivered statement had a perceptible effect on some of the succeeding events of the conference. For example, on September 11 the conference considered a draft article in the Indian proposal to the effect that the International Commission in Laos would act in cooperation with the International Commissions in Cambodia and Vietnam. After I explained the proposal as the representative of India, Chang Han-fu took the floor. While he conceded that there might be some administrative connections between the three identically composed International Commissions in Cambodia, Laos, and Vietnam, he concluded by saying, "My Indian colleague, Mr. Lall, has offered many explanations today on the subject, and I see his point, however I cannot but say frankly that we cannot agree to the formulation in the Indian article as it stands." [53]

Canada supported the Indian proposal, Cambodia suggested a few amendments, and then Averell Harriman suggested a way of bridging the remaining differences:

The explanations of our distinguished colleague from India have perhaps clarified some of the problems which our distinguished colleague from China has in regard to the objections that he raised. He indicated, however, that perhaps there should be some cooperation of a technical nature. . . . I wonder if it would be a helpful suggestion—and I only make it in the attempt of being helpful—that this be referred to the drafting committee, if the Co-Chairmen agree, in order to see whether we can find common language to cover the various points which have been raised.[54]

Averell Harriman's conciliatory remarks and his courteous though formal reference to Chang Han-fu significantly assisted the conference. When Giorgi Pushkin proposed and Malcolm MacDonald (chairman for the day) put to the conference "that the Indian draft should now be sent to the drafting committee for consideration, in the light of the proposals made by Mr. Lall himself and by the representative of Cambodia, and of the comments made by a number of other delegations," [55] this was immediately agreed without demur.

This kind of quick, amicable exchange involving both the United States and China could not and did not occur in the early stages of the Laos Conference. That it could take place after four months of strenuous negotiation was a tribute to the diplomatic skill of the negotiators of these countries, and, to some extent, of their other colleagues at the conference. Even more important, this development is indicative of the beneficial effects on international relations of persisting with the negotiation of difficult issues. It is relevant that it had been originally anticipated that the Laos Conference would last for about six weeks. When such an anticipation becomes fixed in the minds of negotiators there sometimes is a tendency to feel frustrated if a negotiation continues for considerably longer. However at the Laos Conference, though there had been situations when, as we have seen, the fate of the negotiations hung in the balance, the persistence of the delegates won out and gave time for the development of the negotiating mood and deployment of negotiating skills.

The drafting committee was not able to find agreed language for the investigatory and decision-taking procedures of the International Commission. These issues then came before the inner six at their secret meetings and were resolved after many formulations had been tried. Gradually the agreed meaning emerged in words, but only after the factors involved had once again been carefully balanced, taking into account the interests of the various states involved.

The Chinese clung tenaciously to the position that the level of armaments in Laos for its own defense was a matter for the government of the country to decide. In any attempt to find a formulation for activities by the commission to prevent or report on the clandestine entry of arms into Laos he saw a plot to place Laos in one military bloc, or to stifle the Pathet Lao as against the right wing. The solution finally came by putting it to the Chinese that the Laotian government itself might wish the commission to assist it in ensuring that private stocks of arms were not being built up. Since the Chinese had championed the rights of the government of Laos, this was not a suggestion they could reject. It was on this basis that Article 12 of the Protocol [56] was drawn.

Perhaps most difficult of all was the reaching of agreement on the classification of specific issues as ones to be decided unanimously by the commission, or in the alternative by majority vote. Still the Chinese were adamant in the view that a unanimous decision would be necessary before the commission could launch an investigation. Again the Indian idea that the cooperation of the government of Laos was the essential element and not the views of the commission had some effect on the Chinese. But this was not enough, in this matter, to secure agreement. Another issue had to be considered side by side with the investigatory procedure. This was the commission's reporting procedure. The Chinese insisted on unanimous reports. Eventually this was conceded to a large extent: the conclusions and recommendations of the commission resulting from its investigations would be adopted unanimously (Article 15 of the Protocol). On this basis the Chinese were willing to accept investigations of violations of the provisions of the Protocol being launched as a result of a majority vote in the commission. Thus, each side made concessions, but still the relevant articles in the Protocol hung in the balance. Neither side was happy. The United States insisted that a member of the commission should have the right to express its own views in the "agreed reports on investigation."

For meeting after meeting of the six these considerations were carefully weighed and balanced, till in December 1961 and January 1962 agreement was finally reached on them in the language contained in Articles 11 through 16 of the Protocol.[57] By then the United States and China, the United Kingdom and the Soviet Union, and India and France had all taken careful stock of each other, measured each other's intentions and motivation. And these intangible assessments influenced the final formulations. Time and circumstance would show the degree and quality of mutual percipience that had been attained by the negotiators. The agreed words in the Protocol could not be judged in the abstract. Equally, they could not be likened to a steel-clad citadel, but rather to a carefully balanced structure that could endure only if circumstances were not entirely unfavorable.

CHAPTER XIV

The Concluding Rounds at the Laos Negotiation

WE HAVE SEEN how various forces were pushing the conference into greater and greater depths of negotiation till, at last, the cochairmen in consultation with a few delegates devised the format of secret, seemingly social, meetings of the heads of six delegations. It would not have been possible to clinch this development, and to make it, over a period of more than two months, a continuing and most helpful factor if the main negotiators at Geneva had not by this juncture succeeded in establishing some confidence in each other and the requisite degree of negotiating rapport.

Already, when Chang Han-fu spoke at the restricted meeting convened on September 12, 1961, to deal with some of the items remaining on the schedule which had been prepared by the cochairmen,[1] there were indications of the presence of a new factor of mutual tolerance and a modicum of respect between the United States and the Chinese delegations. Even Chang Han-fu, dour and cautious though he was at all sessions of the conference, in his summing up of the situation which the negotiations had reached gave some evidence of this new factor:

We have made some headway, but there are still many questions left in suspense. We have all agreed to recognize and respect the neutrality of Laos and have also reached provisional agreement on most of the basic provisions of the neutrality declaration. However SEATO countries taking part in this Conference are as yet reluctant to remove their protection over Laos, which is incompatible with the very undertakings to recognize and respect the neutrality of Laos.[2]

Commenting next on the Protocol dealing with the functions of the International Commission, Chang Han-fu asked, "How can agreement be reached when pledges are made of respect for the independence and sovereignty of Laos, on the one hand, while conditions totally incompatible with the independence and sovereignty of Laos are put forward and held fast to on the other?" [3]

He concluded by making an appeal to the members of the conference:

My dear colleagues, our Conference can no longer carry on in the old way. We are willing to reach agreement on a reasonable basis but we cannot let the Conference drag out indefinitely. Nor will time stay for us. I sincerely hope that we will make joint efforts to get away from the old track and find a way to speedy agreement.[4]

This moderately stated and reasonable appeal contained much more emphasis on constructive approaches than on forebodings of a breakdown; indeed the latter sentiment was muted. On the constructive side the emphasis was on "joint efforts," a willingness to reach agreement, a "reasonable basis," and the need to "find a way." All these were entirely legitimate and potentially helpful approaches to the final effort to reach agreement.

Averell Harriman spoke immediately after Chang Han-fu. He rebutted the idea that the Western proposals were directed toward infringement of the sovereignty of Laos and then made his own plea to the conference (mainly for the ears of the Chinese): "Let's all assume that we are working to the same end and that we do not attack each other for having motives of some undisclosed nature. . . . We have a right to agree with each other and a right to disagree with each other." [5] He then added:

I fully agree with our Chinese colleague that now we must work together to find a way by which those items which have been set aside can best be discussed. . . . With this spirit which I feel has been engendered in the last few weeks we can look forward to finding a solution to some of the disagreements which seemed to loom rather large a while back.[6]

This was clearly a mood different from that of the distrusts to which William Sullivan had referred. It was a mood that had been engendered by the moves that all sides had been endeavoring to make at the conference table and in informal bilateral talks. "We were moving toward a closer understanding," as Malcolm MacDonald later said to me. This movement also facilitated resort to the admittedly difficult and crucial format of the meetings of the inner six.

Here then, again, was evidence of a negotiating rapport between the United States on the one hand and the Communist countries, including China, on the other. All the countries present at the conference had contributed to the increasingly constructive relationships.

Averell Harriman in closing his remarks expressed the hope that the cochairmen would find a method of furthering the purposes of the conference. The Chinese did not object, and Pushkin, who was in the chair, wisely invoked a paragraph of the rules of procedure to the effect, that, on completion of consideration of proposals in restricted meetings, the cochairmen after consultation with the other delegates would make their suggestions on further procedure for reaching final decision at the conference.

This procedural injunction, together with the increasing mutual tolerance and understanding, encouraged the cochairmen to adopt the tactic of secret meetings of the six. They decided that the overt procedure henceforward would be that they would try to reach agreement on the knotty problems so far left unresolved and would keep all the other members at the conference fully informed of their efforts.

On September 26 the cochairmen reported to the next restricted meeting that certain pending questions had been resolved either because the proposals on which they were based had been withdrawn or that agreement had quickly been reached on them. These were relatively minor questions such as the form of the documents (on which China and the other Communist states had made a concession by withdrawing a proposal that the protion of the Declaration on neutrality containing the obligations to Laos of other states should include provisions relating to the withdrawal of troops), diplomatic immunities for members of the Control Commission, and the release of military and civilian prisoners.

However, the larger issues had not yet been resolved, and this prompted Chang Han-fu to make a vigorous statement. He expressed "disappointment at the attitude of the Western countries," and claimed that the agreements so far reached were "mainly owing to the efforts of the socialist countries." [7]

In this statement Chang Han-fu argued that there was no need to include in the Declaration on neutrality a clause to the effect that the territory of Laos would not be used for interfering in the affairs of other countries. The argument of course was unconvincing. The issue was later a subject of lively discussion among the six and the Chinese gave in. The final wording of the Declaration includes an undertaking on the part of all countries that "they will not use the territory of the Kingdom of Laos for interference in the internal affairs of other countries." [8]

To return to Chang Han-fu's largely unpolemical statement of September 26, 1961, he admitted that the Western countries had made some concessions:

Of course it cannot be said that the Western countries have not made any concessions at all. For instance, on the question of the entry into force of the Agreement [or Protocol] and on the question of the holding of periodic meetings by the ambassadors of the States' members of the Conference as envisaged in the French Draft.[9]

Having been generally reasonable till almost the end, Chang Han-fu back-slid, closing his speech with a strong attack on United States policies in regard to Laos:

I want to mention the latest comments made by President Kennedy of the United States on the Laotian situation. In total disregard of the fact that the present situation in Laos was caused by the U.S. government's supporting the Laotian rebel clique to overthrow the legal government headed by Prince Souvanna Phouma, he ostentatiously asserted that the Laotian situation is a threat to peace. It should be asked: Who, after all, is threatening peace in Laos? The United States and its followers in the SEATO bloc are making use of the interval offered by the cease-fire in Laos to send into Laos large numbers of foreign military personnel and war materials and helping the Laotian rebel clique in arms expansion and war preparations. . . . To call a spade a spade the so-called truly neutral and independent Laos is a Laos which the United States can control both from the outside and from the inside.[10]

Naturally Averell Harriman took the floor "to comment on the statement of the representative of the People's Republic of China."

However instead of rising to the charges made against the United States he regretted "very much the spirit which has motivated him [Chang Han-fu]. If we all could show a little more goodwill and less suspicion of each other, we could get on with our affairs." [11] This was a highly skilled approach in dealing with Chang Han-fu's remarks. It prepared the way for his rejoinder to the charge of United States interference in Laos: "Now they suggest that the United States wants to control the internal affairs of Laos—all I can say is 'utter rot. Nonsense.' " [12] This was less likely to rouse the Chinese and the other Communist delegations to a retort because the United States representative had by his earlier tactics in a sense cleared the way for this vigorous denial of accusations against his country.

He went on to make an entirely reasonable suggestion concerning Souvanna Phouma:

One of the men who is most commonly spoken of as the Prime Minister . . . has been twice to Moscow, twice to Peking, and is a constant visitor to Hanoi. He has not been to the capital of the United States. There are many subjects to discuss with him. I am frank to say my government wants to know whether there are any special privileges or understandings that may exist between Prince Souvanna Phouma and the government which he might lead, with other capitals. The facts of the matter are that we want the new government to look to the non-Communist world in the same manner as it looks to the Communist world —with equal desire for friendship and equal desire for good will and friendship; no more, but no less. And let me repeat that: no more, but— I emphasize—no less. [13]

Harriman then briefly rebutted Chang Han-fu's account of who had started the Laos troubles and he dealt critically but gently with the Chinese insistence that there was no need to say in the agreements that the territory of Laos would not be used for aggression against a third country.

There was no rejoinder by Chang Han-fu to Harriman's statement: the conference was left with both points of view, neither of them stated with too great acrimony. This exchange, though it did not resolve issues, left the other delegates with the impression that the desire of the main protoganists to find a basis of agreement was stronger than their continuing distrusts, and that the remaining knotty problems probably could be resolved.

On November 1, 1961, after a lapse of some five weeks, the conference held its next restricted meeting and Malcolm MacDonald said
that the cochairmen had kept in touch with all delegations on the
unagreed items. He added: "Although we have made quite substantial and, I think, encouraging progress, we are not yet in a position to
put to this meeting any agreed formula. We hope to be able to do so
at the next restricted meeting." [14]

But the meeting was not merely a formal one. Chang Han-fu in the
opening phrases of his statement said, "We had good reason to expect
that today's meeting might be our last [restricted] session," [15] and
went on to identify the factors that had frustrated this anticipation.

The first of these, according to him, was that "the United States-
supported Phoumi Nosavan clique has been creating one obstacle after another," particularly in regard to the formation of a national
government by "demanding such big portfolios as national defense,
interior affairs and foreign affairs, in the future coalition government." [16] However he did not directly attack the United States for
any of its actions in Laos.

The formulation of a coalition government was a crucial step, because till this was accomplished the neutrality declaration of the Laos
government could not be drawn up and final agreement on the other
aspects of the work of the conference could not be reached. In this
connection Harriman mentioned the unhelpful activities of the Pathet
Lao. But he too was conciliatory: "I am not going to place blame for
the delays." [17]

Both the United States and the Chinese, though looking at issues
from very different points of view, had again demonstrated a continuing will to reach agreement. In negotiation the recurrence from time
to time of the confrontation of points of view is not a wholly negative
factor. It provides, in a sense, a test of will to continue the negotiation so as to resolve elements of just that reiterated confrontation.

This was part of the complex setting, with its many contributory
factors, that led the main delegations and the cochairmen of the conference through several weeks of bilateral and trilateral discussions
(in none of which were both the United States and China copartic-
ipants: separate meetings took place with each of these two delega-

tions) to the meetings of the six that we first noted in Chapter XI.
The first of these secret meetings began in an atmosphere that was
almost awesomely conspiratorial. But immediately the six delegates
began to speak a language of frankness that had never been achieved
in the closed conference sessions—whether plenary or restricted.
Soon it became clear without doubt what the minimum requirements
of the main parties were. For example:

"You must understand that we just cannot accept mere paper provisions on good behavior. You will have to agree to provisions in the
Protocol with the kind of substance to them that will give us confidence and assurance," said one delegate, making it clear that the control provisions would have to have at least some teeth.

"But you agree that the ICC is in Laos with the consent of the government of Laos, and can only function in the country with the support of the government?"

"Yes, that is so."

"So it follows that more important than unanimity among the
members of the commission for the initiation of investigations is the
view of the government of Laos about the need for a particular investigation."

Chang Han-fu remained reluctant.

"All right. We agree that the commission's recommendations for
action must be unanimous. After all, we aren't going to agree to action unless the Canadians say yes. We can see that you won't agree to
action unless the Poles say yes," replied his interlocutor.

Thus intractable issues began to be tamed. Some of the movements
forward from both sides were induced partly by new formulations
with which they would be presented by less directly engaged negotiators. These new formulations would in their turn require private discussion by me with Averell Harriman on the one hand and with
Chang Han-fu and Pushkin separately on the other hand. Thus, the
meetings of the six required an intensive underplay of bilateral and
trilateral preparatory negotiation.

When the conference had its next restricted meeting on December
4, 1961, the cochairmen were able to report agreement on several issues, so much so that Chang Han-fu made a brief statement, open-

ing with, "I would like to express my thanks to the two Co-Chairmen for the efforts they have made. As reported by Comrade Pushkin just now, under their Chairmanship, we have surmounted a series of obstacles and at last reached agreement on most of the important questions remaining in our Conference. This is quite a big achievement. We welcome this progress." [18]

Again Chang Han-fu accused the United States of interfering in the internal affairs of Laos, politically through the Boun Oum group and militarily through an enlarged military presence in the country. He was sharp on this occasion: "What the United States has been seeking is absolutely not an independent Laos, but a Laos which can be controlled by the United States, absolutely not a neutral Laos, but a Laos neutral in name while following a pro-American line in practice." [19]

William Sullivan refused to be baited by this accusation or those of the Pathet Lao representative. He said:

I cannot, for the life of me, conceive of any statements more inconsistent with the nature of this Conference, more irrelevant to the purpose of today's meeting, more mischievous in their intent and more meaningless in their content. I can assure you that my Delegation will have absolutely no difficulty in ignoring them altogether.[20]

Thus, the United States–China confrontation continued to be sharp, even if unargued at length. But simultaneously there was the fact of progress. The meetings of the six were inching ahead.

The conference held its next restricted meeting a week later, on December 11, 1961. It was remarkable for the fact that it was entirely devoted to a few businesslike statements, mostly recording progress made and expressing gratification. Chang Han-fu found it unnecessary to make a statement. Indeed, none of the inner six delegations took the floor except for the French, who briefly explained their position regarding their installations in Laos.

Agreements continued to flow from the secret meetings of the inner six supported by secret bilateral and trilateral negotiations. The result was that at the forty-third restricted meeting on December 18, 1961, the cochairmen were able to present to the conference the tentative text of the declaration on the neutrality of Laos and of the accompanying Protocol on the functions of the International Commission. What remained now was for agreement to be reached in Laos on a coalition government so that that government could make its own declaration of neutrality to be fitted into the final documents of the conference. It would also be for that government to express its views of the issue of SEATO protection. These steps took longer than had been anticipated. It was not till the middle of the next year that a national government was formed in Laos and on July 9, 1962, it made its Declaration of Neutrality. Meanwhile the remaining issues had been settled in the concluding meetings of these six. The conference then held its final restricted meeting on July 18, 1962, to incorporate the Laotian Declaration and to reach agreement on the SEATO provisions.

After fourteen months, during which all the work was conducted in closed sessions and much of it in secret sessions open to a limited number of delegates, with a constant going back and forth between individual delegates, the Laos Conference concluded its endeavors, and on July 23, 1962, the final documents were signed for the United States by Dean Rusk and Averell Harriman and for China by Ch'en Yi. It had been shown that starting from widely separated positions, mutual suspicion, and distrust, and dealing with intricate problems on the borders of China including those of infiltration, the expansion of Communist and pro-Communist areas of control, military bases, and military assistance, agreement could be reached on the basis of mutually acceptable arrangements to ensure the neutrality and independence of the country concerned.

The agreement reached on Laos is more eloquent that statements about it. It reflects the peaceful possibilities inherent in the attitudes and relationships of the governments involved. Nevertheless, perhaps the following words of Ch'en Yi in his last statement to the conference on July 21, 1962, are still worthy of some attention:

After more than fourteen months of hard work, the delegations of our fourteen countries have overcome numerous difficulties and finally succeeded in reaching an international agreement on the peaceful settlement of the Laotian question. This is a major contribution to the cause of world peace. The Chinese delegation warmly hails it. . . . The achievements of our Conference also show that acute and complicated international disputes can be settled through negotiations. . . . All negotiations among nations must be conducted under the prerequisite of respect for each other's independence and sovereignty and noninterference in each other's internal affairs. In the course of negotiations, it is necessary both to engage in earnest and serious discussions in order to distinguish right from wrong on each issue, and also to maintain a conciliatory spirit of reaching agreement on a reasonable basis. Only in this way can an agreement acceptable to all be achieved. In this respect our Agreement has set a very good example.[21]

As has been pointed out, all the negotiators at the conference fully realized that the implementation of the Laos Agreement was intimately bound up with the South Vietnamese situation, that, indeed, a settlement of that situation was a necessary concomitant to the Laos settlement. Ch'en Yi, in his concluding statement to the Laos Conference, made some reference to this matter:

We have all broken through a link in the chain of tensions in South-east Asia, and we should enlarge this breakthrough . . . the war flames in Southern Vietnam must be put out through peaceful consultations in line with the 1954 Agreements. So long as the flames of war are kept alive in Southern Vietnam peace in Laos cannot be regarded as consolidated.[22]

Many delegates at the conference, particularly those from neighboring states and all those from the nonaligned countries, expected and hoped that the Laos Conference would, after a few weeks' break, be transformed into a Conference on Vietnam. That event, however, has still to take place. When it does, the patiently constructed agreement on Laos may well shed the tarnish it has been accumulating since 1962. Till then there can be no effective unity in Laos because the Pathet Lao, with the assistance of the North Vietnamese, will defend the area of the Ho Chi Minh trail. For this purpose they will refuse to integrate their separate "fighting forces" into the Lao national army. And these reasons, which are part and parcel of the Vietnamese situation, continue to make nonsense of the very basis of national statehood for Laos. The whole problem awaits the Indochina conference table.

CHAPTER XV

Peking's Negotiations with Three Asian States

THE LAOS CONFERENCE of 1961–1962 remains to this time the only example of a multilateral negotiation involving China and a number of Western states, including the United States, which has resulted in an agreement that the Secretary of State of the United States and the Foreign Minister of the People's Republic of China have signed. Indeed, it is the only negotiation that has resulted in the signatures of these two high functionaries of the United States and China being affixed to an agreed-upon document.

Peking asserts that its whole approach to international affairs is to negotiate disputes between states. Marshal Ch'en Yi did so in his remarks to the conference on Laos, and the *Renmin Ribao* editorial of July 24, 1962, reiterated this view: "The agreements on the peaceful settlement of the Laotian question reached at the enlarged Geneva Conference demonstrate once again that international disputes can be settled through negotiation." [1]

This is a very acceptable sentiment, but it is an overstatement if it tends to convey the impression that China is always willing to negotiate. However, it might be taken as tending to indicate that when a basis for negotiation can be found, and we have noted that in regard to Vietnam Ch'en Yi drew attention to the 1954 agreements as furnishing such a basis, Peking is willing to negotiate.

On the other hand, the shift from the possibilities of negotiation between China and India in 1962 showed that Peking—like other states in the overall area of international relations—could swiftly move to the use of force if its interests so urged it. This statement must not be taken to mean that Peking alone is to be blamed for the armed clash that occurred. The situation was far too complex for so simplistic a summing up. However, certainly Peking's attitudes contributed to the occurrence of the armed clash between China and India.

This brief study of China's current attitudes toward international negotiation requires that some attention be given to Peking's agreements and absences of agreement with states in Asia. The absences of agreement would constitute a study in themselves. Among these, the relations between Peking and Delhi from 1953 to 1967 might be regarded as unfinished business. As to Peking's relations with Tokyo, these too are unresolved, though in this case they are in a phase that might be described as business for the future. Peking's relations with Indonesia have recently dramatically altered their course and it would be unwise to attempt an analysis until the situation settles again in a clearer perspective.

As to relations with other large Asian states, this leaves Peking's relations with Pakistan. These relations have developed into a close friendship. They include agreements on trade and other economic matters, civil aviation, a treaty of friendship, and a settlement of border problems involving the exchange of territory in which China has been a net gainer. However Peking's negotiations with Pakistan cannot be analyzed independently of Peking's and Pakistan's negotiations and general relations with India. Simultaneous antagonisms with Delhi have undoubtedly played a significant role in bringing Peking and Rawalpindi together. On October 23, 1966, Foreign Minister Ch'en Yi, in greeting his colleague from Pakistan, Foreign Minister Mohammad Pirzada, said, as reported in the *Peking Review,* that "the friendly relations between China and Pakistan were based on the vital interests of the two peoples and on the safeguarding of peace and security in this region." [2] This is a clear enough reference, in the language of diplomacy, to the triangularity of relationship between China, India, and Pakistan.

In the foregoing circumstances, China's negotiations or absence of negotiations with the larger states of Asia are both too comprehensive and unresolved to form part of this study. However, if a wide understanding of Peking's attitudes toward negotiation in Asia is to be developed, it is necessary to supplement our analysis of Peking's general policies and postures in negotiation and its performance at the major multi-lateral conference it has attended (that on Laos) by some consideration of bilateral negotiations with individual Asian states. Since no one participated in those negotiations except the representatives of Peking and the countries concerned, and since, moreover, the negotiations were in all cases closed to outsiders and conducted in strict privacy, a detailed analysis of them is not open to us. However, in each case discussed in this chapter I have talked with some of the negotiators of the partners of Peking in those negotiations, and have done so with some personal knowledge of the Chinese negotiators, which perhaps might in some small measure have assisted my own capacity to comprehend the situations that diplomats of other countries have been good enough to talk to me about, to the limited and permissible extent that they felt free to do so. I might add that my own experience of the Chinese was not restricted to my dealings with them at the Laos Conference, but included also an important phase of the bilateral negotiations between China and India that occurred when Marshal Ch'en Yi came to Geneva in July 1962 for the concluding meetings of the Laos Conference and the signing of the Agreement and Protocol on Laos.

The first bilateral negotiation we will briefly examine was one between Peking and Burma. This country, India apart, has the longest border with China among the latter's Asian neighbors. For some 1,500 miles in Southeast Asia the two states have a common frontier. The interrelationship of these two states is inevitably considerable and negotiations between them might therefore be of some special significance.

Nepal is another state sharing a sizable border with China. It is a long, narrow country that lies in the central Himalayan region between China and India and which, impelled by geographic reasons and its long relations with China and India, desires to maintain friendly relations with both these states in spite of their mutual rivalries and unresolved problems. Nepal's negotiations with China are therefore also of interest.

There are states in Asia that are not neighbors of China but still

have entered into close relations with Peking. These include a number
of countries stretching from the United Arab Republic to Cambodia.
Among them, and lying about midway in this wide arc, is the island
state of Ceylon, where a democratic parliamentary form of government, which distinguishes it clearly from the government of Peking,
exists. Indeed, apart from India, Ceylon is the only full-fledged parliamentary democracy in Asia that recognizes and has diplomatic relations with Peking. Its negotiations with China therefore fall into
another category among those of the smaller Asian states and deserve
attention in this study.

Burmese-Chinese Negotiations

The major negotiation between Peking and Rangoon has concerned the settlement of claims and counterclaims to territory along
the long Sino-Burmese border. It was as a by-product of the negotiation of the border dispute that the two countries, simultaneously
with the resolving of territorial claims, signed a treaty of friendship
on January 28, 1960. The border situation between the two states has
therefore been the essence of their negotiations.

Talks on the border situation began in 1954 when U Nu visited
Peking as Prime Minister of Burma. The joint communiqué issued on
December 12, 1954, on the conclusion of U Nu's visit stated: "In
view of the incomplete delimitation of the boundary line between
China and Burma the two Premiers held it necessary to settle this
question in a friendly spirit at an appropriate time through normal
diplomatic channels." [3] However, a border clash on the northern part
of Burma's long eastern frontier with China brought the issue to a
head and instead of using normal diplomatic channels the two governments became involved in intensive negotiations on the boundary
problem. The position was rendered especially difficult for Burma by
the fact that Chinese maps showed large parts of the Kachin State in
northeast Burma as forming part of China. Secondly, a part of the
disputed area had been leased by China to the British government in
1897 and Peking now contended that it was not in consonance with
the new status of the two countries that the lease should be continued, and that the territory should lapse to China, which had never
yielded sovereignty over it.

In this context U Nu went to Peking again in 1956 and in protracted negotiation with Chou En-lai the Chinese made three accommodations: on the northern frontier between China and Burma they accepted the traditional line that was in fact an extension of the watershed line on the northeast Indian frontier and is sometimes called the McMahon Line; in the northeast where their maps had shown significant areas as Chinese territory they accepted instead a line along the watershed between the Salween and N'Mai Kha Rivers. Thirdly, reversing its stand on its demand that the Namwan assigned or leased area be returned to it, China decided to transfer sovereignty to Burma. Burma on its part was willing to let China take over the three villages of Hpimaw, Gawlum, and Kangfang, and U Nu argued that even the British had conceded that China had a case for retaining these three villages.

At the end of U Nu's visit a joint communiqué was drawn up which included the following phrases:

Chairman U Nu held a number of talks with Premier Chou En-lai . . . particularly on the question of [the] boundary line between China and Burma on the basis of the Five Principles of Peaceful Co-existence.

The two parties believe that the present talks have provided a favourable basis for the settlement of the Sino-Burmese boundary question.[4]

On this basis U Nu thought the issue had been settled, and the then Burmese Prime Minister U Ba Swe wrote to Chou En-lai in these terms.[5] Shortly thereafter U Nu resumed the Prime Ministership of Burma and in 1957 he visited Kunming in China. There Chou En-lai visited the Burmese leader and to the surprise of the latter made it clear that China did not regard the border issue as settled. It could not make a gift of the Namwan leased area to Burma without receiving a *quid pro quo*. The territory that China eyed consisted of an area of 86 square miles inhabited by two small tribal groups. This claim led to another long period of negotiation.

During the course of those negotiations Chou En-lai made a detailed report on the question of the Sino-Burmese boundary to the First National People's Congress of China on July 9, 1957. In this statement he, very naturally, defended the Chinese approach to the question. Apart from such expected points as good neighborliness, the Five Principles, historic factors, and treaties, Chou En-lai mentioned two points that were more enlightening.

First, he said: "The stand which our government takes in solving the boundary question between China and Burma is based on a desire to protect our national interests as well as promote Sino-Burmese friendship and the solidarity among Asian and African countries." [6]

This statement frankly puts China's national interests first among the stated bases for its policy on the issue. That China, like most if not all other countries, should approach questions on the basis of its national interests makes its policies more understandable to the rest of the world community than would be the case if an ideological consideration were given primacy of place. In the above citation, the third basis of Chinese policy is ideological: thus this approach, though not excluded in the making of Chinese policy, does not appear in a position of primacy.

The second especially interesting point dealt with nationalities. Chou said:

We know that the boundary line between two countries is often found dividing into two parts a nationality living in compact communities on the borders. This is the result of historical development. On the various sections of the defined boundary between China and Burma and on the borders between China and many other neighbouring countries we find people of the same nationality living on both sides of the boundary line. So when we solve the question of the undefined boundary line between China and Burma, we must realise beforehand that it will be hard to avoid separating the nationalities concerned by the boundary line. In view of this, it is all the more necessary for us to take measures, in consultation with the Burmese government, to make the future defined boundary a boundary of peace and friendship, and further cement the close ties of the peoples of the two countries living on the borders.[7]

In 1959 General Ne Win took over the government of Burma. He led a delegation to Peking at the beginning of 1960 that within a week reached final agreement on the border issue. U Nu in presenting the agreement to the Burmese parliament stated:

Its effect is that the Union of Burma retains all the territory to which she succeeded on January 4, 1948,[8] except that Hpimaw, Kangfang, and Gawlum, the area of which is still to be determined, will be returned to China, and that an area of approximately 60 square miles in the

Panghung and Panglao region of the 1941 line is to be transferred to China in exchange for which the formerly leased Chinese territory of the Namwan Assigned Tract now becomes sovereign Union territory. Considering the long and involved history of the Sino-Burmese boundary, and the fact that our negotiations were in reality a continuation of the uncompleted negotiations between the British and the Chinese, I believe that Burmese interests have been well-served by the conclusion of this Agreement. For the first time in history we shall soon have a well-defined, mutually agreed boundary between Burma and China.[9]

On the same day that the border agreement [10] was signed in Peking, the two governments signed the Treaty of Friendship. It binds the two states to mutual respect for each other's independence, sovereign rights, and territorial integrity. They "undertake to settle all disputes between them by means of peaceful negotiation without resorting to force," [11] and to refrain from taking "part in any military alliance directed against the other contracting party," [12] and to strengthen economic and cultural ties. The treaty is valid for a period of ten years and will presumably be renegotiated at the end of 1969, as the preambular clauses state that the two parties desire "to maintain everlasting peace and cordial friendship."

Two of the Burmese negotiators in the long drawn out talks between Burma and China on the border issue have told the author that in their view the Burmese and Chinese negotiators arrived at a settlement that was fair to both sides. Moreover, in the period succeeding the signing of the border agreement and the Treaty of Friendship, Burma, they have assured me, has had no occasion to regret the agreements arrived at or to complain of any violation.

What appears to emerge from a study of the negotiation is that the initiative in each specific proposal regarding territories to be exchanged came from the Chinese side. It is not unusual in international affairs for the stronger party, when it wants a settlement by changing the status quo, to be the side that takes such initiative. Secondly, it does appear that in some degree China departed from its own claims and maps in arriving at the final agreements. Thirdly, China by acquiring three villages on the Burmese side of the watershed between the Salween and the N'Mai Kha Rivers obtained a position of some vantage in northern Burma. However, taking into account the great difference in military and other power factors between the two countries, perhaps this gain should not be regarded as of great significance to China. It amounts to less than one hundred square miles of territory.

In sum, it would appear that, in the circumstances of the particular case concerned, U Nu's assessment of the agreement reached was broadly correct. It would seem that Peking, in this negotiation, though bargaining hard and insisting on some concessions, responded for its part by making concessions to the Burmese and finally arrived at a mutually acceptable arrangement that did not bear the clear marks of overweening Chinese power.

The Chinese could claim that this negotiation with Burma and their relations thereafter with this neighbor exemplified Chou En-lai's statement on April 19, 1955, at the Afro-Asian Conference at Bandung: "China has no intention whatsoever to subvert the governments of its neighboring countries." [13]

On January 28, 1961, *Renmin Ribao* wrote specifically on the Sino-Burmese and other treaties, under the headline "A Shining Example for the Promotion of Friendly Relations Among Asian and African Countries":

In the past year alone, China has concluded a series of treaties and agreements with Asian and African countries, consolidating and developing thereby its relations of friendship and cooperation with them. Apart from the treaty of friendship and mutual non-aggression with the Union of Burma, we have signed treaties of friendship and mutual non-aggression or treaties of peace and friendship with Yemen, Nepal, Afghanistan, Guinea, and Cambodia.[14]

Ceylon-China Negotiations

When Mao Tse-tung and his party rose to power at Peking, the governing party in Ceylon was generally regarded as being right of center. Nevertheless, it recognized the People's Republic of China as early as January 7, 1950. Indeed, Ceylon has sometimes asserted that it was the first Asian country to recognize the new government at Peking, though Burma also claims priority in extending this form of welcome to Mao's regime. In fact, Burma, India, and Pakistan—in this order—preceded Ceylon by a matter of days.

Trade between the new China and Ceylon started in the early 1950s and since 1952 there have been periodic discussions, negotiations, and agreements on commercial matters. These endeavors and their results have been channeled through normal diplomatic mechanisms.

In 1956, S. W. R. D. Bandaranaike came to power in Ceylon when his party defeated the more conservative United National Party in a general election. This event gave Ceylon a government slightly left of center, working often in close cooperation with Prime Minister Nehru's government in India. Bandaranaike was succeeded by his wife in 1960, after the United National Party had had another brief spell of power. Her government, formed by the Sri Lanka Freedom Party, brought in more left-wing elements than had been contained in the government of her late husband and was generally regarded to be slightly further to the left. This increased the likelihood of closer relations with Peking. However, Mrs. Bandaranaike's government retained its close and friendly relations with India, with other Asian governments, and, indeed, with most governments.

When the Sino-Indian armed clash took place in 1962 it was Mrs. Bandaranaike who, understandably having regard for her good relations with both China and India, took the initiative in convening a six-power conference of Asian and African states to help conciliate the dispute between the two countries. The Colombo Conference, as the meeting of the six governments came to be called, produced a remarkably realistic formula regarding the disposition of forces along the whole length of the Sino-Indian border. This formula very nearly gained complete acceptance by both China and India, and the credit for it must go largely to Mrs. Bandaranaike, who not only took the initiative in convening the conference but journeyed both to Peking and Delhi in order to try to bring together as nearly as possible the points of view of the governments of China and India.

Till that time there had been no major bilateral political negotiations between China and Ceylon regarding their mutual relations. Such negotiations first occurred when, responding to Mrs. Bandaranaike's invitation, a high-level Peking delegation paid an official visit to Ceylon at the end of February 1964. The Chinese delegation consisted of Madame Soong Ching-Ling (the widow of Sun Yat-sen), the vice chairman of the People's Republic of China, Premier Chou En-lai, and Vice Premier Ch'en Yi.

During the stay in Colombo of the Chinese delegation there was a full exchange of views on various issues as well as specific negotiation to strengthen political and trade relations between the two countries. The communiqué issued on February 29, 1964,[15] reflects the degree of mutual understanding and accommodation achieved in these negotiations in which, on the Ceylonese side, all the prominent members of Mrs. Bandaranaike's party took part. The leaders of the two countries expressed their solidarity on such matters as anticolonialism, economic aid without strings of any kind, disarmament, "the restoration to the People's Republic of China of her legitimate rights in the United Nations," [16] and nuclear-free zones.

Matters of more direct concern to both countries figured in the concluding paragraphs of the communiqué because they were resolved toward the very end of the four-day meeting at Colombo.

One of these issues was the holding of international conferences of special interest to both Ceylon and China. Mrs. Bandaranaike, for all her friendship with China, stoutly maintained a nonaligned posture in international affairs. By February 1964, in the inner councils of the nonaligned world, it had been agreed that the nonaligned heads of state and government should hold a second conference, following up their first such meeting, which had taken place at Belgrade in September 1961. Mrs. Bandaranaike was strongly in favor of convening a second such conference. Furthermore, it was known that India was strongly in favor of this move but was not equally enthusiastic about the convening of a second Afro-Asian Conference, a move strongly supported by China, Indonesia, and a number of other countries.

The question of holding one or more of these conferences was fully discussed between the Chinese and the Ceylonese at Colombo, and these discussions took place in a context of promises of aid and expanded trading with China. In these circumstances many expected that in the matter of the conferences—which involved the prestige of China—the joint communiqué would reflect more the point of view of Peking than that of Colombo. However, either Mrs. Bandaranaike

was able to prevail upon Chou En-lai or the Chinese were reluctant to
press their view against that of their hostess, knowing her strong
commitment to nonalignment. The result was a long paragraph in the
communiqué that virtually endorses both conferences, and states that
"the two Prime Ministers also agreed that the Second Non-aligned
Conference and the Second Afro-Asian Conference were not mutually exclusive." [17] Thus if Chou En-lai was able to get the communiqué to say "the Ceylon Prime Minister agreed that such a Conference [a Second Afro-Asian Conference] would serve a useful purpose and indicated that Ceylon would participate in such a Conference," he also had to withdraw his known dislike for a nonaligned
conference where a large number of states would meet, but China
would be absent and her influence would be largely unfelt. He agreed
to sign a communiqué that contained the following sentence: "Both
Prime Ministers hoped that a Second Non-aligned Conference would
contribute to the cause of opposing imperialism and colonialism, of
supporting the national independence movement and safeguarding
world peace." [18]

Since Mrs. Bandaranaike had convened the Colombo Conference
of 1962 regarding the Sino-Indian border dispute, she clearly retained
a strong personal interest in seeing that the recommendations of that
conference succeeded in bringing China and India to the negotiating
table. Mrs. Bandaranaike consequently handled this part of her negotiation with Chou En-lai with special skill, both her convictions and
her international status being in some degree at stake. What emerged
in the communiqué was a deftly worded and useful paragraph that
still has relevance to the Sino-Indian situation. First, "The two Prime
Ministers noted with satisfaction that the situation along the Sino-
Indian border has eased." [19] Then came an important sentence that
expressed overtones not only of peaceful intent but almost of anxiety
to negotiate, on the part of China: "The Chinese Premier expressed
thanks to Ceylon and the other Colombo Conference nations for their
efforts of mediation between China and India, and expressed the
readiness to continue to seek direct negotiations with India on the
basis of the Colombo Proposals for a peaceful settlement of the
Sino-Indian boundary question." [20] This asseveration by Chou

En-lai could have led to tangible results had it not been that India, still inhibited by the Chinese incursion over the Himalayas almost a year and a half earlier, and having taken a position of prior implementation by China of *all* the provisions of the Colombo Conference's suggestions and not just three-fourths of them (which she had done), held back from the direct negotiations for which Peking was ready "on the basis of the Colombo proposals." Finally, in this connection Chou En-lai did not demur when Mrs. Bandaranaike insisted on inserting this sentence in the joint communiqué: "The Ceylon Prime Minister indicated that, together with the other Colombo Conference nations, Ceylon would continue her efforts to promote Sino-Indian reconciliation." [21]

The communiqué next turned to direct Sino-Ceylonese relations and after reaffirming the view that these relations were a demonstration of the fact that countries with different political, economic, and social systems, such as their own, could "live together in peace and harmony and cooperate for their mutual benefit on the basis of the Five Principles of peaceful coexistence and the Ten Principles of Bandung," [22] it proceeded to deal with the tangible questions of trade and aid.

The communiqué reflected satisfaction in the existing good trade relations and "recognized the desirability of further development of trade . . . in new fields, particularly of processed and semi-processed materials to promote the growth of industrialization," [23] an objective dearly prized by Ceylon.

Indeed, the trade aspect of the discussions was highly satisfactory to both sides. Ceylon's supplies of rice from China were stepped up to 200,000 tons per year, while she undertook to supply annually 30,000 tons of rubber to China. Ceylon pays for the rice at the Burma rice price (which is generally favorable to the buyer), while China pays the world market price for rubber. Secondly, the Ceylon government was most anxious that China should agree to export 25,000,000 yards of textiles to Ceylon in time for the Ceylonese New Year. They had little hope of this being feasible but a pressing demand was made. Chou En-lai thought over the matter and said, "Your ration is six yards a year per head, while ours is only four yards. But we will arrange to let you have 25,000,000 yards, and as a token of our friendship and our desire to join in celebrating your New Year we will let you have this supply gratis." Naturally the Ceylon delegation was delighted, and, what is more, the textiles were actually delivered in time for the New Year. This was regarded as a significant gesture of Chinese friendship.

The Bandaranaike government fell early in 1965 and in March 1965 the slightly right-of-center United National Party returned to power under Prime Minister Dudley Senanayake. At the general election that heralded this change, the extreme left in Ceylon—Communists and Trotskyists—were singularly unsuccessful. However, there has been no marked change in Ceylon's foreign policy. A friendly relationship with China has continued though it is possibly a little less warm than in the days of Mrs. Bandaranaike. Trade relations continue as before, and the Chinese Embassy at Colombo continues to be the third largest (so far as diplomatic staff goes), coming after the United States and Soviet Embassies. In national staff the Chinese Embassy is the largest as, following the usual practice of Peking's Foreign Missions, no local staff is employed.

Officials in Ceylon generally believe that the basic attitudes agreed to by China and Ceylon in the negotiations of 1964 are being continued by both countries. In recent years China has been the largest single supplier of aid to Ceylon and in this significant role the Ceylonese state that they have not found their Chinese benefactors to be either arrogant or demanding of favors in return.

China-Nepal Negotiations

Nepal's relations with Tibet, its northern neighbor, as well as with China, which has for considerable periods in the historical past exercised sovereignty over Tibet, are of long standing. As the birth place of the Buddha, Nepal started to attract Chinese visitors about fifteen hundred years ago. There have also been wars, trade, and treaties between China or Tibet and Nepal for some hundreds of years.

After a war from 1790 to 1792, and as a symbol of the peace that resulted, a system of exchange of presents between the Court of Kathmandu and the Imperial Court of China at Peking was established.

This exchange took place once every five years. It has sometimes been described as a tributory system expressing China's overlordship in its relations with Nepal. This view perhaps arises out of a misunderstanding of a general custom in much of Asia whereby the exchange of presents, not only among rulers but among the nobility, is a regularly recurring phenomenon. In a recent monograph, which is well known in China, a modern Nepalese writer described the institution of the exchange of gifts between Nepal and China as follows:

After 1792 the Kingdom of Nepal sent missions to Peking at the interval of roughly five years bearing presents from one sovereign to another. This was done in a purely reciprocal spirit. For the Chinese Emperors in turn loaded the missions with gifts to be taken back to Nepal as a token of friendship and goodwill. In addition the members of the Nepalese mission were allowed to take back with them any amount of Chinese goods without paying anything by way of customs duties. It may be noted that exchange of gifts or presents between the heads of states was one of the most reassuring gestures that the two countries entertained highest regards and respects toward each other. This practice was continued till 1908. But before the next visit was to come off, the revolution led by Dr. Sun Yat-sen overthrew the Manchu dynasty in 1911.[24]

The custom was essentially a courtly and feudal one and naturally ceased when China discarded the monarchical form of government.

The relationship between Nepal and her northern neighbors was by no means a one-way affair. In 1856 Nepal got the better of Tibet in a brief war, and the treaty signed by Nepal and Tibet at its conclusion gave the former the right to establish its own trade emporia in Lhasa, and, over and above this, Article 3 of the treaty provided that "Tibet shall not levy any taxes, duties or rates on the merchandise and subjects of the Kingdom of Nepal." [25]

For the last few decades of the nineteenth century and the first half of the twentieth century Nepal remained very much indrawn, its foreign relations being, in effect, largely guided by the British, whose sway had become fully established in the great Indian subcontinent through which most of Nepal's contacts with the outer world could ordinarily be made.[26]

In 1950–1951, however, the Nepalese people and their heretofore figurehead monarch overthrew the line of hereditary prime ministers who had been in power for many generations. This event marked the re-emergence of Nepal in modern times. Diplomatic contacts were extended, and in 1955, when the present ruler, King Mahendra, ascended the throne he immediately decided to establish diplomatic relations with the Peking government at the level of ambassador.

Since then Sino-Nepalese relations have grown fast. Between the years 1956 and 1961 five formal bilateral agreements or treaties were negotiated and signed. The first of these was an agreement to maintain friendly relations between the two countries and to establish mutually acceptable relations in regard to trade and other forms of intercourse between Nepal and the "Tibet region of China." The path for this agreement had been cleared by the negotiation of 1953–1954 between China and India, which led to a similar arrangement in regard to Tibet. That Sino-Indian treaty set out the first formulation in a modern international document of the *Panch Shila,* the two Sanskrit words that mean the five pillars, by which the Asian formula for coexistence has come to be known.[27] The Sino-Indian treaty went on to extinguish the special trading facilities that India had enjoyed in Tibet since the beginning of the twentieth century.

The first Sino-Nepalese agreement did likewise. It reaffirmed the Panch Shila as "the fundamental principles guiding the relations between the two countries," [28] and went on to extinguish the special facilities acquired by Nepal in Tibet in 1856. Instead it set up, on a basis of reciprocity, trade agencies and markets in Tibet and Nepal. It is noteworthy that the new treaty specifies the towns in Tibet where the Nepalese may establish trade agencies and conduct trade (altogether six towns were so named), whereas there is no specification of the towns in Nepal for Tibetan and Chinese traders: the agreement said that an equal number could be designated later. The point of interest is that the Chinese did not delay the designation of sites in Tibet till such time as they were ready to ask for reciprocal posts in Nepal.

In 1957 Chou En-lai visited Nepal. There were no negotiations during this visit but there were many demonstrations of enthusiastic welcome, which are partly explained by the natural gaiety of the Nepalese people and their love of festive occasions.

By now the situation in Tibet was becoming increasingly tense. The Dalai Lama was being stripped of his powers and large sections of the people resented this. In 1959 open rebellion broke out against the Chinese authorities in Tibet, and the Dalai Lama escaped to India—a perilous venture, which succeeded only because large sections of the Tibetan people, bound to him by strong ties of affection and respect, were able to shelter him all along and from point to point on his journey southward. The Chinese were roused to wrath against India over this episode. There was a swift change in the so-far generally good relations between China and India. The Chinese were suspicious and many of them believed that India had instigated and assisted the escape of the Dalai Lama—which was, in fact, not the case. At Geneva, Chang Han-fu and Ch'iao frequently taunted me with this grave case of interference in the internal affairs of their country.

One of the Chinese responses to these unwelcome events was to intensify their overtures to Nepal. The latter was already convinced of Peking's amity, and its Prime Minister, B. P. Koirala, readily accepted Chou En-lai's invitation to visit China in March 1960. During his stay there of two weeks two agreements were negotiated and signed, and one of these paved the way for the crucial negotiation on the delimitation of the border between Nepal and China (Tibet).

Both agreements were signed at Peking on March 21, 1960. One of them set out agreed guidelines for delineation and demarcation of the Sino-Nepalese border "on the basis of the existing traditional customary line." [29] The treaty stated that this was being done "with a view to bringing about the formal settlement of some existing discrepancies in the boundary line between the two countries and the scientific delineation and formal demarcation of the whole boundary line and to *consolidating and further developing friendly relations between the two countries.*" [30] The points to note here are, first, that the revolts in Tibet, particularly by the Khampas, who were strongly active in southern Tibet, had brought to a head the need to reach clarity as to where precisely the Nepalese-Tibetan frontier lay; [31] and, secondly, that the consolidating of good relations with Nepal, the small but vigilant and martial kingdom bordering on Tibet, and a friend and potential ally (in the Chinese view) of India, the other large neighbor of Nepal and Tibet, was, particularly at this juncture, an objective that the Chinese were anxious to attain.

The border agreement set up a joint committee of the two governments—to meet alternately in Nepal and China—and the Chinese proposed a tripartite division of the problem, which the Nepalese accepted. Category one would deal with sections of the border where the delineation on the maps of the two sides was identical. This category offered no real problem, and the joint committee would send out joint teams to erect boundary markers. The second category would consist of areas of discrepancy on the maps of the two sides but undisputed actual jurisdiction of one side or the other. This category would be dealt with by sending out joint teams to determine the boundary line and erect markers on the basis of topographical contours such as watersheds, valleys, passes, and other concrete features of the terrain, *and* the actual jurisdiction of each side. Since jurisdiction would have to be fitted into the topographical features, there would be considerable scope here for differences of opinion when it came to actual demarcation. The third category was the really contentious one: it consisted of those areas where there were both discrepancies on the maps and disputed jurisdiction. Here joint teams would have to go out and inquire into jurisdictional and territorial claims, and do the best possible job to get agreement. We shall see how this, the core of the border problem, turned out.[32]

Finally, the Chinese proposed, and the Nepalese agreed, that the border area should be immune from the tension of military patroling. It was decided that "each side will no longer dispatch armed personnel to patrol the area on its side within twenty kilometers of the border but only maintain its administrative personnel and civil police there." [33]

While the Nepalese Prime Minister was at Peking the Chinese announced a liberal aid program for Nepal, and this was the subject of the second agreement concluded by the two countries on March 21, 1960. The agreement covered goods, technical services, and training for Nepalese technicians. It provided that the traveling expenses and salaries of Chinese personnel engaged on aid projects in Nepal would not be debited against the agreed quantum of Chinese aid.

Only the living expenses of Chinese experts and technicians "during their period of work in the Kingdom of Nepal shall be paid from the amount of the aid, with their standard of living not exceeding that of personnel of the same level in the Kingdom of Nepal." [34] The amount of Chinese aid was stated in Indian rupees and was fixed at 140,000,000.[35]

The very next month (April 1960) Chou En-lai paid his second visit to Nepal, and on this occasion the two countries signed, at the initiative of China, a Treaty of Peace and Friendship. The reason for China's initiative again seems to have been related to its desire to secure, as far as possible, the faithful and pledged friendship of Nepal. It was not the new substance of the treaty that was of importance. Already (in 1956), as we have noticed, the two countries had affirmed their adherence to Panch Shila, which was a concrete elaboration of friendly relations. In the 1960 treaty the two countries took note of that affirmation, restated it in substantive treaty clauses, and undertook "to settle all disputes between them by means of peaceful negotiation." [36] The diplomatic significance (and the point the Chinese scored in obtaining its inclusion) was that, at any rate by implication, it undercut the view that Prime Minister Nehru had expressed in his analysis in the Indian Parliament of the Treaty of Peace and Friendship signed by India and Nepal on July 31, 1950. Mr. Nehru stated that apart from the treaty, but "as an essential, operative part" of it, there was an exchange of letters between the two governments in identical language. Those two letters included the sentence "Neither Government shall tolerate any threat to the security of the other by a foreign aggressor. To deal with any such threat, the two governments shall consult with each other and devise countermeasures."

Mr. Nehru made this analysis in the Indian Parliament on December 8, 1959,[37] and he did so in a statement that dealt in considerable part with Sino-Indian relations. Now, a few months later, Peking's diplomacy had succeeded in committing Nepal, in the event of a dispute with China, to treat the situation not as a threat (which could attract the provisions of the Indo-Nepalese treaty) but as a matter to be settled by peaceful negotiation. This was not necessarily against Indian interests, but it was, nevertheless, a Chinese achievement.

China did not press, as it had done in the case of Burma, that the treaty should contain a clause requiring that neither side should enter a military alliance directed against the other.[38] This was partly because SEATO, which the Chinese particularly abhorred, was geographically relevant to the case of Burma but not to that of Nepal. The other reason for restraint on this issue could have been that the Chinese felt that the clause cited above had achieved their main purpose of some measure of dissociation between Nepal and India in so far as joint military action might be considered by those states in a dispute between either of them and China. Peking might well have decided that, at any rate for the time being, to push further might also be unwise and could raise suspicions of pressure on its smaller neighbor. In short, the wording of the treaty bears the marks of negotiating restraint and sophistication on the part of China.

This series of agreements in 1960 set the stage for the definitive and substantive negotiation on the border between the two countries. The joint committee set up by the two governments held three fairly protracted sessions. The agreement was that these were to take place alternately in Nepal and China. In this procedural matter, but one that could contain overtones of pressure, the Chinese again showed negotiating sophistication. For the opening session they would come to Kathmandu, the Nepalese capital, instead of assuming that, being by all criteria the major partner, they should play the host. The session at Kathmandu of August 1960 was followed by a second session at Peking in January–February 1961, and the final session took place in August–September 1961 at Kathmandu. To the extent that this was feasible in the high mountains, between the sessions joint teams were busy at work on actual surveying and setting up markers on the frontier.

The leaders of the Nepalese delegation found the Chinese party well prepared and their points backed by documentation generally in the Tibetan script with Chinese translations. Once the first noncontentious category of case had been got out of the way it was found that there were overlapping claims to some 956 square miles of territory. For the most part this was pasture land, but some of it had strategic or tactical value. The main criterion ultimately accepted by both sides in determining the dividing line in these areas was to fol-

low the watershed, sometimes with slight deviation when overstep-
ping it, by one side or the other, was established by long and cogent
custom. On this basis the Chinese acceded to the Nepalese claims
over as much as about 900 square miles of the territory in dispute
and obtained exclusive possession for themselves of only about 56
square miles, and agreed border markers were duly erected.[39]

The border treaty was signed at Peking on October 5, 1961.[40] The
King of Nepal himself went to Peking for the occasion. In his speech
on the day of signature he said:

According to the treaty on the boundary which has been signed, the entire boundary line between the two countries has been delimited on the
basis of the traditional, customary boundary in accordance with the
principles of equality, mutual benefit, friendship and mutual accommodation. All outstanding problems regarding the boundary between the
two countries have been solved to the satisfaction of both parties.[41]

Nepalese diplomats and negotiators have assured me that the
boundary treaty with China has been meticulously observed by the
Chinese—in spite of occasional unsettled conditions in Tibet—and
that there have been no instances of attempts to undo any part of the
agreed demarcation.

On the Chinese side Ch'en Yi and Chang Han-fu frequently said to
me at Geneva that their border settlement with Nepal was another
proof of how "other countries" (the implication was of India's inflexibility) had found it practicable to reach viable territorial settlements
with China.

But there are wider "lessons" that the Chinese seek to read the
world in the kind of dealings with Nepal we have surveyed. Speaking
on February 18, 1967, at a celebration held in Peking of the National
Democratic Day of the Kingdom of Nepal, Ch'en Yi said:

Chairman Mao has also taught us: "In our international relations, we
Chinese people should get rid of great power chauvinism resolutely,
thoroughly, wholly and completely." Acting firmly in accordance with
Chairman Mao's instructions, the Chinese people will strengthen Afro-
Asian solidarity and cement their friendly and good neighborly relations
with Nepal on the basis of the Five Principles of Peaceful Coexistence,
and will fight through to the end to support the revolutionary struggles
of the people of the world and to oppose U.S.-led imperialism and modern revisionism.[42]

Here we find our old friend—for these pages have brought us into a considerable degree of acquaintanceship with him—Ch'en Yi, starting from a not unacceptable sentiment of the need to avoid great-power excesses and then being carried away by his ebullience (of which he has not a little) into fantasies that are surely beyond the reach of any great power at the very height of chauvinism. He sets out a doctrine that states his belief that China will support movements that will be victorious against the United States, the Soviet Union (the revisionists), and all their friends, in which category are contained not only the allies of the superpowers but those nonaligned countries, such as India and Yugoslavia, which for one reason or another have not found favor with Peking.

However, we have seen enough of the Chinese at work in negotiations to have learned that this kind of ideological bombast must not be taken as the major determinant of their attitudes in international relations. When it comes to negotiation they will eventually talk in terms that are related to their national interests, their sense of a viable balance, and the desirability in some cases of the nonalignment and neutralization of areas. These are understandable objectives. Because of China's pursuit of them, negotiation with Peking has at times proved possible both multilaterally and bilaterally, for in the last analysis, even ideological purists and cultural and other revolutionaries—and who knows but that the next phase will not be decentralist revolutionaries—seem to consider that at some point in a situation it might be possible to achieve results by talking matters over. This realization is the beginning of the ancient art of negotiation. In each case that art must find its appropriate idiom. The process brings different accommodations in different times and situations, and that is how it must inevitably be. Moreover, the accommodations reached through negotiation frequently, and in the long run invariably, require to be talked over again, to be up-dated, reaffirmed, or reopened. This too is an inevitable aspect of the interaction of peoples and nations, which will be unending unless and until we attain a cooperative world of voluntarily restricted sovereignties.

Appendixes

APPENDIX 1

Draft Declaration on the Neutrality of Laos

*Submitted by the delegation of the Union of Soviet
Socialist Republics at the third meeting of the
Conference held on 17 May 1961*

THE GOVERNMENTS of the Union of Burma, the Kingdom of Cambodia,
Canada, the People's Republic of China, the Democratic Republic of
Viet-Nam, France, India, the Kingdom of Laos, the Polish People's Republic, the Republic of Viet-Nam, Thailand, the Union of Soviet Socialist Republics, the United Kingdom, and the United States of America,
whose representatives took part in the International Conference on the
Settlement of the Laotian question,

Reaffirming the principles concerning the undertakings to respect the
sovereignty, independence, unity and territorial integrity of Laos and not
to interfere in its internal affairs, and agreeing that these principles constitute a basis for the peaceful settlement of the Laotian problem,

Recognizing that, in conformity with the Geneva Agreements of 1954,
the Kingdom of Laos solemnly pledges itself to observe neutrality, not to
participate in any military alliances, blocs and coalitions, not to associate
itself with any international agreement which directly or indirectly would
involve the Laotian Government in commitments of a military-political
or military nature, and not to permit the establishment on its territory of
foreign military bases or military strong points, not to permit the use of
the territory of Laos by foreign States for any other military purposes,
and not to allow foreign States to introduce troops or military personnel
into Laos,

Considering that these obligations are to be made constitutional by the
supreme legislature of the Kingdom of Laos and to become law, as has
been declared by the representatives of Laos at this Conference,

Profoundly convinced that the independence and neutrality of Laos will promote the peaceful democratic development of Laos and the achievement of national accord and unity therein, and serve the purpose of consolidating peace and security in South-East Asia,

Solemnly declare that they recognize and will respect and observe the independence and neutrality of Laos, will abstain from interfering in the internal affairs of Laos, and will not allow any act that might directly or indirectly impair the sovereignty, independence, neutrality and territorial integrity of that State. They undertake not to impose any political conditions on any assistance that may be given to Laos. They undertake not to involve Laos in any military or other alliance incompatible with the status of neutrality. They undertake not to allow the presence in Laos of any foreign troops or military personnel, not to allow the establishment in Laos of any foreign military base or military strong point, not to resort to force or threat of force, and not to do any other act that might result in the violation of peace in that country.

All foreign troops and military personnel now present in Laos shall be withdrawn within a specified period.

The countries participating in this Conference agree that all provisions of treaties and agreements relating to Laos and conflicting with the independence and neutral status of Laos, including the provisions of the Treaty on the Collective Defence of South-East Asia (SEATO) and the Protocol thereto, cease hereby to have effect.

In universally proclaiming the adoption of the present Declaration, the countries participating in the International Conference on the Settlement of the Laotian Question appeal to all States of the world to recognize and respect the independence and neutrality of Laos, and not to do any act that might violate the independence and neutrality of Laos.

The parties to the present Declaration undertake, in case of violation or a threat of violation of the independence and neutrality of Laos, to hold consultations for the purpose of taking measures to remove that threat.

The present Declaration is an international agreement on the neutrality of Laos, and shall enter into force upon signature. It shall be deposited in the archives of the Governments of the Union of Soviet Socialist Republics and the United Kingdom, which shall furnish certified copies of the Declaration to all States participating in the International Conference on the Settlement of the Laotian Question and to all the other States of the world.

Done in two copies in Geneva on . . . . 1961 in Russian, Chinese, French, English and Laotian, all texts being equally authentic.

Draft Agreement on the Withdrawal of Foreign Troops and Military Personnel from the Territory of Laos and on the Terms of Reference of the International Commission

Submitted by the delegation of the Union of Soviet Socialist Republics at the third meeting of the Conference held on 17 May 1961

HAVING REGARD to the Declaration on the neutrality of Laos of . . . . 1961, the Governments of the States parties to the present Agreement have agreed on the following.

CHAPTER I. WITHDRAWAL OF FOREIGN TROOPS AND MILITARY PERSONNEL

Article 1. All foreign military units and military personnel shall be withdrawn from Laos within 30 days after the entry into force of the present Agreement.

The term "foreign military personnel" shall include all foreign military missions, military advisers, instructors, consultants, observers and any other foreign military persons, including those serving in the armed forces of Laos, and all foreign civilians connected with the supply, maintenance, storing and utilization of war materials.

Article 2. The withdrawal of foreign military units and military personnel from Laos shall be executed along routes and through points to be determined jointly by the representatives of the three political forces in Laos (or by the Government of Laos).

Article 3. It shall be prohibited to introduce into Laos any foreign military units or military personnel to which Article 1 of the present Agreement applies.

Article 4. Upon the entry into force of the present Agreement the introduction into Laos of any kind of armaments, munitions and war materials, except specified quantities of conventional armaments necessary for the defence of Laos, shall be terminated.

CHAPTER II. TERMS OF REFERENCE OF THE
INTERNATIONAL COMMISSION

Article 5. In accordance with the request of the Laotian authorities the International Commission for Supervision and Control in Laos set up in virtue of the Geneva Agreements, 1954, and composed of the representatives of India, Canada and Poland shall exercise supervision and control over the cease-fire in Laos. It shall conduct its work strictly within the limits of the Cease-Fire Agreement entered into by the three political forces of Laos, and in close cooperation with the Laotian authorities.

Article 6. The International Commission shall supervise and control the withdrawal of foreign troops and military personnel as prescribed by Article 1 of the present Agreement.

Article 7. On the instructions of the two Co-Chairmen of the Geneva Conference the International Commission shall investigate cases of violation of the provisions of Article 3 of the present Agreement prohibiting the introduction into Laos of any foreign military units and military personnel.

Article 8. The International Commission shall conduct all its work of supervision and control in cooperation with the Government of Laos, which shall render it all possible assistance in its operations. The Commission shall, in agreement with the Government of Laos, set up suitable groups for the performance of its functions under Article 6.

Article 9. Decisions of the International Commission on all questions shall be unanimous, except that decisions on purely procedural questions shall be adopted by a majority vote.

Article 10. The International Commission shall conduct its work under the general guidance and supervision of the two Co-Chairmen of the Geneva Conference of 1954.

Article 11. The costs of the operations of the International Commission shall be divided among all the States participating in the International Conference. The contribution of each participant shall be determined by special agreement among them.

Article 12. The duration of the operations of the International Commission shall be decided by the Co-Chairmen of the Geneva Conference of 1954 and the Government of Laos, who shall after three years hold due consultations thereon and notify their decisions to all the parties to the present Agreement. If necessary the Government of Laos may raise before the two Co-Chairmen of the Geneva Conference the question whether the operations of the International Commission should end before the expiry of the aforesaid period.

Article 13. The present Agreement shall enter into force upon signature.

It shall be deposited in the archives of the Governments of the Union of Soviet Socialist Republics and the United Kingdom, which shall furnish certified copies of the Agreement to all the States participating in the International Conference on the settlement of the Laotian question.

Done in two copies in Geneva on . . . . 1961 in Russian, Chinese, French, English and Laotian, all the texts being authentic.

APPENDIX 3

Draft Declaration by
the Royal Laotian Government

*Submitted by the delegation of France at the
eighth meeting of the Conference*

THE GOVERNMENT of Laos would reaffirm the principles set forth in the second Declaration made on its behalf at the Geneva Conference on 21 July 1954, expressing its resolve never to participate in an aggressive policy and never to allow Laotian territory to be used to further such a policy.

It would reaffirm the Laotian people's will to live in a sovereign and independent State, to secure respect for the territorial unity and integrity of Laos in accordance with the provisions of the United Nations Charter and to ensure the free operation of their national institutions.

It would express its intention to reconstitute a national force adapted to these ends alone and to limit its acquisitions of war material to the needs of that force.

To the same ends, it would voluntarily proclaim its neutrality and undertake not to enter into military alliances, to tolerate the presence on or passage through its territory of foreign troops in any form whatsoever or to accept bases or installations for the military forces of foreign Powers on its soil or the assistance of foreign military instructors other than that provided for in the Geneva Agreement of 20 July 1954.

It would indicate that it is in order to ensure such neutrality that it intends to sign the Protocol amending and supplementing the Agreement of 20 July 1954 on the Cessation of Hostilities in Laos.

It would take the necessary steps to make the present Declaration a constitutional Law of the Kingdom of Laos.

It would request the Powers represented at the International Conference on the Settlement of the Laotian Question to take note of the present Declaration.

AMENDMENT

SUBMITTED BY THE DELEGATION OF THE REPUBLIC OF VIET-NAM
TO THE DRAFT DECLARATION SUBMITTED BY THE DELEGATION OF
FRANCE ON 23 MAY 1961 (LAOS/DOC/7)

Add the following words between the third and fourth paragraphs: "It would undertake to disarm and dissolve military or para-military forces belonging to the political parties and not integrated in the national army."

APPENDIX 4

Draft Declaration in Reply to the Declaration by the Government of Laos [1]

Revised text submitted by the delegation of France at the sixth restricted meeting of the Conference, held on 27 July 1961

THE GOVERNMENTS of Cambodia, Canada, the People's Republic of China, the Democratic Republic of Viet-Nam, France, India, the People's Republic of Poland, the Republic of Viet-Nam, Thailand, the Union of Burma, the Union of Soviet Socialist Republics, the United Kingdom and the United States of America

Take note of the Declaration by the Government of Laos dated . . 1961 by which it:

. . . .

. . . .

Subscribe to the principles and conditions set forth in that Declaration;

Undertake to do nothing contrary to the principles and conditions set forth above and in particular to refrain from all direct or indirect interference in the internal affairs of Laos;

Undertake, further, to respect the resolve of Laos never to participate in a policy of aggression and never to allow Laotian territory to be used to further such a policy;

Undertake, in accordance with the will of the Laotian people, to respect the sovereignty, independence, unity and territorial integrity of Laos and its determination to ensure the free operation of its national institutions;

Undertake to limit their supplies of war material to the needs of the reconstituted Laotian national forces;

[1] This text replaces Part II of document LAOS/DOC/7 of 23 May 1961.

Undertake to respect the neutrality of Laos and its determination not to enter into military alliances, not to tolerate the presence on or passage through its territory of foreign troops of any kind whatsoever and not to accept on its soil bases or installations for the military forces of foreign Powers or the assistance of foreign military instructors save as provided in the Geneva Agreement of 20 July 1954;

And in order to ensure observance of these undertakings, sign the Protocol amending and supplementing the Agreement of 20 July 1954 on the Cessation of Hostilities in Laos.

AMENDMENT
SUBMITTED BY THE DELEGATION OF THE REPUBLIC OF VIET-NAM
TO THE DRAFT DECLARATION IN REPLY TO THE DECLARATION BY
THE GOVERNMENT OF LAOS, REVISED TEXT SUBMITTED BY THE
DELEGATION OF FRANCE (LAOS/DOC/7/REV.1)

I. Amend the fifth paragraph as follows: "Undertake, further, to respect the resolve of Laos never to participate in a policy of *aggression or of direct or indirect interference in the affairs of other countries* and never to allow Laotian territory or resources to be used to further such a policy."

II. Add the following paragraph between the sixth and the seventh paragraphs: "*Undertake to respect the resolve of Laos to unite the armed forces of the parties in a single national army and disarm and dissolve military or para-military forces belonging to the political parties and not integrated in the national army.*"

III. Add to the existing text of paragraph 7, which reads "Undertake to limit their supplies of war material to the needs of the reconstituted Laotian national forces" the following words: "*and not to contribute directly or indirectly to the maintenance, development or creation of military or para-military forces other than those under the Government of Laos.*"

AMENDMENT
SUBMITTED BY THE DELEGATION OF THE REPUBLIC OF VIET-NAM
TO THE DRAFT DECLARATION IN REPLY TO THE DECLARATION
BY THE GOVERNMENT OF LAOS, REVISED TEXT SUBMITTED BY
THE DELEGATION OF FRANCE (LAOS/DOC/7/REV.1)

After the fifth paragraph, which, according to the amendment presented by the Republic of Viet-Nam on 1 August (see LAOS/AMEND 10), reads as follows: "Undertake, further, to respect the resolve of Laos never to participate in a policy of *aggression or of direct or indirect interference in the affairs of other countries* and never to allow Laotian territory *or resources* to be used to further such a policy", *add* the following paragraph: *"Undertake not to resort to force or the threat of force, not to commit any act which might result in violation of the peace in LAOS, and not to use the territory or the resources of LAOS to further a policy of aggression or of direct or indirect interference in the affairs of other countries."*

APPENDIX 5

Draft Protocol on Control

*Submitted by the delegation of France at the
thirteenth meeting of the Conference*

THE GOVERNMENTS OF . . . .
 Taking note of the cease-fire agreement signed on . . . . . .
 Taking note also of the statements of . . . . . signed on . .
 . . . . on the neutrality of Laos, and . . . . .
 Desiring to supplement the Agreement of 20 July 1954 on the cessa-
tion of hostilities in Laos by provisions designed to ensure that Laotian
neutrality will be effectively protected,
 Have agreed as follows:

Article 1

The International Commission for Supervision and Control established
by Article 25 of the 1954 Agreement shall be responsible for supervision
and control of the application of the provisions of the cease-fire agreement signed on . . . ., the declarations on the neutrality of
Laos signed on . . . . and . . . .
 In performing the duties specified in the present Protocol, the Commission shall act in close co-operation with the Government of Laos.
 The Government of Laos shall assist the Commission. It shall ensure
that the assistance requested by the Commission and its services is provided at all administrative and military levels.

Article 2

The Commission shall set up fixed and mobile inspection teams on
which the three member States shall be equally represented. The absence
of the representative of one of these States shall not prevent the Commission or any of its teams from performing their functions.
 The Commission shall establish for its inspection teams a sufficient
number of operation centres to permit efficient operation of the inspec-

tion system. These centres shall be set up, in particular, at the main points of entry into and exit from the territory.

The Commission may change its centres if need arises.

Article 3

The Commission and its teams shall have all the authority for investigation, inspection and verification necessary for the performance of their duties, including authority to hear witnesses.

To this end they shall, as of right, have free and unrestricted access by land, sea or air to all parts of Laos, and shall have full freedom to inspect, at any time, all aerodromes, installations or establishments and all units, organizations and activities which are or might be of a military nature.

The Commission and its inspection teams shall have access to aircraft and shipping registers, to manifests and other relevant documents relating to all types of aircraft, vehicles and river craft, whether civil or military, domestic or foreign, and shall have the right to check cargoes and passenger lists.

Article 4

The Commission shall have sufficient logistic resources, including all means of transport and communication required for the effective performance of its duties.

The Commission shall have free use of these means of transport and communication, and of the facilities necessary for their maintenance.

Article 5

The Government of Laos shall take all the necessary measures to ensure the safety of the Commission and its inspection teams and, in particular:

(1) it shall grant them full and complete protection including, at their request, the placing of protective forces at their disposal;

(2) it shall take suitable measures to enable them to travel quickly and safely so that they may perform their duties more effectively;

(3) it shall grant them all the privileges and immunities required for the performance of their duties.

Article 6

At the request of the Laotian Government or of one of the members of the Commission, the Commission shall investigate without delay any infringement or threatened infringement of the provisions the application of which is subject to its control.

Investigations may also be carried out by an inspection team at the request of one of its members.

Article 7

Decisions relating to the operations of the Commission or the inspection teams, and all procedural decisions, shall be taken by majority vote.

Article 8

The inspection teams shall report regularly to the Commission on their work. In addition, they shall immediately report any facts which necessitate urgent measures.

The Commission shall send members of the Conference a quarterly report on its work. In case of urgency, it shall send them special reports and suggest the measures it considers appropriate.

In all cases in which the Commission or one of its teams fail to agree on their reports, they shall submit a majority report and a minority report or three separate reports.

Article 9

The Commission shall remain in being until it is agreed by the members of the Conference that it can be terminated, and in any case until 31 July 1964. The Co-Chairmen shall report to the members of the Conference by that date on the question of continuing the Commission's work.

The Government of Laos or the Commission may at any time propose to members of the Conference the arrangements they consider necessary for adapting the activities and resources of the Commission to the needs of the situation.

Article 10

As long as the Commission remains in being, the heads of the diplomatic missions accredited by the States members of the Conference to the Government of . . . . . shall meet to take note of and discuss the reports of the Commission, which shall be transmitted to them direct. They shall also discuss the proposals and reports provided for in preceding article.

These meetings shall take place at least twice a year and, in case of need, at the request of one of the heads of mission, provided that the majority of the members agree.

Article 11

The expenses of the Commission and its services shall be borne by the members of the Conference as follows: . . . .

Article 12

The present Protocol replaces the provisions of articles 26 to 40 inclusive of chapter VI of the 1954 Agreement.

APPENDIX 6

Draft Articles Supplementing the Draft Protocol on Control [1]

*Submitted by the delegation of the United
States of America at the twentieth meeting
of the Conference*

THE FOLLOWING articles, tabled by the representative of the United States
of America on 20 June 1961 are supplementary articles to the draft
Protocol on Control appearing in Appendix 5:

Article 13

(a) The Commission shall initially establish operating centres for its
inspection teams pursuant to the provisions of Article 2 of this Protocol
at all major points of entry into and the principal communication centres
throughout Laos. These places shall include: . . . .

(b) All military personnel and advisers, armaments, munitions and
military equipment shall enter or leave Laos only at such places specified
in paragraph (a) of this Article as may be designated by the Commission. Such entries and departures shall be made only after prior notification to and with the prior approval of the Commission, and in the presence and under the supervision of an inspection team. The Commission
shall withhold its approval of any entry or departure which is inconsistent with any provision the execution of which is subject to its supervision and control.

Article 14

(a) As soon as the Commission has established operating centres at
the places specified in Article 13 of this Protocol, and has determined
that it is able to operate effectively throughout Laos, it shall so notify the
Government of Laos and the members of the Conference.

[1] For the text of the Draft Protocol on Control submitted by the delegation
of France, see Appendix 5.

(b) On the_____day after the date of this notification, Articles 13(b), 16 and 18 of this Protocol shall enter into force.

Article 15

Not later than 30 days after the entry into force of this Protocol, the Parties to the [Cease-Fire Agreement] shall simultaneously inform the Commission of:

(i) the location, organization, strength, and equipment of their forces regular and irregular;

(ii) the location, organization, strength, equipment and nationality of all foreign military and advisory personnel and any foreign armed forces, regular or irregular, associated with their forces; and

(iii) the location and quantity by types of armaments, munitions or military equipment in their possession or under their control, whether with units or in dumps or held in reserve.

Article 16

All foreign military personnel and advisers, other than those whose presence is consistent with the 1954 Agreement, shall be withdrawn from Laos as soon as possible, and in any case not later than_____days after the notification provided for in Article 14 of this Protocol.

Article 17

The Commission shall report to the Government of Laos and to the members of the Conference any armaments, munitions, and military equipment within Laos which appear to be in excess of the needs of the national forces, and shall propose measures for the dispostion of such excess.

Article 18

No armaments, munitions or military equipment in quantities or types inconsistent with the undertaking by the Government of Laos set out in [its declaration on the organization of the national army] shall be introduced into Laos.

Article 19

All prisoners of war and civilian internees, of whatever nationality, captured or interned by any of the Parties to the [Cease-Fire Agreement] during the course of hostilities in Laos and under their control or the control of any member of the Conference shall be released not later than 10 days after the entry into force of this Protocol. Prisoners of war and civilian internees who are not nationals of Laos shall be released to the Commission for repatriation. They shall be given all possible assistance in proceeding to the destination of their choice.

Article 20

There shall be no reprisals or discrimination against any person, group, or organization on account of their activities in connexion with the hostilities in Laos.

Article 21

Articles 9 and 10 of Chapter II of the 1954 Agreement are hereby superseded.

Article 22

Subject to the provisions of Article 14(b), this Protocol shall enter into force on the date of signature.

Note: Certain Articles, in particular Articles 19 and 20, will require further consideration in the light of the Cease-Fire Agreement, when it is signed.

Draft Declaration in Response to the Declaration to Be Made by the Government of Laos

Submitted by the delegation of India at the thirty-fourth meeting of the Conference

THE GOVERNMENTS of the Union of Burma, Cambodia, Canada, the People's Republic of China, the Democratic Republic of Viet-Nam, France, India, the People's Republic of Poland, the Republic of Viet-Nam, Thailand, the Union of Soviet Socialist Republics, the United Kingdom and the United States of America,

1. Take note of the Declaration by the Government of Laos dated . . . . . . 1961 which states as follows: . . . .

. . . .

2. Solemnly declare that they recognize and respect the independence and neutrality of Laos (in accordance with the will and desires of the Government of Laos). In particular, they undertake to refrain from all direct or indirect interference in the internal affairs of Laos, and will not be parties to any act to impair directly or indirectly the sovereignty, independence, neutrality and territorial integrity of that State. They undertake not to attach political conditions to any assistance that they may offer or which Laos may seek, and not to involve Laos in any military alliances or other alliances incompatible with her neutrality. They undertake not to introduce any foreign troops or military personnel in any form or arms into Laos or to establish in Laos military bases or strong points, or in any way to violate or threaten the peace or neutrality of that country.

3. Undertake, in the event of a threat of violation or of violation of he sovereignty, independence or neutrality of Laos, to enter into consul-

tations with the Government of Laos and amongst themselves for the purpose of maintaining the independence, sovereignty and neutrality of Laos.

4. Appeal to all other States to recognize and respect unequivocally the independence and neutrality of Laos and to refrain from any action that might violate such independence and neutrality.

5. State that in order to assist in ensuring observance of these undertakings they are signing the Protocol of the International Conference on the Settlement of the Laotian Question 1961.

AMENDMENT
SUBMITTED BY THE DELEGATION OF THE UNITED STATES OF AMERICA TO THE DRAFT DECLARATION IN RESPONSE TO THE DECLARATION TO BE MADE BY THE GOVERNMENT OF LAOS, SUBMITTED BY THE DELEGATION OF INDIA ON 13 JULY 1961 (LAOS/DOC/23)

In paragraph 2 of the Draft Declaration submitted by the delegation of India on 13 July 1961 (LAOS/DOC/23) *delete the words* "and not to involve Laos in any military alliances or other alliances incompatible with her neutrality" from the third sentence and replace them by the following: "not to invite or encourage Laos to enter into any military alliance or other agreement inconsistent with her neutrality, and not to participate with Laos in any such alliance or agreement."

The third sentence of paragraph 2 would then read: "They undertake .... *not to invite or encourage Laos to enter into any military alliance or other agreement inconsistent with her neutrality, and not to participate with Laos in any such alliance or agreement.*"

AMENDMENT
SUBMITTED BY THE DELEGATION OF THE REPUBLIC OF VIET-NAM TO THE DRAFT DECLARATION SUBMITTED BY THE DELEGATION OF INDIA ON 13 JULY 1961 (LAOS/DOC/23)

Add the following text between the third and fourth sentences of paragraph 2 of this draft: "They undertake not to contribute directly or indirectly to the maintenance, development or formation of military or para-military forces other than those under the authority of the Government of Laos."

AMENDMENT
SUBMITTED BY THE DELEGATION OF THE REPUBLIC OF VIET-NAM TO THE DRAFT DECLARATION SUBMITTED BY THE DELEGATION OF INDIA ON 13 JULY 1961 (LAOS/DOC/23)

Amend the first part of the last sentence of paragraph 2 of the Indian draft as follows: "They undertake to respect the resolve of Laos not to tolerate the presence in or the passage through its territory of any foreign troops, military personnel or, in general, any armed foreign unit, in any form or on any grounds whatsoever; they therefore undertake not to introduce into Laos troops, military personnel, or, in general, any armed unit in any form or on any grounds whatsoever. . . ."

Draft Protocol of Agreement Following the Cessation of Hostilities in Laos, 1961

Submitted by the delegation of India at the thirty-fifth meeting of the Conference held on 14 July 1961

HAVING REGARD to the declarations on the neutrality of Laos dated .   .   .
.   .   . 1961, the Governments of the Union of Burma, Cambodia, Canada, the People's Republic of China, the Democratic Republic of Viet-Nam, France, India, Laos, the People's Republic of Poland, the Republic of Viet-Nam, Thailand, the Union of Soviet Socialist Republics, the United Kingdom and the United States of America, have agreed as follows:

Article 1

Responsibility for the execution of the cease-fire agreement shall rest with the parties to hostilities in Laos, and, after the establishment of a national Government of Laos, with that Government.

Article 2

The International Commission for Supervision and Control, consisting of Canada, India and Poland, with the representative of India as Chairman, established by the Geneva Agreements, 1954, shall supervise and control the execution of the cease-fire agreement in accordance with the provisions of Article 3 of this Agreement.

Article 3

The International Commission for Supervision and Control, on receiving information or reports from the Government of Laos or from such other authorities as may be designated for the purpose, or at its own initiative and in agreement with the Government of Laos, will investigate by visiting and inspecting or in other ways as appropriate such difficulties in regard to the maintenance of the cease-fire as may arise. In making such visits the Commission or its teams may be accompanied by personnel deputed by the Government of Laos, or designated authorities, and will be afforded the facilities needed to carry out its visits and inspections expeditiously and effectively. The Government of Laos will grant to the Commission the following facilities:

(1) Full and complete protection including, if required the placing of protective forces at their disposal.

(2) Agreed privileges and immunities required for the performance of their duties.

Article 4

All foreign military and para-military units and military and para-military personnel and auxiliaries shall be withdrawn from Laos immediately, and in any case such withdrawals shall be completed within . . . . . . days of the entry into force of this Agreement. Withdrawal shall take place along routes and through points to be agreed and indicated by the parties to hostilities in Laos, or the Government of Laos after its formation, to the International Commission for Supervision and Control.

The International Commission for Supervision and Control shall supervise and control these withdrawals.

The introduction or reintroduction of such or similar military personnel is contrary to this Agreement. The International Commission for Supervision and Control shall exercise vigilance to assist in ensuring observance of this prohibition, establishing such machinery as may be necessary for this purpose in agreement with the Government of Laos and in accordance with this Agreement.

Article 5

The retention of French personnel for the purposes of military training of the Laotian security force as provided in the Geneva Agreements, 1954, may be mutually agreed between the Governments of France and Laos.

It shall not be open to the French Government to transfer or delegate its functions or powers to any other Government or authority excepting the Government of Laos, or to recruit any personnel other than French or Laotian in respect of these arrangements.

Article 6

The Government of Laos having themselves declared their neutrality, it follows that its preservation and the consequent exclusion of outside interference in their internal affairs is their concern, interest and obligation.

The International Commission for Supervision and Control shall assist in the preservation of the neutrality of Laos, establishing such machinery as may be necessary in agreement with the Government of Laos and in accordance with this Agreement.

Article 7

The introduction into Laos of arms and war material generally, except as required for the defence and security forces of Laos, is contrary to this Agreement. It shall be the duty of the International Commission for Supervision and Control to exercise vigilance to assist in preventing any attempts at unauthorized or illegitimate entry into Laos of arms or other war material, and shall have machinery for this purpose as provided in Article 4 of this Agreement.

Article 8

The International Commission for Supervision and Control shall decide major questions by agreement among its members.

Article 9

The International Commission for Supervision and Control will report to the Co-Chairmen as and when necessary. It will in any case send reports whenever it investigates an incident or takes other important or major steps in pursuance of this Agreement.

The Co-Chairmen will circulate the reports of the Commission to members of this Conference.

Article 10

The International Commission for Supervision and Control shall function in close co-operation with the Government of Laos which shall extend to it the necessary facilities and assistance for the implementation of this Agreement, and consistent with it.

Article 11

The International Commission for Supervision and Control shall act in co-operation with the International Commissions in Cambodia and Viet-Nam, in accordance with the Geneva Agreements, 1954.

Article 12

The Co-Chairmen shall, after the expiry of three years, or earlier if so requested by the Government of Laos, report to the members of this Conference on the question of the termination or substantial modification of the operations of the International Commission for Supervision and Control.

Article 13

The personnel required by the International Commission for Supervision and Control shall consist exclusively of the nationals of Canada, India and Poland or Laos, as appropriate.

Article 14

The administrative control of personnel and equipment at the disposal of the International Commission for Supervision and Control for the purposes of the discharge of its functions in accordance with this Agreement vests, to the extent necessary for such purposes, in the Commission.

Article 15

The expenses of the Commission and its services shall be borne by the members of the Conference on the basis of the principles governing contributions towards the expenses of the United Nations.

Joint Communiqué of the Three Princes of Laos on the Problem of Achieving National Agreement by the Formation of a Government of National Union (the Zurich Communiqué of June 22, 1961)

THE THREE PRINCES, Souvanna Phouma, Boun Oum and Souphanouvong, high representatives of the three existing forces in Laos, met in Zurich from 19 June, as was agreed among them on 18 June, to discuss the problem of realising national accord through the formation of a Government of national union. Since that date the three Princes have discussed the political programme of the provisional Government of national union and its immediate tasks. On these two points the three Princes have agreed as follows:

1. POLITICAL PROGRAMME

The Kingdom of Laos is resolved to follow the road of peace and neutrality in conformity with the interests and aspirations of the Laotian people and with the 1954 Geneva Agreements with a view to building a peaceful, neutral, independent, democratic, unified and prosperous Laos. A provisional Government of national union will be formed, which will apply this policy of peace and neutrality in carrying out the following political programme.

Internal Policy

(1) Execute the cease-fire agreement agreed by the three interested parties in Laos and see to it that peace is re-established in the country.

(2) Apply strictly democratic liberties to the benefit of the people and abrogate all provisions of law which are contrary to this, and restore the laws of these democratic liberties of the citizens and the electoral law approved in 1957 by the National Assembly.

(3) Defend the unity, neutrality, independence and national sovereignty of Laos.

(4) Ensure justice and peace to all citizens of the kingdom in order to achieve peace and national accord without discrimination of origin or political obedience.

(5) Realise the unification of the armed forces of the three parties in a single National Army according to a programme agreed by the parties.

(6) Develop agriculture, industry and handicrafts, create lines of communication and transport, develop culture and pay full attention to the improving of the standard of living of the people.

External Policy

(1) Apply resolutely the five principles of peaceful co-existence in foreign relations, build amicable relations and develop diplomatic relations with all countries, in the first place with the neighbouring countries, on the basis of equality and sovereignty of Laos.

(2) Not to participate in any military alliance or coalition, not to permit the establishment of any foreign military base on the territory of Laos, it being understood that those bases which figure in the 1954 Geneva Agreements will be the object of a special study; not to permit any country to use Laotian territory for military ends, not to recognize the protection of any military alliance or coalition.

(3) Not to permit any foreign interference in the internal affairs of Laos in any form, demand the withdrawal from Laos of all foreign troops and all foreign military personnel and not to permit the introduction into Laos of any foreign troops and military personnel.

(4) Accept direct and unconditional aid from all countries which desire to help Laos in building an autonomous national economy on the basis of respect for the sovereignty of Laos.

(5) Respect the treaties and agreements which have been signed in conformity with the interest of the Laotian people and the policy of peace and neutrality of the kingdom, notably the 1954 Geneva Agreements, and abrogate all those treaties and agreements which are contrary to these principles.

2. IMMEDIATE TASKS

The provisional Government of national union will carry out the following immediate tasks:

(1) Form a Governmental delegation to participate in the International Conference for the Settlement of the Laotian Question.

(2) Realise a cease-fire and restore peace to the whole country.

(3) Honour commitments undertaken in the name of Laos at the International Conference for the Settlement of the Laotian Question and

carry out seriously the agreements concluded among the three interested parties in Laos.

(4) Set free all political prisoners and detainees.

(5) Organise general elections for the National Assembly with a view to forming a definite Government.

(6) During the period of transition the administrative organs established during the hostilities will be left in place provisionally.

Concerning the formation of a Government of national union, the three Princes have agreed on the following principles:

(1) The Government of national union will comprise the representatives of the three parties and will have a provisional character.

(2) It will be formed according to a special procedure by direct designation and nomination by HM the King without passing through the National Assembly. The exchange of views is continuing among the three Princes on this question and will be the object of a new meeting with the aim of achieving national reconciliation as soon as possible.

Done in Zurich on 22 June, 1961.

(Signed) Prince Souvanna Phouma
       Prince Boun Oum
       Prince Souphanouvong

APPENDIX 10

Declaration on the Neutrality of Laos

(July 23, 1962)

THE GOVERNMENTS of the Union of Burma, the Kingdom of Cambodia, Canada, the People's Republic of China, the Democratic Republic of Vietnam, the Republic of France, the Republic of India, the Polish People's Republic, the Republic of Vietnam, the Kingdom of Thailand, the Union of Soviet Socialist Republics, the United Kingdom of Great Britain and Northern Ireland and the United States of America, whose representatives took part in the International Conference on the Settlement of the Laotian Question, 1961–1962;

Welcoming the presentation of the statement of neutrality by the Royal Government of Laos of July 9, 1962, and taking note of this statement, which is, with the concurrence of the Royal Government of Laos, incorporated in the present Declaration as an integral part thereof, and the text of which is as follows:

The Royal Government of Laos, being resolved to follow the path of peace and neutrality in conformity with the interests and aspirations of the Laotian people, as well as the principles of the Joint Communiqué of Zurich dated June 22, 1961, and of the Geneva Agreements of 1954, in order to build a peaceful, neutral, independent, democratic, unified and prosperous Laos solemnly declares that:

(1) It will resolutely apply the five principles of peaceful coexistence in foreign relations, and will develop friendly relations and establish diplomatic relations with all countries, the neighboring countries first and foremost, on the basis of equality and of respect for the independence and sovereignty of Laos;

(2) It is the will of the Laotian people to protect and ensure respect

for the sovereignty, independence, neutrality, unity, and territorial integrity of Laos;

(3) It will not resort to the use or threat of force in any way which might impair the peace of other countries, and will not interfere in the internal affairs of other countries;

(4) It will not enter into any military alliance or into any agreement, whether military or otherwise, which is inconsistent with the neutrality of the Kingdom of Laos; it will not allow the establishment of any foreign military base on Laotian territory, nor allow any country to use Laotian territory for military purposes of interference in the internal affairs of other countries, nor recognize the protection of any alliance or military coalition, including SEATO;

(5) It will not allow any foreign interference in the internal affairs of the Kingdom of Laos in any form whatsoever;

(6) Subject to the provisions of Article 5 of the Protocol, it will require the withdrawal from Laos of all foreign troops and military personnel, and will not allow any foreign troops or military personnel to be introduced into Laos;

(7) It will accept direct and unconditional aid from all countries that wish to help the Kingdom of Laos build up an independent and autonomous national economy on the basis of respect for the sovereignty of Laos;

(8) It will respect the treaties and agreements signed in conformity with the interests of the Laotian people and of the policy of peace and neutrality of the Kingdom of Laos, in particular the Geneva Agreements of 1962, and will abrogate all treaties and agreements which are contrary to those principles.

This statement of neutrality by the Royal Government of Laos shall be promulgated constitutionally and shall have the force of law.

The Kingdom of Laos appeals to all the States participating in the International Conference on the Settlement of the Laotian Question, and to all other States, to recognize the sovereignty, independence, neutrality, unity and territorial integrity of Laos, to conform to these principles in all respects, and to refrain from any action inconsistent therewith.

Confirming the principles of respect for the sovereignty, independence, unity and territorial integrity of the Kingdom of Laos and noninterference in its internal affairs which are embodied in the Geneva Agreements of 1954;

Emphasizing the principle of respect for the neutrality of the Kingdom of Laos;

Agreeing that the above-mentioned principles constitute a basis for the peaceful settlement of the Laotian question;

Profoundly convinced that the independence and neutrality of the Kingdom of Laos will assist the peaceful democratic development of the Kingdom of Laos and the achievement of national accord and unity in that country, as well as the strengthening of peace and security in Southeast Asia;

1. Solemnly declare, in accordance with the will of the Government and people of the Kingdom of Laos, as expressed in the statement of neutrality by the Royal Government of Laos of July 9, 1962, that they recognize and will respect and observe in every way the sovereignty, independence, neutrality, unity and territorial integrity of the Kingdom of Laos.

2. Undertake, in particular, that

    (a) they will not commit or participate in any way in any act which might directly or indirectly impair the sovereignty, independence, neutrality, unity or territorial integrity of the Kingdom of Laos;

    (b) they will not resort to the use or threat of force or any other measures which might impair the peace of the Kingdom of Laos;

    (c) they will refrain from all direct or indirect interference in the internal affairs of the Kingdom of Laos;

    (d) they will not attach conditions of a political nature to any assistance which they may offer or which the Kingdom of Laos may seek;

    (e) they will not bring the Kingdom of Laos in any way into any military alliance or any other agreement, whether military or otherwise, which is inconsistent with her neutrality, nor invite or encourage her to enter into any such alliance or to conclude any such agreement;

    (f) they will respect the wish of the Kingdom of Laos not to recognize the protection of any alliance or military coalition, including SEATO;

    (g) they will not introduce into the Kingdom of Laos foreign troops or military personnel in any form whatsoever, nor will they in any way facilitate or connive at the introduction of any foreign troops or military personnel;

    (h) they will not establish nor will they in any way facilitate or connive at the establishment in the Kingdom of Laos of any foreign military base, foreign strong point or other foreign military installation of any kind;

    (i) they will not use the territory of the Kingdom of Laos for interference in the internal affairs of other countries;

    (j) they will not use the territory of any country, including their own, for interference in the internal affairs of the Kingdom of Laos.

3. Appeal to all other States to recognize, respect and observe in every way the sovereignty, independence and neutrality, and also the unity and territorial integrity, of the Kingdom of Laos and to refrain from any action inconsistent with these principles or with other provisions of the present Declaration.

4. Undertake, in the event of a violation or threat of violation of the sovereignty, independence, neutrality, unity or territorial integrity of the Kingdom of Laos, to consult jointly with the Royal Government of Laos and among themselves in order to consider measures which might prove to be necessary to ensure the observance of these principles and the other provisions of the present Declaration.

5. The present Declaration shall enter into force on signature and together with the statement of neutrality of the Royal Government of Laos of July 9, 1962, shall be regarded as constituting an international agreement. The present Declaration shall be deposited in the archives of the Governments of the United Kingdom and the Union of Soviet Socialist Republics, which shall furnish certified copies thereof to the other signatory States and to all the other States of the world.

In witness whereof, the undersigned Plenipotentiaries have signed the present Declaration.

Done in two copies in Geneva this twenty-third day of July one thousand nine hundred and sixty-two in the English, Chinese, French, Lao and Russian languages, each text being equally authoritative.

U Thi Han (Burma), Nhiek Tioulong (Cambodia), H. C. Green (Canada), Chen Yi (China), Ung Van Khiem (Democratic Republic of Vietnam), M. Couve de Murville (France), V. K. Krishna Menon (India), A. Rapacki (Poland), Vu Van Mau (Republic of Vietnam), Direck Jayanama (Thailand), A. Gromyko (Union of Soviet Socialist Republics), Home (United Kingdom), Dean Rusk (United States)

PROTOCOL TO THE DECLARATION ON THE NEUTRALITY OF LAOS

The Governments of the Union of Burma, the Kingdom of Cambodia, Canada, the People's Republic of China, the Democratic Republic of Vietnam, the Republic of France, the Republic of India, the Kingdom of Laos, the Polish People's Republic, the Republic of Vietnam, the Kingdom of Thailand, the Union of Soviet Socialist Republics, the United Kingdom of Great Britain and Northern Ireland and the United States of America;

Having regard to the Declaration on the Neutrality of Laos of July 23, 1962;

Have agreed as follows:

Article 1. For the purposes of this Protocol

(a) the term "foreign military personnel" shall include members of foreign military missions, foreign military advisers, experts, instructors, consultants, technicians, observers and any other foreign military persons, including those serving in any armed forces in Laos, and foreign civilians connected with the supply, maintenance, storing and utilization of war materials;

(b) the term "the Commission" shall mean the International Commission for Supervision and Control in Laos set up by virtue of the Geneva Agreements of 1954 and composed of the representatives of Canada, India and Poland, with the representative of India as Chairman;

(c) the term "the Co-Chairmen" shall mean the Co-Chairmen of the International Conference for the Settlement of the Laotian Question, 1961–1962, and their successors in the offices of Her Britannic Majesty's Principal Secretary of State for Foreign Affairs and Minister for Foreign Affairs of the Union of Soviet Socialist Republics respectively;

(d) the term "the members of the Conference" shall mean the Governments of countries which took part in the International Conference for the Settlement of the Laotian Question, 1961–1962.

Article 2. All foreign regular and irregular troops, foreign para-military formations and foreign military personnel shall be withdrawn from Laos in the shortest time possible and in any case the withdrawal shall be completed not later than thirty days after the Commission has notified the Royal Government of Laos that in accordance with Articles 3 and 10 of this Protocol its inspection teams are present at all points of withdrawal from Laos. These points shall be determined by the Royal Government of Laos in accordance with Article 3 within thirty days after the entry into force of this Protocol. The inspection teams shall be present at these points and the Commission shall notify the Royal Government of Laos thereof within fifteen days after the points have been determined.

Article 3. The withdrawal of foreign regular and irregular troops, foreign para-military formations and foreign military personnel shall take place only along such routes and through such points as shall be determined by the Royal Government of Laos in consultation with the Commission. The Commission shall be notified in advance of the point and time of all such withdrawals.

Article 4. The introduction of foreign regular and irregular troops, foreign para-military formations and foreign military personnel into Laos is prohibited.

Article 5. Note is taken that the French and Laotian Governments will conclude as soon as possible an arrangement to transfer the French military installations in Laos to the Royal Government of Laos.

If the Laotian Government considers it necessary, the French Government may as an exception leave in Laos for a limited period of time a precisely limited number of French military instructors for the purpose of training the armed forces of Laos.

The French and Laotian Governments shall inform the members of the Conference, through the Co-Chairmen, of their agreement on the question of transfer of the French military installations in Laos and of the employment of French military instructors by the Laotian Government.

Article 6. The introduction into Laos of armaments, munitions and war material generally, except such quantities of conventional armaments as the Royal Government of Laos may consider necessary for the national defense of Laos, is prohibited.

Article 7. All foreign military persons and civilians captured or interned during the course of hostilities in Laos shall be released within thirty days after the entry into force of this Protocol and handed over by the Royal Government of Laos to the representatives of the Governments of the countries of which they are nationals in order that they may proceed to the destination of their choice.

Article 8. The Co-Chairmen shall periodically receive reports from the Commission. In addition the Commission shall immediately report to the Co-Chairmen any violations or threats of violations of this Protocol, all significant steps which it takes in pursuance of this Protocol, and also any other important information which may assist the Co-Chairmen in carrying out their functions. The Commission may at any time seek help from the Co-Chairmen in the performance of its duties, and the Co-Chairmen may at any time make recommendations to the Commission exercising general guidance.

The Co-Chairmen shall circulate the reports and any other important information from the Commission to the members of the Conference.

The Co-Chairmen shall exercise supervision over the observance of this Protocol and the Declaration of the Neutrality of Laos.

The Co-Chairmen will keep the members of the Conference constantly informed and when appropriate will consult with them.

Article 9. The Commission shall, with the concurrence of the Royal Government of Laos, supervise and control the cease-fire in Laos.

The Commission shall exercise these functions in full cooperation with the Royal Government of Laos and within the framework of the Cease-Fire Agreement or cease-fire arrangements made by the three political forces in Laos, or the Royal Government of Laos. It is understood that responsibility for the execution of the cease-fire shall rest with the three parties concerned and with the Royal Government of Laos after its formation.

Article 10. The Commission shall supervise and control the withdrawal of foreign regular and irregular troops, foreign para-military formations and foreign military personnel. Inspection teams sent by the Commission for these purposes shall be present for the period of the withdrawal at all points of withdrawal from Laos determined by the Royal Government of Laos in consultation with the Commission in accordance with Article 3 of this Protocol.

Article 11. The Commission shall investigate cases where there are reasonable grounds for considering that a violation of the provisions of Article 4 of this Protocol has occurred.

It is understood that in the exercise of this function the Commission is acting with the concurrence of the Royal Government of Laos. It shall carry out its investigations in full cooperation with the Royal Government of Laos and shall immediately inform the Co-Chairmen of any violations or threats of violations of Article 4, and also of all significant steps which it takes in pursuance of this Article in accordance with Article 8.

Article 12. The Commission shall assist the Royal Government of Laos in cases where the Royal Government of Laos considers that a violation of Article 6 of this Protocol may have taken place. This assistance will be rendered at the request of the Royal Government of Laos and in full cooperation with it.

Article 13. The Commission shall exercise its functions under this Protocol in close cooperation with the Royal Government of Laos. It is understood that the Royal Government of Laos at all levels will render the Commission all possible assistance in the performance by the Commission of these functions and also will take all necessary measures to ensure the security of the Commission and its inspection teams during their activities in Laos.

Article 14. The Commission functions as a single organ of the International Conference for the Settlement of the Laotian Question, 1961–1962. The members of the Commission will work harmoniously and in cooperation with each other with the aim of solving all questions within the terms of reference of the Commission.

Decisions of the Commission on questions relating to violations of Articles 2, 3, 4, and 6 of this Protocol or of the cease-fire referred to in Article 9, conclusions on major questions sent to the Co-Chairmen and all recommendations by the Commission shall be adopted unanimously. On other questions, including procedural questions, and also questions relating to the initiation and carrying out of investigations (Article 15), decisions of the Commission shall be adopted by majority vote.

Article 15. In the exercise of its specific functions which are laid down in the relevant articles of this Protocol the Commission shall conduct investigations (directly or by sending inspection teams), when there are reasonable grounds for considering that a violation has occurred. These investigations shall be carried out at the request of the Royal Government of Laos or on the initiative of the Commission, which is acting with the concurrence of the Royal Government of Laos.

In the latter case decisions on initiating and carrying out such investigations shall be taken in the Commission by majority vote.

The Commission shall submit agreed reports on investigations in which differences which may emerge between members of the Commission on particular questions may be expressed.

The conclusions and recommendations of the Commission resulting from investigations shall be adopted unanimously.

Article 16. For the exercise of its functions the Commission shall, as necessary, set up inspection teams, on which the three member-states of the Commission shall be equally represented. Each member-state of the Commission shall ensure the presence of its own representatives both on the Commission and on the inspection teams, and shall promptly replace them in the event of their being unable to perform their duties.

It is understood that the dispatch of inspection teams to carry out various specific tasks takes place with the concurrence of the Royal Government of Laos. The points to which the Commission and its inspection teams go for the purpose of investigation and their length of stay at those points shall be determined in relation to the requirements of the particular investigation.

Article 17. The Commission shall have at its disposal the means of communication and transport required for the performance of its duties. These as a rule will be provided to the Commission by the Royal Government of Laos for payment on mutually acceptable terms, and those which the Royal Government of Laos cannot provide will be acquired by the Commission from other sources. It is understood that the means of communication and transport will be under the administrative control of the Commission.

Article 18. The costs of the operations of the Commission shall be borne by the members of the Conference in accordance with the provisions of this article.

(a) The Governments of Canada, India and Poland shall pay the personal salaries and allowances of their nationals who are members of their delegations to the Commission and it subsidiary organs.

(b) The primary responsibility for the provision of accommodation for the Commission and its subsidiary organs shall rest with the Royal Government of Laos, which shall also provide such other local services as may be appropriate. The Commission shall charge to the Fund referred to in sub-paragraph (3) below any local expenses not borne by the Royal Government of Laos.

(c) All other capital or running expenses incurred by the Commission in the exercise of its functions shall be met from a Fund to which all the members of the Conference shall contribute in the following proportions:

The Governments of the People's Republic of China, France, the Union of Soviet Socialist Republics, the United Kingdom and the United States of America shall contribute 17.6 per cent each.

The Governments of Burma, Cambodia, the Democratic Republic of Vietnam, Laos, the Republic of Vietnam and Thailand shall contribute 1.5 per cent each.

The Governments of Canada, India and Poland as members of the Commission shall contribute 1 per cent each.

Article 19. The Co-Chairmen shall at any time, if the Royal Government of Laos so requests, and in any case not later than three years after the entry into force of this Protocol, present a report with appropriate recommendations on the question of the termination of the Commission to the members of the Conference for their consideration. Before making such a report the Co-Chairmen shall hold consultations with the Royal Government of Laos and with the Commission.

Article 20. This Protocol shall enter into force on signature. It shall be deposited in the archives of the Governments of the United Kingdom and the Union of Soviet Socialist Republics, which shall furnish certified copies thereof to the other signatory States and to all other States of the world.

In witness whereof, the undersigned Plenipotentiaries have signed this Protocol.

Done in two copies in Geneva this twenty-third day of July one thousand and nine hundred and sixty-two in the English, Chinese, French, Lao and Russian languages, each text being equally authoritative.

U Thi Han (Burma), Nhiek Tioulong (Cambodia), H. C. Green (Canada), Ch'en Yi (China), Ung Van Khiem (Democratic Republic of Vietnam), M. Couve de Murville (France), V. K. Krishna Menon (India), A. Rapacki (Poland), Vu Van Mau (Republic of Vietnam), Direck Jayanama (Thailand), A. Gromyko (Union of Soviet Socialist Republics), Home (United Kingdom), Dean Rusk (United States), Q. Pholsena (Laos)

Agreement between the Government of the People's Republic of China and the Government of the Union of Burma on the Question of the Boundary between the Two Countries

(January 28, 1960)

THE GOVERNMENT of the People's Republic of China and the Government of the Union of Burma,

With a view to promoting an over-all settlement of the Sino-Burmese boundary question and to consolidating and further developing friendly relations between China and Burma,

Have agreed to conclude the present Agreement under the guidance of the Five Principles of Peaceful Co-existence and have agreed as follows:

Article I

The Contracting Parties agree to set up immediately a joint committee composed of an equal number of delegates from each side and charge it, in accordance with the provisions of the present Agreement, to discuss and work out solutions on the concrete questions regarding the Sino-Burmese boundary enumerated in Article II of the present Agreement, conduct surveys of the boundary and set up boundary markers, and draft a Sino-Burmese boundary treaty. The joint committee shall hold regular meetings in the capitals of the two countries or at any other places in the two countries.

Article II

The Contracting Parties agree that the existing issues concerning th Sino-Burmese boundary shall be settled in accordance with the followin provisions:

(1) With the exception of the area of Hpimaw, Gawlum and Kang-fang, the entire undelimited boundary from the High Conical Peak to the western extremity of the Sino-Burmese boundary shall be delimited along the traditional customary line, that is to say, from the High Conical Peak northward along the watershed between the Taiping, the Shweli, the Nu (Salween) and the Tulung (Taron) Rivers on the one hand and the Nmai Hka River on the other, up to the place where it crosses the Tulung (Taron) River between Chingdam and Nhkumkang, and then along the watershed between the Tulung (Taron) and the Tsayul (Zayul) Rivers on the one hand and all the upper tributaries of the Ir-rawaddy River, except for the Tulung (Taron) River, on the other, up to the western extremity of the Sino-Burmese boundary. The joint commit-tee shall send out joint survey teams composed of an equal number of persons from each side to conduct surveys along the above-mentioned watersheds so as to determine the specific alignment of this section of the boundary line and to set up boundary markers.

(2) The Burmese Government has agreed to return to China the area of Hpimaw, Gawlum and Kangfang which belongs to China. As to the extent of this area to be returned to China, it is to be discussed and de-termined by the joint committee in accordance with the proposals put forward and marked on maps by the Governments of Burma and China on February 4, 1957 and July 26, 1957 respectively. After determining the extent of this area to be returned to China, the joint committee shall send out joint survey teams composed of an equal number of persons from each side to conduct on-the-spot survey of the specific alignment of this section of the boundary line and to set up boundary markers.

(3) In order to abrogate the "perpetual lease" by Burma of the Meng-Mao triangular area (Namwan Assigned Tract) at the junction of the Namwan and the Shweli Rivers, which belongs to China, the Chinese Government has agreed to turn over this area to Burma to become part of the territory of the Union of Burma. In exchange, the Burmese Gov-ernment has agreed to turn over to China to become part of Chinese ter-ritory the areas under the jurisdiction of the Panhung and Panlao tribes, which are west of the boundary line from the junction of the Nam Ting and the Nampa Rivers to the No. 1 marker on the southern delimited section of the boundary as defined in the notes exchanged between the Chinese and the British Governments on June 18, 1941. As to the extent of these areas to be turned over to China, the Chinese and the Burmese Governments put forward proposals marked on maps on July 26, 1957 and June 4, 1959 respectively. The area where the proposals of the two Governments coincide will definitely be turned over to China. Where the proposals of the two Governments differ as to the area under the juris-diction of the Panhung tribe, the joint committee will send out a team

composed of an equal number of persons from each side to ascertain on the spot as to whether it is under the jurisdiction of the Panhung tribe, so as to determine whether it is to be turned over to China. After the extent of the areas under the jurisdiction of the Panhung and Panlao tribes to be turned over to China has been thus determined, the joint committee will send out joint survey teams composed of an equal number of persons from each side to conduct on-the-spot survey of the specific alignment of this section of the boundary line and to set up boundary markers.

(4) Except for the adjustment provided for in paragraph (3) of this Article, the section of the boundary from the junction of the Nam Ting and the Nampa Rivers to the No. 1 marker on the southern delimited section of the boundary shall be delimited as defined in the notes exchanged between the Chinese and the British Governments on June 18, 1941. The joint committee shall send out joint survey teams composed of an equal number of persons from each side to carry out delimitation and demarcation along this section of the boundary line and set up boundary markers.

Article III

The Contracting Parties agree that the joint committee, after working out solutions for the existing issues concerning the Sino-Burmese boundary as enumerated in Article II of the present Agreement, shall be responsible for drafting a Sino-Burmese boundary treaty, which shall cover not only all the sections of the boundary as mentioned in Article II of the present Agreement, but also the sections of the boundary which were already delimited in the past and need no adjustment. After being signed by the Governments of the two countries and coming into effect, the new boundary treaty shall replace all old treaties and notes exchanged concerning the boundary between the two countries. The Chinese Government, in line with its policy of being consistently opposed to foreign prerogatives and respecting the sovereignty of other countries, renounces China's right of participation in mining enterprises at Lufang of Burma as provided in the notes exchanged between the Chinese and the British Governments on June 18, 1941.

Article IV

(1) The present Agreement is subject to ratification and the instruments of ratification will be exchanged in Rangoon as soon as possible.

(2) The present Agreement will come into force immediately on the exchange of the instruments of ratification and shall automatically cease to be in force when the Sino-Burmese boundary treaty to be signed by the two Governments comes into force.

Done in duplicate in Peking on the twenty-eighth day of January

1960, in the Chinese and English languages, both texts being equally authentic.

For the Government of the	For the Government of
People's Republic of China:	*the Union of Burma:*
(Signed) CHOU EN-LAI	(Signed) NE WIN

APPENDIX 12

Treaty of Friendship and Mutual Non-Aggression between the People's Republic of China and the Union of Burma

(January 28, 1960)

THE GOVERNMENT of the People's Republic of China and the Government of the Union of Burma,

Desiring to maintain everlasting peace and cordial friendship between the People's Republic of China and the Union of Burma,

Convinced that the strengthening of good neighbourly relations and friendly co-operation between the People's Republic of China and the Union of Burma is in accordance with the vital interests of both countries,

Have decided for this purpose to conclude the present Treaty in accordance with the Five Principles of Peaceful Co-existence jointly initiated by the two countries, and have agreed as follows:

Article I

The Contracting Parties recognize and respect the independence, sovereign rights and territorial integrity of each other.

Article II

There shall be everlasting peace and cordial friendship between the Contracting Parties who undertake to settle all disputes between them by means of peaceful negotiation without resorting to force.

Article III

Each Contracting Party undertakes not to carry out acts of aggression against the other and not to take part in any military alliance directed against the other Contracting Party.

Article IV

The Contracting Parties declare that they will develop and strengthen the economic and cultural ties between the two States in a spirit of friendship and co-operation, in accordance with the principles of equality and mutual benefit and of mutual non-interference in each other's internal affairs.

Article V

Any difference or dispute arising out of the interpretation or application of the present Treaty or one or more of its Articles shall be settled by negotiations through the ordinary diplomatic channels.

Article VI

(1) The present Treaty is subject to ratification and the instruments of ratification will be exchanged in Rangoon as soon as possible.

(2) The present Treaty will come into force immediately on the exchange of the instruments of ratification and will remain in force for a period of ten years.

(3) Unless either of the Contracting Parties gives to the other notice in writing to terminate it at least one year before the expiration of this period, it will remain in force without any specified time limit, subject to the right of either of the Contracting Parties to terminate it by giving to the other in writing a year's notice of its intention to do so.

In witness whereof the Premier of the State Council of the People's Republic of China and the Prime Minister of the Union of Burma have signed the present Treaty.

Done in duplicate in Peking on the twenty-eighth day of January 1960, in the Chinese and English languages, both texts being equally authentic.

For the Government of the
People's Republic of China:
(Signed) CHOU EN-LAI

For the Government of
the Union of Burma:
(Signed) NE WIN

APPENDIX 13

Ceylon-China Joint Communiqué

AT THE INVITATION of the Prime Minister of Ceylon, Mrs. Sirimavo R.D. Bandaranaike, Her Excellency Madame Soong Ching Ling, Vice-Chairman of the People's Republic of China, and His Excellency Mr. Chou En-Lai, Premier of the State Council of the People's Republic of China, paid an official visit to Ceylon from February 26th to 29th 1964.

2. They were accompanied by Marshal Chen Yi, Vice-Premier of the State Council and Minister of Foreign Affairs, and high ranking officials.

3. The distinguished visitors received a warm and enthusiastic welcome, expressive of the feelings of deep friendship which the people of Ceylon have for the Chinese people and their representatives.

4. In the course of the visit, the Premier of the State Council of the People's Republic of China had meetings and conversations with the Prime Minister of Ceylon. Taking part in these talks on the Chinese side were:

Marshal Chen Yi, Vice-Premier and Foreign Minister;

Kung Yuan, Deputy Director of the Office in charge of Foreign Affairs, State Council;

Huang Chen, Vice-Minister of Foreign Affairs;

Tung Hsiao-Peng, Chief of the Secretariat of the Premier of the State Council;

and high officials of the Chinese Government.

On the Ceylon side were:

Hon. C. P. de Silva, Minister of Lands, Irrigation & Power;

Hon. T. B. Ilangaratne, Minister of Finance;

Hon. Maitripala Senanayake, Minister of Commerce and Industries;

Hon. Felix R. Dias Bandaranaike, Minister of Agriculture, Food and Co-operatives and Parliamentary Secretary to the Minister of Defence and External Affairs;

and high officials of the Government of Ceylon.

5. The talks were held in an atmosphere of cordiality and friendship which characterise the relationship between the two countries. The two parties exchanged opinions on a wide range of internationl problems of common interest as well as on the problems relating to the further strengthening and development of Sino-Ceylonese relations.

6. The two Prime Ministers noted with deep satisfaction the emergence into freedom and national independence of many countries in Asia and Africa. They expressed their firm opposition to colonialism in all its forms and manifestations and hoped that its last vestiges would soon be eradicated.

The two leaders agreed that the national Governments of countries that have newly won national independence should be helped in their endeavours to attain full economic independence as rapidly as possible. They were of the view that aid so given without any political conditions or privileges, and on a basis of equality and mutual benefit, respect for the sovereignty of the recipient countries and non-interference in their internal affairs, would help to strengthen their national independence and serve the cause of world peace and security.

7. The Prime Ministers of Ceylon and China considered that disarmament is an important problem of our time. They expressed their determination to strive, in co-operation with other nations, for general disarmament and for complete prohibition and destruction of nuclear weapons.

8. The Prime Minister of Ceylon declared her Government's continued support for the restoration to the People's Republic of China of her legitimate rights in the United Nations. She also re-affirmed Ceylon's view that Taiwan is an integral part of China. The Chinese Prime Minister expressed his appreciation of Ceylon's stand.

9. The two leaders supported the establishment of nuclear free zones in various parts of the world and held that nuclear Powers should undertake due obligations towards such zones. In this connection, the Chinese Prime Minister commended the initiative taken by the Ceylon Prime Minister to refuse entry into Ceylon's territorial waters, ports and airfields of ships and aircraft carrying nuclear weapons or equipped for nuclear warfare. They expressed the hope that other States would take appropriate action on these lines.

10. The Ceylon Prime Minister explained to the Chinese Prime Minister Ceylon's active interest in the holding of a Second Non-aligned Conference. Both Prime Ministers hoped that a Second Non-aligned Conference would contribute to the cause of opposing imperialism and colonialsm, of supporting the national Independence movement and safeguarding world peace.

The two Prime Ministers noted that since the First Afro-Asian Conference held in Bandung in 1955 more than 30 new nations in Asia and Africa had attained freedom and independence, and that the cause of Afro-Asian solidarity had been greatly advanced. The Chinese Prime Minister was of the opinion that the time was right for convening a Second Afro-Asian Conference and that active preparations should be made for that purpose. The Ceylon Prime Minister agreed that such a Conference would serve a useful purpose and indicated that Ceylon would participate in such a Conference.

The two Prime Ministers also agreed that the Second Non-aligned Conference and the Second Afro-Asian Conference were not mutually exclusive.

11. The two Prime Ministers noted with satisfaction that the situation along the Sino-Indian border has eased. The Chinese Premier expressed thanks to Ceylon and the other Colombo Conference nations for their efforts of mediation between China and India, and expressed the readiness to continue to seek direct negotiations with India on the basis of the Colombo Proposals for a peaceful settlement of the Sino-Indian boundary question. The Ceylon Prime Minister indicated that, together with the other Colombo Conference nations, Ceylon would continue her efforts to promote Sino-Indian reconciliation.

12. The two Prime Ministers expressed great satisfaction that the friendly relations between Ceylon and China have continued to grow. They considered it a demonstration of the fact that countries with different political, economic and social systems can live together in peace and harmony and co-operate for their mutual benefit on the basis of the Five Principles of peaceful co-existence and the Ten Principles of Bandung.

13. Trade relations between the two countries were reviewed and the two leaders agreed that the trade between the two countries which had been based on the principles of equality and mutual benefit had expanded satisfactorily over the last ten years. They recognized the desirability of further development of trade between the two countries in new fields, particularly of processed and semi-processed materials to promote the growth of industrialisation.

14. The two delegations also reviewed the present position with regard to economic aid. They discussed and decided upon new items of economic aid by China to Ceylon including assistance for the construction of an International Conference Hall and related buildings and for the supply of textiles and rice. The Ceylon Prime Minister thanked the Chinese Prime Minister for these generous offers of assistance.

15. Both parties stressed the value of personal contacts between leaders of the two countries in contributing towards the strengthening of friendship and unity between Ceylon and China. The visit of Vice Chairman Soong Ching Ling, Premier Chou En-Lai and other distin

guished members of the Chinese Delegation has helped to bring the two countries and peoples closer together.

Sgd: Chou En-Lai

Premier of the State Council

of the People's Republic of

China.

Colombo, 29th February, 1964.

Sgd: Sirimavo R.D. Bandaranaike

Prime Minister of

Ceylon.

*Agreement to Maintain the Friendly
Relations between the Kingdom of Nepal
and the People's Republic of China
and on Trade and Intercourse
between the Kingdom of Nepal
and the Tibet Region of China*

THE GOVERNMENT of the Kingdom of Nepal and the Government of the People's Republic of China,

Being desirous of further developing the friendly relations between the two countries as good neighbours on the basis of the long-standing friendship between the two peoples, reaffirm that the Five Principles (Panch Shila) of,

1. Mutual respect for each other's territorial integrity and sovereignty,
2. Non-aggression,
3. Non-interference in each other's internal affairs for any reason of an economic, political or ideological character,
4. Equality and mutual benefit, and
5. Peaceful co-existence,

should be the fundamental principles guiding the relations between the two countries,

The two Parties have resolved to conclude the present Agreement in accordance with the above-mentioned principles and have for this purpose appointed as their respective Plenipotentiaries:

The Government of the Kingdom of Nepal, His Excellency Chuda Prasad Sharma, Minister for Foreign Affairs of the Kingdom of Nepal; the Government of the People's Republic of China, His Excellency Pan Tzu-li, Ambassador Extraordinary and Plenipotentiary of the People's

Republic of China to the Kingdom of Nepal, who, having examined each others' credentials and finding them in good and due form, have agreed upon the following:

Article I

The High Contracting Parties declare that peace and friendship shall be maintained between the Kingdom of Nepal and the People's Republic of China.

Article II

The High Contracting Parties hereby re-affirm their decision to mutually exchange diplomatic representatives on ambassadorial level.

Article III

All treaties and documents which existed in the past between Nepal and China including those between Nepal and the Tibet Region of China are hereby abrogated.

Article IV

In order to maintain and develop the traditional contacts between the peoples of Nepal and the Tibet Region of China, the High Contracting Parties agree that the nationals of both Parties may trade, travel and make pilgrimage in those places in each other's territory as agreed upon by both Parties, and the two Parties agree to safeguard the proper interests of the nationals of the other Party in its territory in accordance with the laws of the country of residence, and for this purpose the High Contracting Parties agree to do as follows:

Paragraph I. The High Contracting Parties mutually agree to establish Trade Agencies:

1. The Chinese Government agrees that the Government of Nepal may establish Trade Agencies at Shigatse, Kyerong and Nyalam;
2. The Government of Nepal agrees that the Chinese Government may establish an equal number of Trade Agencies in Nepal, the specific locations of which will be discussed and determined at a later date by both Parties;
3. The Trade Agencies of both Parties shall be accorded the same status and same treatment. The Trade Agents of both Parties shall enjoy freedom from arrest while exercising their functions, and shall enjoy in respect of themselves, their wives and their children who are dependend on them for livelihood freedom from search.

The Trade Agencies of both Parties shall enjoy the privileges and immunities for couriers, mail-bags and communications in code.

Paragraph II. The High Contracting Parties agree that traders of both countries may trade at the following places:

1. The Chinese Government agrees to specify (1) Lhasa, (2) Shigatse, (3) Gyantse and (4) Yatung as markets for trade;

2. The Government of Nepal agrees that when with the development of Chinese trade in Nepal, it has become necessary to specify markets for trade in Nepal, the Government of Nepal will specify an equal number of markets for trade in Nepal.
3. Traders of both countries known to be customarily and specifically engaged in border trade between Nepal and the Tibet Region of China may continue trade at the traditional markets for such trade.

Paragraph III. The High Contracting Parties agree that pilgrimage by religious believers of either country to the other may continue according to religious custom. Personal baggages and articles used for pilgrimage carried by the pilgrims of either Party shall be exempted from taxation by the other Party.

Paragraph IV. For travelling across the border between Nepal and the Tibet Region of China, the High Contracting Parties agree that the nationals of both countries shall use the customary routes.

Paragraph V. For travelling across the border by the nationals of the two countries, the High Contracting Parties agree to adopt the following provisions:

1. Diplomatic personnel and officials of the two countries and nationals of the two countries except those provided by sub-paragraphs 2, 3 and 4, who travel across the border between Nepal and the Tibet Region of China, shall hold passports issued by their respective countries and visaed by the other Party. Nationals of the two countries who enter Nepal or the Tibet Region of China through a third country shall also hold passports issued by their respective countries and visaed by the other Party.
2. Traders of the two countries known to be customarily and specifically engaged in trade between Nepal and the Tibet Region of China, their wives and children dependent on them for livelihood and their attendants, not covered by sub-paragraph 3 of this Paragraph, who enter into Nepal or the Tibet Region of China as the case may be for the purposes of trade, shall hold passports issued by their respective countries and visaed by the other Party, or certificates issued by their respective Government or by organs authorized by their respective Governments.
3. Inhabitants of the border districts of the two countries who cross the border to carry on petty trade, to visit friends or relatives, or for seasonal changes of residence, may do so as they have customarily done heretofore and need not hold passports, visas or other documents of certification.
4. Pilgrims of either Party who travel across the border between Nepal and the Tibet Region of China for the purposes of pilgrimage need not hold passports, visas or other documents of certification, but shall

register at the border checkposts or the first authorized Government office of the Party, and obtain permits for Pilgrimage therefrom.

5. Notwithstanding the provisions of the foregoing sub-pargaraphs of this Paragraph, either Government may refuse entry to any particular person.
6. Nationals of either country who enter the territory of the other Party in accordance with the foregoing sub-paragraphs of this Paragraph may stay within the territory only after complying with the procedures specified by the other Party.

Article V
This Agreement shall be ratified. It shall come into effect after mutual notice of ratifications, and remain in force for eight years. Extension of the present Agreement may be negotiated by the two Parties if either Party requests for it six months prior to the expiry of the Agreement and the request is agreed to by the other Party.

Done in Kathmandu on the 20th day of September, 1956, in duplicate in Nepalese, Chinese and English languages, all texts being equally authentic.

Plenipotentiary of His
Majesty's Government
of Nepal

Plenipotentiary of the
Government of the
People's Republic of
China

APPENDIX 15

Agreement between His Majesty's
Government of Nepal and the
Government of the People's Republic of China
on the Boundary between the Two Countries

HIS MAJESTY'S GOVERNMENT of Nepal and the Government of the People's Republic of China have noted with satisfaction that the two countries have always respected the existing traditional customary boundary line and live in amity. With a view to bringing about the formal settlement of some existing discrepancies in the boundary line between the two countries and the scientific delineation and formal demarcation of the whole boundary line, and to consolidating and further developing friendly relations between the two countries, the two Governments have decided to conclude the present Agreement under the guidance of the Five Principles of peaceful co-existence and have agreed upon the following:

Article I

The Contracting Parties have agreed that the entire boundary between the two countries shall be scientifically delineated and formally demarcated through friendly consultations, on the basis of the existing traditional customary line.

Article II

In order to determine the specific alignment of the boundary line and to enable the fixing of the boundary between the two countries in legal form, the Contracting Parties have decided to set up a joint committee composed of an equal number of delegates from each side and enjoin the Committees, in accordance with the provisions of Article III of the present Agreement, to discuss and solve the concrete problems concerning the Nepalese-Chinese boundary, conduct survey of the boundary, erect markers, and draft a Nepalese-Chinese boundary treaty. The joint committee will hold its meetings in the capitals or other places of Nepal and China.

Article III

Having studied the delineation of the boundary line between the two countries as shown on the maps mutually exchanged and the information furnished by each side about its actual jurisdiction over the area bordering on the other country, the Contracting Parties deem that, except for discrepancies in certain sections, their understanding of the traditional customary line is basically the same. The Contracting Parties have decided to determine concretely the boundary between the two countries in the following ways in accordance with three different cases:

1. Sections where the delineation of the boundary line between the two countries on the maps of the two sides is identical.

In these sections the boundary line shall be fixed according to the identical delineation on the maps of the two sides. The joint committee will send out joint survey teams composed of an equal number of persons from each side to conduct survey on the spot and erect boundary markers.

After the boundary line in these sections is fixed in accordance with the provisions of the above paragraph, the territory north of the line will conclusively belong to China, while the territory south of the line will conclusively belong to Nepal, and neither Contracting Party will any longer lay claim to certain areas within the territory of the other Party.

2. Sections where the delineation of the boundary line between the two countries on the maps of the two sides is not identical, whereas the state of actual jurisdiction by each side is undisputed.

The joint committee will send out joint survey teams composed of an equal number of persons from each side to conduct survey on the spot, determine the boundary line and erect boundary markers in these sections in accordance with concrete terrain features (watersheds, valleys, passes, etc.) and the actual jurisdiction by each side.

3. Sections where the delineation of the boundary line between the two countries on the maps of the two sides is not identical and the two sides differ in their understanding of the state of actual jurisdiction.

The joint committee will send out joint teams composed of an equal number of persons from each side to ascertain on the spot the state of actual jurisdiction in these sections, make adjustments in accordance with the principles of equality, mutual benefit, friendship and mutual accommodation, determine the boundary line and erect boundary markers in these sections.

Article IV

The Contracting Parties have decided that, in order to ensure tranquillity and friendliness on the border, each side will no longer dispatch armed personnel to patrol the area on its side within twenty kilometers of the border but only maintain its administrative personnel and civil police there.

Article V

The present Agreement is subject to ratification and the instruments of ratification shall be exchanged in Kathmandu as soon as possible.

The present Agreement will come into force immediately on the exchange of the instruments of ratification and will automatically cease to be in force when the Nepalese-Chinese boundary treaty to be signed by the two Governments comes into force.

Done in duplicate in Peking on the twenty first day of March, 1960, in Nepalese, Chinese and English languages, all texts being equally authentic.

Plenipotentiary of His
Majesty's Government
of Nepal

Plenipotentiary of the
Government of the
People's Republic of
China

*Agreement between His Majesty's
Government of Nepal and the
Government of the People's Republic of China
on Economic Aid*

HIS MAJESTY'S GOVERNMENT of Nepal and the Government of the People's Republic of China for the purpose of further promoting the friendly relations and of strengthening the economic and technical co-operation between the two countries have, on the basis of the Five Principles of peaceful co-existence, concluded the present Agreement, the articles of which are as follows,

Article I

With a view to helping His Majesty's Government of Nepal to develop its economy, the Government of the People's Republic of China is willing to give His Majesty's Government of Nepal, within a period of three years as from the date of coming into force of the present Agreement, a free grant of economic aid without any conditions or privileges attached. The amount of the aid is 100,000,000 (one hundred million) Indian Rupees. This amount, together with the remaining 40,000,000 (forty million) Indian Rupees, provided under the Agreement between Nepal and China on Economic Aid of 1956, which has not yet been used by His Majesty's Government of Nepal, making a total of 140,000,000 (one hundred and forty million) Indian Rupees, shall be utilized by instalments during the period of validity of the present Agreement by His Majesty's Government of Nepal in accordance with the items of economic aid to be agreed upon by both sides.

Article II

The economic aid to be given by the Government of the People's Republic of China to His Majesty's Government of Nepal shall cover equipment, machinery and materials, technique and other commodities.

Article III

According to the requirement of His Majesty's Government of Nepal, the Government of the People's Republic of China is willing to supply, on basis of the principles of economy and usefulness, equipment, machinery and materials and designs relating to the items of aid, in order to help develop the economy of the Kingdom of Nepal.

Article IV

At the request of His Majesty's Government of Nepal, the Government of the People's Republic of China agrees to dispatch a necessary number of experts and technicians to help the Kingdom of Nepal in the construction of the items of aid to be specified under the present Agreement. The travelling expenses of the Chinese experts and technicians to the Kingdom of Nepal and back to China and their salaries during their period of work in the Kingdom of Nepal shall be borne by the Government of the People's Republic of China; the living expenses of the Chinese experts and technicians during their period of work in the Kingdom of Nepal shall be paid from the amount of the aid, with their standard of living not exceeding that of personnel of the same level in the Kingdom of Nepal.

At the request of His Majesty's Government of Nepal, the Government of the People's Republic of China agrees to accept trainees dispatched by His Majesty's Government of Nepal to learn technical skill in China. The expenses of the trainees shall be paid from the amount of the aid.

Article V

The items of aid to be given by the Government of the People's Republic of China to His Majesty's Government of Nepal and the methods of their implementation, in accordance with Article II of the present Agreement, shall be discussed and decided upon separately in a protocol to be concluded by the representatives to be appointed by the two Governments.

Article VI

The organs to carry out the present Agreement shall be the Ministry of Finance of His Majesty's Government of Nepal for Nepal, and the Ministry of Foreign Trade of the People's Republic of China for the People's Republic of China.

Article VII

The present Agreement will come into force on the date of its signing and remain in force for a period of three years. At the expiry of the present Agreement, if the amount of the aid is not yet used up, the period of validity of the present Agreement may be extended by agreement of two Governments.

Done in duplicate in Peking on the twenty first day of March, 1960, in Nepalese, Chinese and English languages, all texts being equally authentic.

Plenipotentiary of His
Majesty's Government
of Nepal

Plenipotentiary of the
Government of the
People's Republic of
China

APPENDIX 17

Treaty of Peace and Friendship between the Kingdom of Nepal and the People's Republic of China

HIS MAJESTY the King of Nepal and the Chairman of the People's Republic of China, desiring to maintain and further develop peace and friendship between the Kingdom of Nepal and the People's Republic of China,

Convinced that the strengthening of good-neighbourly relations and friendly co-operation between the Kingdom of Nepal and the People's Republic of China is in accordance with the fundamental interests of the peoples of the two countries and conducive to the consolidation of peace in Asia and the world,

Have decided for this purpose to conclude the present Treaty in accordance with the Five Principles of peaceful co-existence jointly affirmed by the two countries, and have appointed as their respective plenipotentiaries:

His Majesty the King of Nepal: Prime Minister Bishweshwar Prasad Koirala,

The Chairman of the People's Republic of China: Premier Chou En-lai of the State Council.

The above-mentioned Plenipotentiaries, having examined each other's credentials and found them in good and due form, have agreed upon the following:

Article I

The Contracting Parties recognize and respect the independence, sovereignty and territorial integrity of each other.

Article II

The Contracting Parties will maintain and develop peaceful and friendly relations between the Kingdom of Nepal and the People's Republic of China. They undertake to settle all disputes between them by means of peaceful negotiation.

Article III

The Contracting Parties agree to develop and further strengthen the economic and cultural ties between the two countries in a spirit of friendship and co-operation, in accordance with the principles of equality and mutual benefit and of the non-interference in each other's internal affairs.

Article IV

Any difference or dispute arising out of the interpretation or application of the present Treaty shall be settled by negotiation through normal diplomatic channels.

Article V

This present Treaty is subject to ratification and the instruments of ratification will be exchanged in Peking as soon as possible.

The present Treaty will come into force immediately on the exchange of the instruments of ratification and will remain in force for a period of ten years.

Unless either of the Contracting Parties gives to the other notice in writing to terminate the Treaty at least one year before the expiration of this period, it will remain in force without any specified time limit, subject to the right of either of the Contracting Parties to terminate it by giving to the other in writing a year's notice of its intention to do so.

Done in duplicate in Kathmandu on the twenty-eighth day of April 1960 in Nepalese, Chinese and English languages, all texts being equally authentic.

Plenipotentiary of the
Kingdom of Nepal

Plenipotentiary of the
People's Republic of
China.

APPENDIX 18

Boundary Treaty between the Kingdom of Nepal and the People's Republic of China

HIS MAJESTY the King of Nepal and the Chairman of the People's Republic of China,

Being of the agreed opinion that a formal settlement of the question of the boundary between Nepal and China is of fundamental interest to the peoples of the two countries;

Noting with satisfaction that the friendly relations of long standing between the two countries have undergone further development since the establishment of diplomatic relations between the two countries and that the two Parties have, in accordance with the Five Principles of peaceful co-existence and in a spirit of fairness, reasonableness, mutual understanding and mutual accommodation, smoothly achieved an overall settlement of the boundary question between the two countries through friendly consultations;

Firmly believing that the formal delimitation of the entire boundary between the two countries and its consolidation as a boundary of peace and friendship not only constitute a milestone in the further development of the friendly relations between Nepal and China, but also are a contribution towards strengthening peace in Asia and the world;

Have resolved for this purpose to conclude the present Treaty on the basis of the Agreement Between His Majesty's Government of Nepal and the Government of the People's Republic of China on the Question of the Boundary Between the Two Countries of March 21, 1960 and have agreed upon the following:

Article I

The Contracting Parties, basing themselves on the traditional customary boundary line and having jointly conducted necessary on-the-spot investigations and surveys and made certain adjustments in accordance with the principles of equality, mutual benefit, friendship and mutual accommodation, hereby agree on the following alignment of the entire boundary line from west to east, Nepalese territory being south of the line and Chinese territory north thereof:

(1) The Nepalese-Chinese boundary line starts from the point where the watershed between the Kali River and the Tinkar River meets the watershed between the tributaries of the Karnali (Mapchu) River on the one hand and the Tinkar River on the other hand, thence it runs southeastwards along the watershed between the tributaries of the Karnali (Mapchu) River on the one hand and the Tinkar River and the Seti River on the other hand, passing through Lipudhura (Niumachisa) snowy mountain ridge and Lipudhura (Tinkarlipu) Pass to Urai (Pehlin) Pass.

(2) From Urai (Pehlin) Pass, the boundary line runs along the mountain ridge southeastwards for about 500 meters, then northeastwards to Height 5655 meters, thence continues to run along the mountain ridge northwestwards to Tharodhunga Tuppa (Tojang), then northeastwards passing through Height 5580.6 meters to Chimals Pass, thence it runs generally northwestwards, passing through Chimala to Numoche Tuppa (Lungmochiehkuo); thence the boundary line runs generally eastwards, passing through Kitko Tuppa (Paimowotunkuo) and then runs along Kitko (Chokartung) mountain spur down to the Yadangre (Chilungpa) stream, then it follows the Yadangre (Chilungpa) stream northwards to its junction with the Karnali (Mapchu) River, then it follows the Karnali (Mapchu) River generally eastwards to Hilsa (Yusa). At Hilsa (Yusa), the boundary line departs from the Karnali (Mapchu) River and runs northeastwards along the mountain spur up to Takule (Chialosa), then along the mountain ridge, passing through Kumalapche (Kumalatse), Ghanbochheko (Kangpaochekuo) and Manepamango (Mainpaimikuo) to Kangarje (Kangkuona), then northwards passing through Kandumbu (Kangchupeng) and Height 6550 meters to Nalakankar.

(3) From Nalakankar, the boundary line runs generally northeastwards along the watershed between the tributaries flowing into the Manasarowar Lake and the tributaries of the Humla Karnali River passing through Nalakankar Pass to Lapche (Letsela) Pass; thence it runs generally southeastwards along the watershed between the tributaries flowing into the Manasarowar Lake and the tributaries of the Machuan River on the one hand and the tributaries of the Humla Karnali River, the Mugu Karnali River and the Panjang Koola on the other hand, passing through Changla mountain, Namja Pass, Thau (Khung) Pass and Marem Pass to Pindu Pass, then it continues to run southeastwards along the watershed between the tributaries of the Machuan River on the one hand the the tributaries of the Barbung River and the Kali Gandaki

River on the other hand gradually turning northeastwards to Height 6214.1 meters.

(4) From Height 6214.1 meters, the boundary line runs northeastwards along the mountain spur, passing through Height 5025 meters and crossing the Angarchhu (Angarchubo) stream to Height 5029 meters; thence it runs generally eastwards along Thukchu (Tuchu) mountain spur, passing through Height 4730 meters and Panglham (Bungla) to the foot of Tingli Bhodho spur at its northwestern end, then turns northeastwards and runs along the southern bank of the Rhamarchhushu (Roumachushui) seasonal stream to the foot of Tingli Bhodho spur at its northeastern end; thence turns southeastwards, crosses the junction of two seasonal streams flowing northwards, and runs to the junction of three seasonal streams flowing northwards, and then up the eastern stream of the above three seasonal streams to Height 4697.9 meters, then turns southwestwards crossing a seasonal stream to Height 4605.8 meters; thence it runs generally southeastwards passing through Phumphula (Pengpengla) and then along Chhukomapoj (Chukomaburi) mountain ridge, passing through Height 4676.6 meters and Height 4754.9 meters to Height 4798.6 meters, thence along the mountain ridge northeastwards passing through Hsiabala, then generally eastwards passing through Height 5044.1 meters to Chaklo.

(5) From Chaklo, the boundary line runs generally southwards along the watershed between the tributaries of the Yalu Tsangpo River and the tributaries of the Kali Gandaki River, passing through Height 6724 meters to Lugula Pass, thence it runs generally eastwards along Lugula snowy mountain and the watershed between the tributaries of the Yalu Tsangpo River and the tributaries of the Marshiyangdi River to Gyala (Gya) Pass.

(6) From Gyala (Gya) Pass, the boundary line runs along the mountain ridge eastwards to Height 5782 meters, then southeastwards to Lajing Pass, then it runs along Lajing mountain ridge, passing through Height 5442 meters and Lajung (Lachong) Pass to Height 5236 meters, then turns southwestwards to Sangmudo snowy mountain; thence generally southeastwards and continues to run along Lajing mountain ridge, passing through Height 6137 meters, to Height 5494 meters, and then in a straight line crosses the Tonn (Dougar) River to Height 5724 meters; thence the boundary line runs generally northeastwards along the snowy mountain ridge, passing through Height 6010 meters, Height 5360 meters and Height 5672 meters to Thaple Pass.

(7) From Thaple Pass, the boundary line runs generally northeastwards along the snowy mountain ridge, passing through Tsariyangkang snowy mountain to Khojan; thence it continues to run generally south-

wards along the snowy mountain ridge, passing through Mailassaching Pass, Pashuo snowy mountain and Langpo snowy mountain to Yangra (Yangrenkangri) snowy mountain.

(8) From Yangra (Yangrenkangri) snowy mountain, the boundary line runs along the mountain ridge southwards to Tsalasungkuo and then generally eastwards and then northeastwards along a dry stream bed and passes through Kerabas (Jirapo) to reach the Sanjen (Sangching) River, then follows that river southeastwards, passes through its junction with the Bhrayange (Changchieh) River and continues to follow the Sanjen (Sangching) River to a point where a small mountain spur south of Pangshung (Genjungma) pasture ground and north of Chhaharey pasture ground meets with the Sanjen (Sangching) River; then it runs along the above small mountain spur eastwards and then southeastwards to Height 4656.4 meters, then runs eastwards to the Black Top; thence it runs along a mountain spur to the junction of the Bhurlung River and the Khesadhang (Tanghsiaka) stream, then runs eastwards along the Bhurlung River to its junction with the Kyerong River; thence follows the Kyerong River southwards and then eastwards to its junction with the Lende (Tungling Tsangpo) River; then runs northeastwards up the Lende (Tungling Tsangpo) River, passing through Rasua Bridge to the junction of the Lende (Tungling Tsangpo) River and the Jambu (Guobashiachu) stream; thence turns eastwards up the Jambu (Guobashiachu) stream, passing through the junction of the Chusumdo Tsangpo River and the Pheriphu Tsangpo River, both the tributaries of the upper Jambu (Guobashiachu) stream, to reach the boundary marker point at Chusumdo.

(9) From the boundary marker point at Chusumdo, the boundary line runs generally southeastwards along the ridge of Seto Pokhari (Tsogakangri) snowy mountain, Langtang snowy mountain, Dorley mountain and Phurbo Ghyachu (Gulinchin) mountain to Kharaney (Chakesumu) mountain; thence runs down to reach the Kharaney (Changnibachu) River and then follows that river southwards to its junction with the Bhote Kosi (Bhochu) River; then follows the Bhote Kosi (Bhochu) River southwards, passing through Bhaise (Dalaima) Bridge to the junction of the Bhote Kosi (Bhochu) River and the Jum (Junchu) River; thence eastwards up the Jum (Junchu) River to its source at Jum Khola Ko Sir Ko Tuppa (Tsaie mountain); thence the boundary line runs generally northwards along the mountain ridge to Height 6208.8 meters (Chomo Pamari).

(10) From Height 6208.8 meters (Chomo Pamari), the boundary line runs generally northwards along the mountain ridge to Height 5914.8 meters, then generally northeastwards along Sudemo (Shondemo

Kangri) snowy mountain passing through Height 5148 meters, and then crosses two tributaries of the Shongdemo (Shondemo Chu) stream, passing through Sudemo (Shondemo) which lies between the above two tributaries to Gyanbayan, then it runs along Gyanbayan mountain spur downwards, crosses the western tributary of the Lapche River (Pinbhu Tsangpo River), and then along the mountain spur up to Height 5370.5 meters at Korland Pari Ko Tippa (Sebobori); thence the boundary line turns southeastwards along the mountain spur downwards, crosses the eastern tributary of the Lapche River (Lapche Khung Tsangpo River), then it runs along Piding (Bidin Kangri) snowy mountain to Height 5397.2 meters; thence the boundary line turns westwards along the mountain ridge to Height 5444.2 meters at Raling (Kabobori), then generally southwards along Rishinggumbo (Rasumkungpo) mountain ridge to Niule (Niehlu) Bridge.

(11) From Niule (Niehlu) Bridge, the boundary line runs generally eastwards to Gauri Shankar (Chajenma), and then eastwards along the mountain ridge and then northwards along the watershed between the Rongshar River and the Rongbuk River on the one hand and the tributaries of the Dudhkosi River on the other hand to Nangpa Pass, and then runs generally southeastwards along the mountain ridge, passing through Cho Oyu mountain, Ghire Langur (Pumoli mountain), Sagar Matha (Mount Jolmo Lungma) and Lhotse, to Makalu mountain; then runs southeastwards and then eastwards along the mountain ridge to Popti Pass.

(12) From Popti Pass, the boundary line runs along the mountain ridge eastwards passing through Kepu Dada (Tsagala) to Khade Dada (Kharala), and then generally northeastwards passing through Lhenakpu (Lanapo) and Chhipung (Chebum) to the source of the Shumjung (Sunchunchu) River; then it follows the Shumjung (Sunchunchu) River to its junction with the track leading from Kimathangka to Chentang, then it runs along the track to the bridge on the Kama (Karma Tsangpo) River; thence it runs generally southeastwards along the Kama (Karma Tsangpo) River passing through its junction with the Arun River, and then along the Arun (Pengchu) River to its junction with the Nadang River, then continues to follow the Arun (Pengchu) River westwards to its junction with the Chhokang (Tsokangchingpo) River; thence the boundary line departs from the Arun (Pengchu) River and runs generally eastwards along a mountain spur passing through Angde and Tale (Dalai) Pass to Tale (Dalaila), and then runs along the mountain ridge passing through Dukan (Jungkan), Khachunkha (Kaijungkan), Relinbu (Renlangbu) and Sulula to reach Rakha (Ragla) Pass.

(13) From Rakha (Ragla) Pass, the boundary line runs generally

eastwards along the watershed between the tributaries of the Nadang River and the tributaries of the Yaru River on the one hand and the tributaries of the Tamur River on the other hand, passing through Ombak (Ombola) Pass, Tiptala (Theputala) Pass, Kangla (Yangma-khangla) Pass and Chabukla to the terminal point where the watershed between the Khar River and the Chabuk River meets the watershed between the Khar River and the Lhonak River.

The entire boundary line between the two countries as described in the present Article is shown on the 1:500,000 maps of the entire boundary attached to the present Treaty; the location of the temporary boundary markers erected by both sides and the detailed alignment of certain sections of the boundary are shown on the 1:50,000 maps of those sections attached to the present Treaty.

Article II

The Contracting Parties have agreed that wherever the boundary follows a river, the midstream line shall be the boundary. In case a boundary river changes its course, the original line of the boundary shall remain unchanged in the absence of other agreements between the two Parties.

Article III

After the signing of the present Treaty, the Nepalese-Chinese Joint Boundary Committee constituted in pursuance of the Agreement of March 21, 1960 between the two Parties on the question of the boundary between the two countries shall set up permanent boundary markers as necessary on the boundary line between the two countries, and then draft a protocol setting forth in detail the alignment of the entire boundary line and the location of the permanent boundary markers, with detailed maps attached thereto showing the boundary line and the location of the permanent boundary markers. The above-mentioned protocol, upon being signed by the Governments of the two countries, shall become an annex to the present Treaty and the detailed maps shall replace the maps now attached to the present Treaty.

Upon the signing of the above-mentioned protocol, the tasks of the Nepalese-Chinese Joint Boundary Committee shall be terminated, and the Agreement of March 21, 1960 between the two Parties on the question of the boundary between the two countries shall cease to be in force.

Article IV

The Contracting Parties have agreed that any dispute concerning the boundary which may arise after the formal delimitation of the boundary between the two countries shall be settled by the two Parties through friendly consultations.

Article V

The present Treaty shall come into force on the day of the signing of the Treaty.

Done in duplicate in Peking on October 5, 1961, in the Nepalese, Chinese and English languages, all three texts being equally authentic.

Sd/-	Sd/-
His Majesty the King of Nepal	Chairman of the People's Republic of China

Notes

Chapter I. THE NATURE OF THE CHINESE PRESENCE IN NEGOTIATION

1. Mao Tse-tung, *Selected Works* (New York, International Publications, (1945–1949), Vol. 5, p. 433.
2. U.S. Department of State Publication 3573.
3. *Ibid.,* p. 453, fn. 1.
4. *Peking Review,* Vol. 9, No. 24 (June 10, 1966), p. 16.
5. Mao Tse-tung, *Selected Works,* Vol. 5, p. 166.
6. *Ibid.,* p. 161.   7. *Ibid.,* Vol. 1, p. 109.
8. See Nehru's account of his written record of Chou En-lai's remarks regarding the McMahon Line in Jawaharlal Nehru, *India's Foreign Policy: Selected Speeches, September 1946–April 1961* (New Delhi, Government of India Publications Division, 1961), pp. 350–51.

Chapter II. THE BACKGROUND AND TRAINING OF CHINESE NEGOTIATORS

1. Franz Schurmann, *Ideology and Organization in Communist China* (Berkeley, University of California Press, 1966), p. 165.
2. *Ibid.,* p. 167.
3. Mao Tse-tung, *Selected Works* (New York, International Publications, 1945–1949), Vol. 2, p. 259.
4. For further facts on in-service education, see John Lewis, *Leadership in Communist China* (Ithaca, N.Y., Cornell University Press, 1963), p. 146 ff.
5. Quoted by John Lewis in *Leadership in Communist China,* p. 153.

6. Ch'en Yi is also vice chairman of the National Defense Council, former chairman of the Commission for Scientific Planning, member of the Central Committee of the Chinese Communist Party, and member of the Politburo of the Chinese Communist Party.

7. Mao Tse-tung, *Selected Works,* Vol. 1, p. 74.

8. *Ibid.,* Vol. 3, p. 225.

9. *Ideology and Organization,* pp. 173–74. For a detailed account of the structure of the Chinese Foreign Ministry, see Donald W. Klein's forthcoming book on this subject.

Chapter III. THE GENERAL APPROACH AND ATTITUDE OF COMMUNIST CHINA TOWARD INTERNATIONAL NEGOTIATION

1. Mao Tse-tung, *Selected Works* (New York, International Publications, 1945–1949), Vol. 4, p. 209.

2. Ch'en Po-ta, *Mao Tse-tung on the Chinese Revolution* (Peking, Foreign Languages Press, 1953), p. 83.

3. *Mao Tse-tung, An Anthology of His Writings,* ed. Anne Fremantle (New York, New American Library, 1962), p. 267.

4. Text published in the *Peking Review* and the *New York Times,* July 5, 1963, p. 7.

5. *Ibid.*   6. *Ibid.*

7. *Le Monde,* July 1, 1966.

8. From *Resolution on India Adopted by the Afro-Asian Writers Emergency Meeting,* held in July 1966 at Peking; see *Peking Review,* Vol. 9, No. 29 (July 15, 1966), pp. 41–42.

9. On August 3, 1966, Foreign Minister Adam Malik of Indonesia conferred on the outgoing Pakistani Ambassador the high honor of Mahaputra, Second Class, and expressed appreciation for the Ambassador's services in strengthening relations and friendship between the two countries. See *News & Views* (New York, Consulate General of Indonesia), No. 187, Aug. 5, 1966.

10. CCP letter of June 14, 1963, to the CPSU, *New York Times,* July 5, 1963, p. 7.

11. On the "Current Handling of Contradictions Among the People," by Mao Tse-tung, see *Mao Tse-tung,* p. 266.

12. Lin Yutang, *The Wisdom of China and India* (New York, Random House, 1942), p. 568: "So far as any systematic epistemology or metaphysics is concerned, China had to import it from India." And, again, "India has as rich a culture, as creative an imagination and wit and humor as any China has to offer, and India was China's teacher in religion and imaginative literature, and the world's teacher in trigonome-

try, quadratic equations, grammar, phonetics, Arabian Nights, animal fables, chess, as well as in philosophy, . . . she inspired Boccaccio, Goethe, Herder, Schopenhauer, Emerson and probably also old Aesop" (pp. 3–4).

13. The time-honored imperial policy of divide and rule—with the Indian subcontinent divided, for the first time in Asia's long history China has been able to exert force in the area and to achieve influence in it.

14. See Joint Statement of China and Albania (dated Peking, May 11, 1966), *Peking Review*, Vol. 9, No. 21 (May 20, 1966), p. 10.

15. *Ibid.*, p. 9.

16. Translation of *Renmin Ribao* editorial in the *New York Times*, April 7, 1966, p. 12.

17. *Peking Review*, Vol. 9, No. 21 (May 20, 1966), p. 11.

18. *Ibid.*

19. Mao Tse-tung, *Selected Works*, Vol. 5, p. 104.

20. *Ibid.*   21. *Ibid.*

22. *Peking Review*, Vol. 8, No. 36 (Sept. 3, 1965), pp. 9–30.

23. From Secretary Rusk's statement on China policy, March 16, 1966, at a closed session of the Far East Subcommittee of the House Foreign Affairs Committee. See the *New York Times*, April 17, 1966, p. 34.

24. *U.S. Policy with Respect to Mainland China*, Hearings before the Committee on Foreign Relations, U.S. Senate, March 1966, p. 26.

25. *Ibid.*, p. 371.

26. *Peking Review*, Vol. 8, No. 36 (Sept. 3, 1965), p. 28.

27. *Ibid.*, Vol. 9, No. 24 (June 10, 1966), pp. 6–7.

28. *Ibid.*, p. 7.   29. *Ibid.*

30. Mao Tse-tung, *Selected Works*, Vol. 3, p. 125.

31. *Ibid.*, p. 135.

32. *Peking Review*, Vol. 9, No. 30 (July 22, 1966), p. 19.

33. *Ibid.*, p. 20.

34. Liu Shao-ch'i, *Internationalism and Nationalism* (Peking, Foreign Languages Press, 1949), p. 32 (italics added).

35. Mao Tse-tung, *Selected Works*, Vol. 5, p. 59 (italics added).

36. *Ibid.*, p. 87 (italics added).

37. *Ibid.* It should be noted that these remarks were at first recorded in an innerparty document. Almost two years later the full text was issued as public document by the Central Committee of the CCP (in January 1948). This is important as it indicates full endorsement of Mao's earlier view.

38. See text of Chinese letter in *New York Times*, July 5, 1963, p. 7.

39. Mao Tse-tung, *Selected Works*, Vol. 4, p. 9.

40. *Ibid.*, Vol. 1, p. 180.   41. *Ibid.*, p. 193.

42. *Ibid.*, Vol. 4, p. 158.   43. *Ibid.*, Vol. 5, p. 15.

44. *Ibid.*, Vol. 2, p. 254.   45. *Ibid.*, Vol. 1, p. 110.

46. *Peking Review*, Vol. 9, No. 22 (May 27, 1966), p. 6.

47. Mao Tse-tung, *Selected Works*, Vol. 1, p. 179.

48. *Ibid.*, p. 110; Vol. 2, p. 254.

49. Franz Schurmann, *Ideology and Organization in Communist China* (Berkeley, University of California Press, 1966), p. 141.

50. *Ibid.*, p. 180.   51. *Ibid.*, p. 173.

Chapter IV. *THE PEKING GOVERNMENT AND THE CONVENING OF THE INTERNATIONAL CONFERENCE ON LAOS, MAY 1961*

1. The final declaration of the Geneva Conference of July 21, 1954, stated: "The conference . . . expresses its conviction that the execution of the provisions set out in the present declaration and in the agreements on the cessation of hostilities will permit Cambodia, Laos, and Viet Nam henceforth to play their part, in full independence and sovereignty, in the peaceful community of nations."

In paragraph five of the same declaration the conference also took note "of the declaration of the governments of Cambodia and Laos to the effect that they will not join in any agreement with other states if this agreement includes the obligation to participate in a military alliance not in conformity with the principles of the Charter of the United Nations."

2. *Peking Review*, Vol. 4, No. 1 (Jan. 6, 1961), p. 19.

3. The United States reaction to developments in Cuba following Fidel Castro's growing closeness to the Soviet Union is a case in point.

4. *Peking Review*, Vol. 4, No. 1 (Jan. 6, 1961), p. 19.

5. *Ibid.*, p. 20.

6. *Ibid.*, Vol. 4, No. 3 (Jan. 20, 1961), p. 7.

7. *Department of State Bulletin*, XLIV, 1126 (Jan. 23, 1961), pp. 115–17.

8. *Ibid.*, p. 117.   9. *Ibid.*

10. *Peking Review*, Vol. 4, No. 6 (Feb. 10, 1961), p. 7.

11. *Ibid.*

12. For text of British aide-mémoire, see *Documents on American Foreign Relations, 1961* (New York, Council on Foreign Relations, 1962), pp. 306–07.

13. *Ibid.*, pp. 305–06.   14. *Ibid.*

15. *Department of State Bulletin*, XLIV, 1138 (April 17, 1961), p. 544.

16. *Ibid.*, p. 308, fn. 12.   17. *Ibid.*, p. 309.

18. *Ibid.,* p. 308.

19. For text see *Peking Review,* Vol. 4, No. 9 (March 3, 1961), p. 8.

20. *Ibid.,* p. 7.

21. See above, pp. 36–37.

22. See the author's book *Modern International Negotiation, Principles and Practice* (New York, Columbia University Press, 1966), pp. 40, 45, 46.

23. *Documents on American Foreign Relations, 1961,* p. 310.

24. *Department of State Bulletin,* XLIV, 1142 (May 15, 1961), p. 710.

25. *United Kingdom Government White Paper,* "International Conference on the Settlement of Laotian Question" (London, Her Majesty's Stationery Office), Command Paper 1828, p. 8.

26. Laos/Doc/1, dated May 17, 1961. First Report of the International Commission, dated May 12, 1961.

27. SCMP (Survey of the China Mainland Press; Hong Kong, American Consulate General), No. 2421, Jan. 20, 1961, pp. 22–23.

28. *Peking Review,* Vol. 4, No. 7 (Feb. 19, 1961), p. 19.

Chapter V. THE NEGOTIATING CONFRONTATION AT THE OPENING OF THE LAOS CONFERENCE

1. The meetings were closed, but texts of all major statements were freely distributed. For convenience the symbols of the verbatim records circulated by the U.S. delegation will be used in these notes. The above remarks by Lord Home are in USVR/1, p. 23.

2. USVR/1, May 16, 1961, p. 34.

3. *Ibid.,* pp. 35–36 (italics added).

4. *Ibid.,* p. 25. 5. *Ibid.,* p. 26. 6. *Ibid.,* p. 27.

7. *Ibid.,* p. 31. 8. *Ibid.* 9. *Ibid.,* p. 32.

10. USVR/2, May 17, 1961, p. 4. 11. *Ibid.,* p. 5. 12. *Ibid.*

13. *Ibid.,* pp. 5–6. 14. *Ibid.,* p. 3.

15. *Ibid.,* pp. 3–4. 16. *Ibid.,* p. 4.

17. It was not till the leaders of the three factions had met at Zurich and reached agreement (June 22, 1961) that Prince Boun Oum sent Phoui Sananikone (an ex-Prime Minister of Laos) to represent him at the conference.

18. USVR/2, May 17, 1961, p. 7.

19. *Ibid.* 20. *Ibid.,* p. 8. 21. See above, p. 53.

22. USVR/2, May 17, 1961, p. 10.

23. USVR/1, May 16, 1961, p. 31.

24. USVR/2, May 17, 1961, p. 11.   25. *Ibid.*, p. 12.
26. USVR/3, May 17, 1961, p. 17.
27. USVR/7, May 22, 1961, p. 17.
28. *Ibid.*   29. *Ibid.*   30. *Ibid.*, p. 18.   31. *Ibid.*
32. *Ibid.*, pp. 18–19.   33. *Ibid.*, p. 19.
34. *Ibid.*, p. 20.   35. *Ibid.*

Chapter VI. *WAS THE SINO-AMERICAN CONFRONTATION
AT THE LAOS CONFERENCE NEGOTIABLE?*

1. USVR/9, May 24, 1961, p. 5.
2. USVR/4, May 18, 1961, p. 55.
3. USVR/9, May 24, 1961, p. 2.
4. The United States had, in fact, submitted no draft of proposals to the conference; it had expressed views.
5. USVR/9, May 24, 1961, p. 3.   6. *Ibid.*, p. 4.
7. *Ibid.*   8. *Ibid.*, pp. 9–10.   9. *Ibid.*, pp. 11–12.
10. *Ibid.*, p. 14.   11. *Ibid.*, p. 15.
12. USVR/10, May 31, 1961, p. 7.
13. Laos/Doc/5, May 17, 1961, article 12 (see Appendix 2).
14. USVR/10, May 31, 1961, p. 28.
15. USVR/11, June 1, 1961, p. 14.
16. *Ibid.*, p. 15.   17. *Ibid.*, p. 16.
18. *Ibid.*, p. 17.   19. *Ibid.*
20. USVR/12, June 5, 1961, p. 1.
21. USVR/13, June 6, 1961, p. 3.   22. *Ibid.*, p. 30.
23. These were generally regarded to be the delegates of China, France, India, the United Kingdom, the Soviet Union, and the United States.
24. USVR/14, June 12, 1961, p. 1.   25. *Ibid.*, p. 3.
26. *Ibid.*, p. 5.   27. *Ibid.*, p. 6.   28. *Ibid.*, pp. 7–8.
29. This was an important statement announcing Thailand's withdrawal from the conference till a representative of the Boun Oum wing could be seated. The other two Laotian wings, the Centrists and the Pathet Lao, had been at the conference table from the opening session.
30. USVR/14, June 12, 1961, p. 31.
31. *Ibid.*, p. 33.   32. *Ibid.*
33. *Ibid.*, p. 38.   34. *Ibid.*
35. *Ibid.*, p. 19.   36. *Ibid.*
37. Laos/Doc/11, June 6, 1961, p. 2 (see Appendix 5).
38. USVR/14, June 12, 1961, p. 39.
39. *Ibid.*, p. 40.   40. *Ibid.*
41. Laos/Doc/4, May 17, 1961, p. 2 (see Appendix 1).

42. Laos/Doc/5, May 17, 1961, p. 2. Article 1 of the Soviet proposal said, "All foreign military units and military personnel shall be withdrawn from Laos within 30 days after the entering into force of the present Agreement." See Appendix 2.

43. USVR/14, June 12, 1961, p. 40.

44. *Ibid.*, p. 41 (italics added).

45. *Ibid.*, p. 42.   46. *Ibid.*, p. 43.   47. *Ibid.*, pp. 43–44.

48. Jawaharlal Nehru, *India's Foreign Policy Selected Speeches, September 1946–April 1961* (New Delhi, Government of India Publications Division, 1961), p. 89.

49. USVR/14, June 12, 1961, p. 44. The high-level talks referred to by Ch'en Yi were to take place at a meeting then being arranged between the three princes, Souvanna Phouma, Boun Oum, and Souphanouvong. This meeting took place at Zurich June 19–22, 1961, and resulted in a most important agreement (see Appendix 9).

50. USVR/14, June 12, 1961, p. 45.

Chapter VII. THE FIRST FRUITS OF CHINA'S WILLINGNESS TO NEGOTIATE

1. USVR/15, June 13, 1961, p. 20.

2. At the Bilateral Summit Conference in June 1961.

3. USVR/15, June 13, 1961, p. 22.

4. Mr. Menon was of course well known for his very long statements. He holds the record at the United Nations, having spoken for about eight hours before the Security Council on the Kashmir issue.

5. USVR/15, June 13, 1961, p. 37.

6. *Ibid.*, p. 47.   7. *Ibid.*, p. 58.

8. For the American proposals, see Appendix 6.

9. The United States proposal read: "The Commission shall report to the Government of Laos and to the members of the Conference any armaments, munitions, and military equipment within Laos which appear to be in excess of the needs of the national forces, and shall propose measures for the disposition of such excess." See Appendix 6.

10. USVR/23, June 26, 1961, p. 3.

11. *Ibid.*, p. 4.   12. See above, pp. 36–37.

13. A *Renmin Ribao* editorial on July 1, 1966, stated, "Our party is a great, glorious and correct party" (*Peking Review*, Vol. 9, No. 27 [July 1, 1966], p. 5).

14. *Ibid.*, Vol. 9, No. 22 (May 27, 1966).

15. USVR/23, June 26, 1961, pp. 6–7.   16. *Ibid.*, p. 10.

17. Mao Tse-tung, *Selected Works* (New York, International Publications, 1945–1949), Vol. 1, p. 74.

18. *Ibid.,* Vol. 3, p. 225.
19. USVR/23, June 26, 1961, p. 10 (italics added).
20. For terms of the agreement, see Appendix 9.
21. USVR/23, June 26, 1961, p. 13.   22. *Ibid.,* p. 14.
23. *Ibid.,* p. 15.   24. *Ibid.,* p. 19.   25. *Ibid.,* pp. 21–22.

Chapter VIII. A SETBACK IN NEGOTIATION

1. Appendix 9.   2. USVR/27, July 3, 1961, p. 2.
3. *Ibid.,* p. 10.   4. See above, p. 85.
5. USVR/27, July 3, 1961, pp. 10–11.
6. *Ibid.,* p. 11.   7. *Ibid.,* p. 13.
8. *Ibid.,* p. 14.   9. *Ibid.,* p. 13.   10. *Ibid.,* p. 33.
11. USVR/28, July 4, 1961, p. 20.
12. *Ibid.,* p. 27.   13. *Ibid.,* p. 34.   14. *Ibid.,* p. 35.
15. USVR/30, July 6, 1961, pp. 4–5.
16. *Ibid.*   17. *Ibid.,* p. 30.   18. Appendix 9.
19. Laos/Doc/22, July 4, 1961. The commission's report itself was dated June 27, 1961, but was distributed to the conference about a week later.
20. *Peking Review,* Vol. 4, No. 28 (July 14, 1961), pp. 12–13.
21. USVR/31, July 10, 1961, p. 2.
22. USVR/32, July 11, 1961, p. 7.
23. USVR/34, July 13, 1961, pp. 24–25.
24. USVR/35, July 14, 1961, p. 41.
25. Cf. p. 97 above. The commission's next report was dated on July 26, 1961, and on the question of the cease-fire it said, "The Commission is pleased to note that since 27 June the number of complaints received was considerably smaller than at any time since the Commission's arrival in Laos."
26. USVR/35, July 14, 1961, p. 43.
27. *Ibid.,* p. 44.   28. *Ibid.*   29. *Ibid.,* pp. 44–45.
30. Chester Ronning for Canada, Jerzy Michalowski for Poland, and myself for India.
31. USVR/35, July 14, 1961, pp. 46–47.
32. USVR/28, July 4, 1961, p. 23.
33. *Ibid.*   34. *Ibid.,* p. 48.   35. *Ibid.*
36. *Ibid.,* p. 50.   37. *Ibid.*
38. *Ibid.,* p. 52 (italics added).
39. *Ibid.*   40. *Ibid.,* p. 53.
41. Mao Tse-tung, *Selected Works* (New York, International Publications, 1945–1949), Vol. 5, pp. 103–06.
42. *Peking Review,* Vol. 9, No. 39 (Sept. 23, 1966), p. 28.

Chapter IX. THE DEADLOCK BREAKS

1. USVR/32, July 11, 1961, pp. 7–8.
2. See Laos/Doc/5, July 20, 1961.
3. USVR/36, July 19, 1961, p. 3.
4. *Ibid.,* p. 4.   5. *Ibid.*   6. *Ibid.,* p. 6.   7. *Ibid.,* p. 57.

Chapter X. SUBSTANTIVE NEGOTIATION IS UNDER WAY

1. See Appendix 1.
2. USVR/1 (Restricted), July 20, 1961, p. 35.
3. *Ibid.,* p. 36.
4. Chang Han-fu said: "I would like to refer to the statement made by Mr. Lall, the Representative of India, to the effect that we already have a Zurich communiqué. The three Princes of Laos have already reached agreement on their external and domestic policy, insofar as our Conference is concerned" (*ibid.*).
5. *Ibid.,* p. 38.   6. *Ibid.,* p. 41.
7. USVR/2 (Restricted), July 21, 1961, p. 2.
8. *Ibid.,* p. 22.
9. Now (1967) Ambassador of the United States in Laos.
10. USVR/2 (Restricted), July 21, 1961, p. 24.
11. USVR/3 (Restricted), July 24, 1961, p. 6.
12. *Ibid.,* p. 24.   13. See above, pp. 28–31.
14. USVR/3 (Restricted), July 24, 1961, p. 27.
15. *Ibid.,* pp. 28–29.
16. USVR/5 (Restricted), July 26, 1961, p. 7.

Chapter XI. THE QUESTION OF SEATO

1. This is the wording of the Indian proposal. That of the Soviet Union was almost precisely the same. The French proposal used slightly different language.
2. USVR/5 (Restricted), July 26, 1961, p. 29.
3. *Ibid.,* p. 31.
4. Laos/Doc/4, May 17, 1961, p. 2 (see Appendix 1).
5. USVR/5 (Restricted), July 26, 1961, p. 35.
6. *Ibid.,* p. 36.   7. *Ibid.*   8. *Ibid.,* p. 37.

9. *Ibid.*   10. *Ibid.*, pp. 37–38.   11. *Ibid.*, p. 39.
12. *Ibid.*, p. 45.   13. *Ibid.*, p. 46.
14. USVR/7 (Restricted), July 28, 1961, p. 9.
15. *Ibid.*, p. 10.   16. *Ibid.*, pp. 10–11.   17. *Ibid.*, pp. 1–2.
18. *Peking Review*, Vol. 4, No. 31, (Aug. 4, 1961), p. 17.
19. *Ibid.*, p. 18.   20. *Ibid.*   21. See above, p. 121.
22. See Appendix 9.   23. USVR/39, Sept. 26, 1961, p. 15.
24. *Ibid.*, p. 18.   25. *Ibid.*
26. USVR/40 (Restricted), Nov. 1, p. 15.
27. *Ibid.*, pp. 16–17.   28. *Ibid.*, p. 23.   29. *Ibid.*, pp. 24–25.
30. USVR/41 (Restricted), Dec. 4, 1961, pp. 19–20. There were a few other unresolved issues such as the French military establishments in Laos and the details of the procedure for investigation and report by the International Control Commission.
31. *Ibid.*, p. 29. In referring to the work that had been accomplished Sullivan must have had in mind mainly the steady progress that had been made in some sixty sessions of the drafting committee which had succeeded in reaching agreement on the wording of a number of clauses of the texts of an agreement or a protocol.
32. Laos/Doc/7, Sept. 14, 1961.
33. USVR/37, Dec. 18, 1961, p. 14.
34. *Ibid.*, p. 15.   35. *Ibid.*, p. 14.
36. *Ibid.*, p. 40.   37. *Ibid.*, p. 46.
38. USVR/39, Jan. 23, 1962, p. 33.
39. *Ibid.*   40. *Ibid.*, pp. 41–42.
41. Li Ch'ing-ch'üan remained the Peking Ambassador to Berne till March 17, 1966, when he was recalled. However, his French and German and related cultural traits appear not to have developed beyond the limits of acceptance by Peking. There is evidence that he remains in good standing with the Mao people there.
42. He said, "Now there is only one question remaining before our Conference and that is the abolition of SEATO 'protection' over Laos" (United Kingdom Verbatim Record of 40th Plenary Session, July 2, 1962, p. 15).
43. *Ibid.*   44. *Ibid.*, p. 16.   45. *Ibid.*, pp. 21–22.
46. *Ibid.*, pp. 9–10.   47. UKYR/41, July 9, 1962, p. 2.
48. *Ibid.*, p. 3.   49. *Ibid.*, p. 7.   50. *Ibid.*
51. UKVR/44 (Restricted), July 18, 1962, p. 4.
52. *Ibid.*   53. See above, pp. 122–124.
54. See the author's *Modern International Negotiation, Principles and Practice* (New York, Columbia University Press, 1966), pp. 47–54.

Chapter XII. *THE WITHDRAWAL FROM LAOS OF FOREIGN FORCES AND MILITARY PERSONNEL*

1. See above, p. 75. 2. See Appendix 9.
3. See Appendices 2, 6, and 8.
4. USVR/17 (Restricted), Aug. 11, 1961, p. 3.
5. The British recital of the facts too supported the view that there were no Chinese elements in Laos. Malcolm MacDonald, in making his statement on the issue, said the following: "I assure you that we, in the British delegation, want all foreign troops and all foreign military personnel, without any exception, to be withdrawn. We have no partiality in the matter. We want to see the Americans withdrawn. We want to see the military personnel from the Democratic Republic of Vietnam withdrawn. We want to see the Soviet airmen and air crews withdrawn. We want to see all the Chiang Kai-shek troops withdrawn" (USVR/18 [Restricted], Aug. 14, 1961, p. 9).
6. *Ibid.*, pp. 3–4.   7. *Ibid.*, p. 17.   8. *Ibid.*, p. 22.
9. *Ibid.*, p. 21.   10. *Ibid.*, pp. 21–22.   11. *Ibid.*, p. 22.
12. *Ibid.*   13. *Ibid.*, pp. 23–24.
14. USVR/19 (Restricted), Aug. 15, 1961, p. 30.
15. *Ibid.*, p. 31.   16. *Ibid.*   17. *Ibid.*, p. 32.
18. *Ibid.*, pp. 31, 34.   19. *Ibid.*, p. 35.   20. *Ibid.*, p. 36.
21. *Ibid.*, pp. 35–36.   22. *Ibid.*, pp. 47–48.
23. USVR/20 (Restricted), Aug. 16, 1961, p. 10.
24. Article 2 of the Protocol reads as follows: "All foreign regular and irregular troops, foreign para-military formations and foreign military personnel shall be withdrawn from Laos in the shortest time possible and in any case the withdrawal shall be completed not later than thirty days after the Commission has notified the Royal Government of Laos that in accordance with Articles 3 and 10 of this Protocol its inspection teams are present at all points of withdrawal from Laos. These points shall be determined by the Royal Government of Laos in accordance with Article 3 within thirty days after the entry into force of this Protocol. The inspection teams shall be present at these points and the Commission shall notify the Royal Government of Laos thereof within fifteen days after the points have been determined." See Appendix 10.
25. Article 3 of the Protocol to the Declaration on the Neutrality of Laos. See Appendix 10.
26. Article IV in Laos/Doc/24, July 14, 1961, p. 2. See Appendix 8.

Chapter XIII. *CONTROL "OVER" OR "IN" LAOS*

1. The author.
2. USVR/23 (Restricted), Aug. 21, 1961, p. 13.
3. *Ibid.*, p. 14.   4. *Ibid.*, p. 15.   5. *Ibid.*, p. 14.
6. *Ibid.*, p. 15.   7. *Ibid.*   8. *Ibid.*   9. *Ibid.*   10. *Ibid.*
11. Laos/Doc/5, May 17, 1961, p. 2 (see Appendix 2).
12. USVR/24 (Restricted), Aug. 22, 1961, p. 37.
13. *Ibid.*, p. 38.   14. *Ibid.*, p. 40.
15. *Ibid.*, p. 14. Sullivan was referring to the ICC's report of July 26, 1961, Laos/Doc/28, dated August 1, 1961, in which the commission said, "From general observation it would appear, however, that some build-up of war-like equipment and other measures of military preparedness are proceeding on both sides. The possibility that either or both sides might resort to force in default of satisfactory agreements, cannot, in the view of the Commission, be excluded."
16. USVR/24 (Restricted), Aug. 22, 1961, p. 41.
17. *Ibid.*, pp. 41–42.   18. *Ibid.*, p. 42.   19. *Ibid.*
20. *Ibid.*   21. *Ibid.*, p. 43.
22. USVR/25 (Restricted), Aug. 23, 1961, p. 2.
23. Appendices 5 and 6.
24. USVR/25 (Restricted), Aug. 23, 1961, p. 21.
25. *Ibid.*, p. 22.   26. *Ibid.*, p. 23.   27. *Ibid.*
28. *Ibid.*, p. 24.   29. *Ibid.*   30. *Ibid.*, p. 25.
31. *Ibid.*, pp. 12–13. Regarding the armed forces the Zurich communiqué of the three Princes, dated June 22, 1961, said: "Cinq. Réaliser l'unification des forces armées des trois parties en une armée nationale unique suivant un programme fixé d'accord parties."
32. *Ibid.*, p. 25.
33. *Peking Review,* Vol. 4, No. 35 (Sept. 1, 1961), p. 9.
34. *Ibid.*   35. USVR/26 (Restricted), Aug. 24, 1961, p. 9.
36. *Ibid.*, p. 10.   37. *Ibid.*, p. 12.   38. *Ibid.*
39. *Ibid.*, pp. 20–25. And, besides, it could act only when so instructed by the cochairmen—which meant that both the British (or more broadly the West) and the Soviets (or more broadly the Communist states) could veto investigations.
40. USVR/32 (Restricted), Sept. 1, 1961, p. 3.
41. *Ibid.*, p. 4.
42. USVR/34 (Restricted), Sept. 5, 1961, p. 11.
43. Harriman said, "We are very fortunate to have as the Chairman

of this Commission, the Indian representative and they have shown themselves to be impartial in the past and we can count upon their being impartial in the future" (*ibid.*, pp. 11–12).

44. *Ibid.*, p. 17.

45. The ICC had left in 1958, at the request of the Laotian government. It returned by agreement at the beginning of the 1961–1962 Laos Conference.

46. USVR/34 (Restricted), Sept. 5, 1961, p. 15.

47. *Ibid.* 48. *Ibid.*, p. 17.

49. *Ibid.*, p. 16, and cf. Mao Tse-tung, *Selected Works* (New York, International Publications, 1945–1949), Vol. 1, p. 110; Vol. 2, p. 254.

50. USVR/34 (Restricted), Sept. 5, 1961, p. 16.

51. *Ibid.*, pp. 17–18. 52. See Appendix 10.

53. USVR/36 (Restricted), Sept. 11, 1961, p. 8.

54. *Ibid.*, p. 11. 55. *Ibid.*, p. 16.

56. Appendix 10. 57. *Ibid.*

Chapter XIV. THE CONCLUDING ROUNDS AT THE LAOS NEGOTIATION

1. These items related to technical minutiae such as the date of entry into force of the new agreement on Laos, the relationship between the new agreement and the 1954 agreement, and arrangements for the deposit of the new agreement.

2. USVR/37 (Restricted), Sept. 12, 1961, p. 49.

3. *Ibid.*, pp. 49–50. 4. *Ibid.*, p. 51.

5. *Ibid.*, p. 53. 6. *Ibid.*

7. USVR/39 (Restricted), Sept. 26, 1961, p. 10.

8. Article 2(i) of the Declaration on the Neutrality of Laos (Appendix 10).

9. USVR/39 (Restricted), Sept. 26, 1961, p. 13.

10. *Ibid.*, pp. 14–15. 11. *Ibid.*, p. 18.

12. *Ibid.*, p. 19. 13. *Ibid.*, pp. 19–20.

14. USVR/40 (Restricted), Nov. 1, 1961, p. 11.

15. *Ibid.*, p. 14. 16. *Ibid.*, p. 15. 17. *Ibid.*, p. 25.

18. USVR/41 (Restricted), Dec. 4, 1961, p. 16.

19. *Ibid.*, pp. 19–20. 20. *Ibid.*, p. 28.

21. United Kingdom Delegation Verbatim Record of 42nd Plenary Session, July 21, 1962, pp. 27, 29.

22. *Ibid.*, p. 31.

Chapter XV. *PEKING'S NEGOTIATIONS WITH THREE ASIAN STATES*

1. *Peking Review,* Vol. 5, No. 30 (July 27, 1962), p. 6.
2. *Ibid.,* Vol. 9, No. 44 (Oct. 28, 1966), p. 5.
3. Communiqué on Talks between Chinese and Burmese Premiers, Dec. 12, 1954, contained in *A Victory for the Five Principles of Peaceful Co-existence* (Peking, Foreign Languages Press, 1960), p. 5.
4. *Ibid.,* pp. 6–7. Between China and Burma the first reference to the Five Principles was made in the Joint Statement of the Premiers of China and Burma, June 29, 1954, when Chou En-lai visited Rangoon on his way back from the first Geneva Conference on Indochina. In that Joint Statement the Five Principles are referred to as follows: "In regard to the principles agreed upon between China and India to guide relations between the two countries, namely [then the five principles are stated] the Prime Ministers agreed that those should also be the guiding principles for relationship between China and Burma." The early Sino-Indian negotiations had left a legacy which China was to use time and again in its relations with other states.
5. Speech of U Nu in the Chamber of Deputies, Rangoon, April 28, 1960, published by the Director of Information, Union of Burma, 1960, pp. 14–15.
6. Communiqué on Talks between Chinese and Burmese Premiers, Dec. 12, 1954, in *A Victory for the Five Principles of Co-existence,* p. 24.
7. *Ibid.,* p. 26.
8. The date on which Burma regained its independence from Britain.
9. Speech of U Nu, Rangoon, April 28, 1960, pp. 25–26.
10. For text, see Appendix 11.
11. Article II of Treaty of Friendship and Mutual Non-Aggression between the People's Republic of China and the Union of Burma. For text, see Appendix 12.
12. Article II of the treaty. *Renmin Ribao* alluded to this clause in its editorial of February 1, 1960, saying, "This affirmation is of great significance. Since United States imperialism is now doing its utmost to expand its aggressive military blocs, this article deals a stunning blow against the United States plot."
13. *The Chinese Communist World Outlook,* Department of State Publication 7379; Far Eastern Series 112, Bureau of Intelligence and Research, Sept. 1962, p. 84.
14. *Ibid.,* p. 85.   15. See Appendix 13.

16. See Appendix 13, paragraph 8.   17. *Ibid.,* paragraph 10.
18. *Ibid.*   19. *Ibid.,* paragraph 11.   20. *Ibid.*
21. *Ibid.*   22. *Ibid.,* paragraph 12.   23. *Ibid.,* paragraph 13.
24. Tirtha R. Tuladhan, *Nepal-China, A Study of Friendship* (Kathmander, Department of Publicity and Broadcasting, n.d.), pp. 8–9.
25. *Ibid.,* p. 9.
26. Before this happened, and foreseeing the danger, an outstanding Prime Minister of Nepal, Bhim Sen Thapa, wrote to both Peking and Ranjit Singh, the ruler of the Punjab, urging joint action against the spread of foreign rule in Asia, but neither responded with deeds to this proposal (1816).
27. The five pillars are (1) mutual respect for each other's territorial integrity and sovereignty; (2) nonaggression; (3) noninterference in each other's internal affairs for any reason of an economic, political, or ideological character; (4) equality and mutual benefit; and (5) coexistence.
28. Tuladhan, *Nepal-China,* p. 32. See also Appendix 14.
29. Agreement between Nepal and the People's Republic of China on the Boundary between the Two Countries, dated March 21, 1960, Article I. For text, see Appendix 15.
30. *Ibid.,* Preamble (italics added).
31. That this appeared to be the main, if not the sole, motivation of the Chinese tended to come out in the actual border delimitation to which we will come later in this chapter.
32. For the wording in the agreement regarding these three categories, see Article III.
33. Article IV.
34. Agreement between the Kingdom of Nepal and the People's Republic of China on Economic Aid, dated March 21, 1960, Article IV. For text, see Appendix 16.
35. Nepal unlinked the value of its rupee from that of the Indian rupee when in 1966 India, for reasons which Nepal considered inapplicable to itself, devalued its currency.
36. Treaty of Peace and Friendship between the Kingdom of Nepal and the People's Republic of China, dated April 28, 1960, Article II. For text, see Appendix 17.
37. Jawaharlal Nehru, *India's Foreign Policy: Selected Speeches, September 1946–April 1961* (New Delhi, Government of India Publications Division, 1961), pp. 373–74.
38. Treaty of Friendship and Non-Aggression between Burma and China, dated Jan. 28, 1960 (Appendix 12).
39. In his statement to the United Nations General Assembly on Nov. 28, 1966, Ambassador Khatri said that the boundary agreement brought

back to Nepal 300 square miles of territory which was formerly in dispute (U.N. General Assembly Document A/PV.1480d. Nov. 28, 1966). This calculation uses the words "in dispute," but the Chinese claimed a large area in which, because of the facts of clear jurisdiction on the ground, they did not press their claims. These figures are based on the wider claims of the Chinese as given me by Nepalese officials.

40. See Appendix 18.

41. *Statement of Principles, Major Foreign Policy Speeches* by His Majesty King Mahendra (Nepal, Department of Publicity, 1964), 2d ed., p. 43.

42. *Peking Review,* Vol. 10, No. 9 (Feb. 24, 1967), pp. 27–28.

Index